Additional Praise for *Goddess and God in* the World

"*Goddess and God* makes clear that women's experience and perspectives enrich and transform theology and also that some of the central theological debates continue. Do we think of God as the impersonal ground of everything or as the personal embodiment of cosmic love? Is one view more feminine or more feminist than the other?"

—John B. Cobb Jr., professor emeritus and cofounding director of the Center for Process Studies, Claremont School of Theology
Author of *Process Theology* and *For the Common Good*

"What is most striking about this book is the sustained engagement with one another of two brilliant thinkers with radically divergent theologies. They are, of course, still committed feminists, but this book presents a model of theological conversation that challenges all of us, not just women, to reflect deeply on our own understanding of the divine."

—Christine Downing, professor of mythological studies, Pacifica Graduate Institute
Author of *The Goddess* and *Women's Mysteries*

"*Goddess and God in the World* is essential reading. Carol P. Christ and Judith Plaskow bring their formidable intellects and compassionate imaginations to the difficult, necessary work of thinking constructively about the Divine. Their exploration ranges widely, reaches deeply, and offers resources to us all."

—Kecia Ali, associate professor of religion, Boston University
Author of *Sexual Ethics and Islam* and *The Lives of Muhammad*

"The engaging narratives and conversations in *Goddess and God in the World* brilliantly model the authors' conviction that divinity is to be found within our lives and in our shared experience. Carol P. Christ and Judith Plaskow have given us a unique gift: the record of a long and evolving friendship between two of our foremost feminist foremothers. I am thrilled with this book."

—Marcia Falk, author of *The Book of Blessings* and *The Days Between*

Goddess and God in the World offers readers the chance to sit in a cozy room with two of the greats of feminist theology. In this work, Carol P. Christ and Judith Plaskow answer all the questions you would pose if you had an audience with them. You overhear them laugh, reminisce, pontificate, argue and laugh again. They share their theological journeys with academia, philosophy, theological traditions and Scripture. Beautifully weaving together their personal paths with the histories of Judaism, Christianity, Western philosophy and Goddess traditions, Plaskow and Christ offer distinct theologies that wrestle with the depth and breadth of patriarchy. They emerge different than how they entered, and yet maintaining deep and meaningful faiths. Most importantly, they engage each other in a way that is quickly disappearing from the academy: they note their differences, critique one another other, revel in their similarities, and debate without needing to convert. May this work be a model for all dialogical theology!"

—Monica A. Coleman, professor and codirector of the Center for
Process Studies, Claremont School of Theology
Author of *Making a Way Out of No Way* and *Bipolar Faith*

Goddess and God in the World

Goddess and God in the World

Conversations in Embodied Theology

Carol P. Christ and Judith Plaskow

Fortress Press

Minneapolis

GODDESS AND GOD IN THE WORLD

Conversations in Embodied Theology

Cover image: "The Tree of Life" by Judith Shaw

Cover design: Joe Reinke

Library of Congress Cataloging-in-Publication Data

Print ISBN: 978-1-5064-0118-8

eBook ISBN: 978-1-5064-0119-5

The paper used in this publication meets the minimum requirements of American National Standard for Information Sciences — Permanence of Paper for Printed Library Materials, ANSI Z329.48-1984.

Manufactured in the U.S.A.

This book was produced using Pressbooks.com, and PDF rendering was done by PrinceXML.

This book is dedicated

to

the power of female friendship

with thanks to

friends who read and commented on our manuscript

and helped us to see what it could become

Christine Downing, Martha Ackelsberg, Nicola Morris,

Joyce Zonana, and Elizabeth Chloe Erdmann

Contents

Part II. Theological Conversations

Introduction: Goddess and God in Our Lives

People who reject the popular image of God as an old white man who rules the world from outside it often find themselves at a loss for words when they try to articulate new meanings and images of divinity.[1] Speaking about God or Goddess is no longer as simple as it once was. Given the variety of spiritual paths and practices people follow today, theological discussions do not always begin with shared assumptions about the nature of ultimate reality. In the United States, the intrusion of religion into politics has led many people to avoid the subject of religion altogether. In families and among friends, discussions of religion often culminate in judgment, anger, or tears. Sometimes the conversation is halted before it even begins when someone voices the opinion that anyone who is interested in religion or spirituality is naive, unthinking, or backward—or, alternatively, that religious views are matters of personal preference and not worth discussing at all.

Talking about divinity is also surprisingly intimate. Unless we simply repeat what we have been taught, it is not possible to speak about what we believe about Goddess or God without saying something important about ourselves. Revealing our deepest convictions can leave us feeling vulnerable and exposed. Moreover, many otherwise well-informed adults whose religious educations were nonexistent or stopped with

---

1. Though educated people might say that they do not think of God in this way, the combination of traditional imagery and classical metaphysics in this picture, along with its equation of power with masculinity and masculine power with transcendence and omnipotence, continues to influence the theological imagination in both direct and subtle ways.

Sunday school lack a vocabulary for intelligent discussion of religion. Without new theological language, we are likely to be hesitant, reluctant, or unable to speak about the divinity we struggle with, reject, call upon in times of need, or experience in daily life. Yet ideas about the sacred are one of the ways we orient ourselves in the world, express the values we consider most important, and envision the kind of world we would like to bring into being. Our ideas about divinity are also intimately connected to questions that trouble us in the night about whether life has purpose and what that purpose might be.

Theology and Women

Theology is an important way to address these questions and this why we are drawn to it. We began our graduate studies in theology in an era when theologians and theology students were almost all men. We had been taught that the sex and gender of a theologian—or for that matter of any other writer—was irrelevant. But we came to understand that the exclusion of female voices does make a difference, not only on questions about women, but on other questions as well. As we developed our feminist perspectives in conversation with each other, we became instrumental in founding the feminist study of women and religion.

Our book *Womanspirit Rising* was the first collection of readings in the emerging field of feminist theology.[2] It included contributions from Christians, Jews, and Goddess feminists and has been widely used in university and graduate courses, as well as in church, synagogue, and unaffiliated study groups. "Why Women Need the Goddess," Carol's keynote address at the Great Goddess Re-Emerging Conference at the University of Santa Cruz, was influential in launching the Goddess movement, while Judith's speech, "The Jewish Feminist: Conflict in Identities," at the first national Jewish feminist conference helped to catalyze the transformation of Judaism.[3] Our second coedited book,

2. Carol P. Christ and Judith Plaskow, eds., *Womanspirit Rising: A Feminist Reader in Religion* (San Francisco: Harper & Row, 1979).
3. Carol P. Christ, "Why Women Need the Goddess," was first published in *Heresies* (Spring, 1978) and is the final chapter in *Womanspirit Rising*, 273–87; Judith Plaskow, "The Jewish Feminist: Conflict in

Weaving the Visions, brought together a growing chorus of diverse voices and shaped yet another decade of the study of women and religion.[4] Carol supported Judith when she undertook the daunting task of writing *Standing Again at Sinai*,[5] the first Jewish feminist theology, while Judith supported Carol when she later began, with even fewer resources to draw upon, to conceive *Rebirth of the Goddess*, the first feminist thealogy.[6] It would be an understatement to say that our friendship sustained us through many difficult and rewarding times.

An Important Disagreement

We began working on this book because—although we agree about many things—we disagree about the nature of Goddess and God. After working together for decades, we found it quite a shock to come face-to-face with a difference on such a major theological issue as the nature of divinity. Our theological conversations have long been rooted in a critique of the God of biblical traditions as a dominating male other. This God has traditionally been understood to transcend the world: to reside above, beyond, or outside of nature and finite embodied life. The transcendent God has been seen as omnipotent: to be in control of everything that happens in the world. We believe that this God has justified not only the domination of women but other forms of domination as well, including slavery, colonialism, war, and environmental degradation. We have both rejected traditional views of divine transcendence and omnipotence. *We find divinity in the world, in*

Identities," in *The Jewish Woman: New Perspectives*, ed. Elizabeth Koltun (New York: Schocken, 1976), 3–10; reprinted in Judith Plaskow, *The Coming of Lilith: Essays on Feminism, Judaism, and Sexual Ethics, 1972–2003*, ed. with Donna Berman (Boston: Beacon Press, 2005), 31–32, 35–39.

4. Judith Plaskow and Carol P. Christ, eds., *Weaving the Visions: New Patterns in Feminist Spirituality* (San Francisco: Harper & Row, 1989).

5. Judith Plaskow, *Standing Again at Sinai: Judaism from a Feminist Perspective* (San Francisco: Harper & Row, 1990).

6. Carol P. Christ, *Rebirth of the Goddess: Finding Meaning in Feminist Spirituality* (New York: Routledge, 1998 [1997]). Carol used the term "thealogy" from *thea*, "Goddess," and *logos*, "meaning," to refer to reflection on the meaning of the Goddess in *Rebirth of the Goddess*. "Theology," from *theos* or God, is a male generic. She did not insist on the use of dual terms to refer to the thea-theo-logical enterprise in this book, because, here, she wanted to underscore the fact that she and Judith share a commitment to a common enterprise of *feminist* theology.

finite, embodied life. This insight means that our embodied lives matter. Understanding that God is not in control of everything means that our choices contribute to the future of life on earth. Given that we agree on so much, we were surprised to find that as we thought further about the nature of divinity, our views diverged.

> *Judith views God as an impersonal power of creativity that is the ground of all being and becoming, including all good and all evil.*
>
> *Carol understands Goddess as the intelligent embodied love that is in all being, a personal presence who cares about the world.*[7]

There are two major differences between us. First, Judith thinks of divinity as an impersonal creative power, while Carol thinks of divinity as an individual who cares about and loves the world. Second, Carol thinks of divinity as intelligent, loving, and good, while Judith thinks of divinity as encompassing all that is, including and supporting both good and evil. As we will discuss, these two views are not ours alone, but reflect significant divides in the ways people have imagined and thought about divinity in both the East and the West.

Embodied Theological Method

We both can give reasons for our views, and in the course of these chapters, we discuss many of them. But the fact that neither of us has been able to persuade the other to change her mind led us to conclude that the philosophical, theological, and moral reasons we offer in justification of our views are only part of the story. All of the reasons we give are situated in our individual bodies and in our communities, societies, and histories. Different kinds of experiences do not lead directly or necessarily to different theological positions, but experiences are the matrix from which we all begin to think theologically. As we develop our theological perspectives, we

---

7. Carol arrived at this wording of her definition of the nature of divinity in the course of writing this book, as she discusses in chapters 9 and 11.

constantly test them against our experiences, asking if they ring true, if they help us make sense of our personal, communal, and social lives.

Recognizing that our experiences have contributed to our different understandings of the nature of God, we decided to write in a hybrid form that combines theological autobiography with rigorous philosophical, theological, and ethical reflection. This book is an experiment in *embodied theology* that seeks both to demonstrate the connection of theology to experience and to show the complexity of the relationship between them. Combining theology and autobiography is not easy. On the one hand, it has become common for theological others (but not for those who are white and male) to name the social locations from which we write. Situating theology is important, but sometimes it becomes a formulaic preface not explicitly connected to theological methods and conclusions. On the other hand, when personal experiences are shared, they often become primary and theology secondary. We have tried to achieve a balance. We reveal and discuss many intimate aspects of our own stories, but always with a focus on their theological implications. Our intention is to give our theologies flesh, to show how they emerge out of and in turn shape the embodied realities of our lives. We hope this approach will help readers more easily navigate the difficult waters of theological concepts and language.

While we connect our theologies to our stories, we do not intend to reduce theology to autobiography. Ideas that are rooted in experience can be discussed, queried, and defended on rational and moral grounds. This is possible because, though experience is always personal, it is also situated in a world that is shared. Our ideas about divinity must make sense not only of our personal experiences, but also of the world. The ethical implications of our views of Goddess and God can and must be considered because our understandings of divinity shape our understandings of what is right, just, and possible in the world. Not all theological ideas are equal. Thinking through our different perspectives, questioning each other's ideas, and trying to defend our own has been one of the central—and exciting—challenges in writing this book.

We approached the second part of the book, where we take issue with each other's views, with some trepidation because we have been taught that there are always winners and losers in arguments about ideas. Yet, as we articulated our theologies and reflected on them together, we found that we could probe and question each other's deeply held convictions without losing respect for each other. We discovered that, as we thought deeply about how we differed, our own views became clearer. At the outset, we each believed that ours was the best solution to the problems created by traditional views of God. In the process of conversing with each other, we concluded that more than one—but not every—view of the nature of divinity can provide a theological foundation for the more just and harmonious world we envision.

Our Book

In the chapters that follow, we begin with experience, move on to theological reflection, proceed through dialogue and questioning, and return to experience. The first part of the book (chapters 1–2, 4–5, 7–8) describes our journeys toward our views of Goddess and God, beginning with our childhoods, moving through early adulthood, up to the present day.[8] In two jointly written chapters (chapters 3 and 6), we set our positions in larger theological contexts: in relation to the history of theology and to the theological environment of the mid-twentieth century in which we began our studies (chapter 3); and in relation to major themes in feminist theology that have shaped our work (chapter 6). In the second part of the book (chapters 9–10, 11–12), we challenge each other's perspectives and respond to each other's questions. We wrote our individual chapters in pairs: thus chapter 2 is not a response to chapter 1, nor is chapter 10 a response to chapter 9; however, in chapters 9 and 10 each of us responds to issues raised in

---

8. The order of the chapters and of our names on the cover and title page were decided by a toss of a coin.

the first part of the book, while in chapters 11 and 12, we each respond to questions posed by the other in chapters 9 and 10. In the final chapter (chapter 13), we call attention to the common ground that underlies our theological differences, suggesting that it could provide the starting point for wider conversations about the nature of divine power both within and across religious boundaries. These conversations are important because, as we show, the ways we think and speak about divine power have implications for the way we imagine the future of our world.

Questions to Ponder

We hope this book will stimulate others to think and speak about divinity in their lives and provide a vocabulary for doing so. We invite our readers to embark with us on a theological journey: asking what you believe about the nature of Goddess or God; pondering the relation of theology to your own experiences; reflecting on how theologies make sense of our common world; asking which theologies provide the orientation we need as we seek to create a more just and harmonious world. Before you continue, you might like to reflect on the questions that lie at the heart of our book.

Is God or Goddess to be found outside the world, or within it?

Are we called to a life beyond the body and nature, or is this world our home and our bodily life the only life we have?

Is there someone listening to us when we worship, pray, or meditate, or is addressing Goddess or God a metaphoric way of speaking?

Is everything that happens in the world the will of Goddess or God, or is the world shaped by chance and a multiplicity of wills?

Is Goddess or God good, or does the divine power include both good and evil?

Does the idea that divinity loves the world inspire us to promote the flourishing of all, or does the notion that divine power includes both good and evil encourage greater human responsibility for the fate of the earth?

Should we speak of Goddess, God, neither, or both?

Is what each of us believes about divine power a personal choice with only private meaning, or do our beliefs matter because they shape the world we share?

You might want to answer these questions again after you read our book, reflect on your own theology, and enter with us into a wider conversation about divinity and the world.

PART I

Embodied Theologies

1

For the Beauty of the Earth

Carol P. Christ

I was brought from the Huntington Hospital just before Christmas to my grandmother's home on Old Ranch Road in Arcadia, California. Peacocks from the adjacent Los Angeles County Arboretum screeched on the roof. There was another baby in the house, my cousin Dee, born a few months earlier. My mother and her sister were living with their mother. The Second World War was over, and they were anticipating the return of their husbands from the Pacific Front. My earliest memory, recovered during a healing energy session, is visual and visceral. I am lying crossways in a crib next to the other baby. There is a soft breeze. The other baby is kicking its legs, and I am trying to do the same. I look up and see three faces looking down at us. Although the faces are blurry in the vision I see, I feel them as female and loving.

My parents had what was called a mixed marriage. My father's family was Roman Catholic and my mother's was Christian Science.

This was at a time when Roman Catholics were viewed with suspicion in the United States. We were brought up in local Protestant churches in the postwar tract home suburbs of Southern California where my parents hoped we would all fit in. In church, I learned about the love of God without much mention of judgment. God was the one who made the ivy twine; He looked for the one lost sheep, and His love was divine, all loves excelling.[1] I knew what this meant, because I never doubted my grandmothers' love for me. There was something about worship that attracted me, and I often begged my parents to get up to take me to church when they would have liked to stay in bed on a Sunday morning. I preferred the grown-ups' service to Sunday school, and I enjoyed the uplifting feeling that enveloped me while singing hymns with the whole congregation. I loved thanking God "For the beauty of the earth, for the glory of the skies, for the love that from our birth, over and around us lies."[2]

My grandmothers were more spiritual than my parents. When we stayed overnight with our grandmother Lena Marie Searing Bergman in Arcadia, we sat on the living room floor and played cards or dominoes while she listened to "The Christian Science Hour" on the radio or read from Mary Baker Eddy's *Science and Health.* My mother didn't discuss Christian Science with us except to say that she had felt embarrassed to have been seen as different in school. Our grandmother did not speak to us about her faith, but we knew that she did not believe in doctors or medicine and that she almost always had a positive attitude toward life. We listened with her to stories of miraculous faith healings, and we were quiet while she read and prayed. Although we got the measles, mumps, and chicken pox, my brother and I were rarely sick and often had perfect attendance records at school. We were raised with the assumption of health.

Grandmother Bergman had been raised on a farm in Michigan and

---

1. In my individual chapters, I capitalize pronouns used to refer to divinity in order to call attention to the male gender of the traditional God and the disruptive power of the female gender of the Goddess.
2. The refrain of this rousing hymn is, "Lord of All to thee we raise, this our hymn of grateful praise." With "Lord of All" changed to "Goddess in All," this hymn still expresses my theology. http://www.hymnsite.com/lyrics/umh092.sht.

was sturdy and tall—I got my height from her German, English, and Huguenot ancestors. Her garden was filled with roses and camellias that always graced her table at much-loved family meals. I can still picture her with a pitchfork in her hand turning over compost in the fruit orchard. Her pantry was filled with fruits and jellies she had preserved. When we were small, there was no fence separating her backyard from the arboretum, and she often took us on special walks through it. Even after the fence was put up, a hole emerged, and she showed us how to crawl through it with her. Grammy taught us that the world was a beautiful and magical place, and the peacocks that spread their tails for us in her garden and the peahens that brought their chicks to her back door convinced us that this was indeed true.

When I was six years old, I went to stay with my father's parents in San Francisco. What was supposed to have been a short visit expanded into a whole summer. My grandparents adored me, and I was probably glad not to have to share the attention of adults with my younger, demanding brother. My grandmother Mary Rita Inglis Christ, who took the name Mae to avoid becoming Mary (the mother of Jesus) Christ, was delicate and tiny, much less than five feet tall. Though I would far surpass her in height, I inherited her Irish freckled skin, strawberry blonde hair, blue-green eyes, and facial structure. She and I would get up early to drive my grandfather Irv to the train he took to work in the mornings. Afterward, we sometimes went to Lake Merced to see the ducks. Other mornings we went to the Pacific Ocean beach where my little grandmother removed her shoes and stockings to run with me in the sand. Usually we also stopped at the local Catholic Church where my Nannie lit a candle in a blue glass vase for Uncle Bobby who was away in the Korean War. We sat together in the still dark church while she prayed the rosary on her lavender faceted beads. She spoke often of the Blessed Virgin. I delighted in her love of life and absorbed her faith without the need of many words.

Discord and Death

My childhood world was not all rosy. Our father was strict and sometimes angry, and I was an awkward, quiet, tall, smart child who didn't always feel at home with the other kids, especially after we moved to a lower-middle-class neighborhood where being smart was not valued, but playing spin the bottle at the age of nine and ten out of the sight of parents was. In the church we joined after our move, I was not fully accepted by the other girls because we were newcomers in town and lived on the wrong side of the railroad tracks. Their mothers refused to let me join their daughters' Girl Scout troop. My father's family time was given to Little League and incessant baseball practice limited to my brother only. My mother had a baby when I was ten years old, and I threw myself into the role of second mother. I fed and diapered the new baby and treated him like he was my own. I started babysitting and prided myself on being able to put five kids under the age of five to bed all by myself.

When I was fourteen, my world fell apart. My father's mother was diagnosed with cancer and kept alive on tubes much longer than she should have been. My mother vowed that this would never happen to her. Our maternal grandfather, who had been bedridden at home for a long time following a stroke, died the same year. Then the second baby my mother and I were planning to raise together died without even having been brought home from the hospital. The only time I saw him was in the open coffin. While he was dying, I promised God that I would never fight with my other brother again if the baby lived. God did not answer my prayer. My mother fell into a depression that lasted for years. Before I was nineteen, I had also lost my other grandfather in a fire, and one of my only two aunts to a tragic prescription drug overdose. While other students may have felt carefree in their college years, I was struggling to understand the meaning of a life that included so much death.

Entering into Western Culture

I went to Stanford because my high school guidance counselor told my parents that, with my grades and scores, I should not go to the local junior college, but somewhere that would challenge my mind. My parents would not let me apply out of state. I got into Stanford with a partial California State Scholarship, worked summers as a telephone solicitor, and my parents made personal sacrifices to pay the difference. When they sent me to college, my parents expected me to get a teaching credential, teach for a few years before I got married, and have a profession to fall back on if my husband died. I probably would have followed this path if I had started dating in my first year of college. I did not know any women who spoke about careers and had no ambition to have one. However, because I was over six feet tall, extremely shy, and quite overwhelmed by college, I did not start dating, much to my chagrin. I also was totally unprepared for Stanford, because I had never even heard of Plato and Aristotle or the Middle Ages. At some point, I looked around me and saw that most of the other girls were dating as well as getting better grades than I was. I did not know how to make the boys ask me out, but, I figured, at least I could improve my grades. Because of my lack of background, this meant studying pretty much night and day and during weekends and holidays.

I spent six months of my sophomore year at Stanford-in-Florence. There we read Augustine and Dante and visited Christian churches and immersed ourselves in Christian art. I think living in close connection to monuments of Christian history gave me an embodied sense that Christianity had a history and was much more than the social club it often seemed to be for my parents and their friends. I spent many hours in churches meditating on the frescoes and praying where so many others had prayed before me. I did not always know the questions I was asking, but I sensed that all the feelings of my heart were taken up into the shadowy darkness.

The book that most impressed me that year was Augustine's

Confessions.[3] I not only read it but reread it many times. I identified with Augustine's search for God and his struggle to understand God's presence in his daily life. His was a spiritual passion combined with intellectual acuity and persistence that I had never experienced before. Until that time, I had often been told that I was thinking too much or that my questions about God didn't really matter. Reading Augustine, I began to see that there was a way to combine my grandmothers' spiritual intensity with my own intellectual curiosity and desire to make sense of the questions that had arisen in my life. I wanted to know why my brother had died, and I wanted to understand why I so often felt alone with my questions. In Augustine, I felt a spiritual kinship that I did not find in church or among my contemporaries at Stanford. I would continue to read and reread Augustine during my undergraduate and graduate school years and use him as a model for bringing full engagement of mind and body, heart and head, to theological questions. In those days, I understood Augustine's struggle with the flesh symbolically and did not identify with the woman he viewed as an impediment to his relationship with God.

Falling in Love with God

When I returned to Stanford, I enrolled in an Old Testament course for background. The professor presented the Bible as a book that raised more questions than it answered. I fell in love with the Old Testament and idolized the professor who taught it. During Christmas break, I learned enough Hebrew on my own to join the second quarter class. I suppose I thought that if I could read the Bible in God's own language I would understand Him better. I was fascinated with a God who did not stay in the heavens but came down to earth to enter into a covenant with His own special people. The Hebrew people did not hold God in awe, but dared to converse and even disagree with Him. God's people, our professor loved to point out, were a "stiff-necked people," but God loved them anyway. God's on-again off-again relationship with His

3. Augustine, *Confessions*, trans. R. S. Pine-Coffin (London: Penguin Books, 1961).

people echoed my father's stormy relationship with me and seemed to hold a clue to the relation of life and death. I needed to believe in a God whose "steadfast love" was overflowing with a compassion that stemmed his judgment and anger. I needed a God whose love conquered death. I was deeply moved by the prophets' understanding that God cares about the widow at the gate and that the proper way to worship Him is to care for her. In my senior year, I chose to write my thesis on "Nature Imagery in Hosea and Second Isaiah" because the images of the trees of the field clapping their hands on the day of redemption resonated with my grandmothers' and my spiritual feelings in nature. At my oral, I stumbled when I was asked if the prophets' imagery was a pathetic fallacy. I did not know the meaning of the term, and it had never crossed my mind that the prophets did not intend to say that God loves and redeems trees as well as people. As in my reading of Augustine, I failed to recognize the significance for me as a woman of the fact that Hosea portrayed female sexuality as source and symbol of evil.

I studied theology with Roman Catholic Michael Novak, whose *Belief and Unbelief*[4] shaped my future study of religion. Novak defined a process of understanding he called "intelligent subjectivity" that incorporates mind, body, and feeling. I was extremely lucky to have been taught to question the widely accepted ideal of scholarly objectivity so early in my career. Through Novak, I was introduced to the idea that all thinking is situated in personal, cultural, and historical experience, long before standpoint theory became popular. Novak gave me the tools I would need to combine head and heart in my studies and to resist ideas and ways of thinking that did not make sense in my own life. He also taught me that theologies need to be open to the world, as advocated by Vatican II. In *Belief and Unbelief,* Novak asked existential theological questions—questions about the meaning of life. He entered into dialogue with Dr. Rieux of Albert Camus's *The Plague*.[5] For Dr. Rieux the pervasiveness of death and undeserved suffering in

---

4. Michael Novak, *Belief and Unbelief* (New York: New American Library, 1965).
5. Albert Camus, *The Plague*, trans. Stuart Gilbert (New York: Alfred A. Knopf, 1948).

the world argued against the existence of God. The questions raised in *The Plague* haunted me too, and I would introduce students to them when I began teaching. Novak came very close to agreeing with Camus, but in the end concluded that because we humans "sometimes love and understand," there is reason to believe in a God who loves and understands.

My favorite theologian was Martin Buber, whose idea that the meaning of life was found in the I-Thou relationship with other human beings, with nature, and with God[6] affirmed my own feelings about life and the view of God I was learning through my study of the Old Testament. Although I had not studied or practiced Judaism, my view of God was in many ways as Jewish as it was Christian. When I prayed, I prayed to God the Father who I understood as the God of the Old Testament. I had very little interest in the New Testament or in Jesus as a teacher, prophet, companion, or savior. I suspect that I never really understood the Trinitarian controversies when I later studied them because I had always been a radical monotheist—I believed God is one, not three-in-one. Though I had become consumed by the study of religion, I did not ever think of becoming a minister, and I certainly did not want to become a dowdy spinster director of Christian education, the only role in the church I had ever seen a woman hold. I had declined confirmation in the Presbyterian Church at age thirteen because I felt the other kids were just going through the motions. I thought we should have been taught something about other denominations and religions before making a choice for one of them. While studying religion in college, I decided to become confirmed in my home church. I remember telling our intellectual and liberal minister that I was not sure if I believed in the divinity of Christ. He said not to worry too much about that. When he confirmed me, he asked if I believed in God, but he did not ask me if I believed in Christ. I will never know if this was intentional or accidental on his part.

During my junior year, my advisor in the Humanities Honors

---

6. Martin Buber, *I and Thou*, trans. Ronald Gregor Smith (New York: Charles Scribners' Sons: 1958 [1937]).

Program called me into his office to discuss my future. With my grades, he said, I could go on to graduate school anywhere I wanted and with a full fellowship. He suggested that I should become a university professor of religious studies, not a high school teacher. When I told my parents my new plans on the way home from the airport at spring break, my mother started to cry, saying I would never get married if I pursued my studies. My father said curtly that I had wasted the money he spent on my education. He did not speak to me or look at me again for the whole two weeks I was home. This was a time when fellowships for graduate study were plentiful, and a year later, I managed to win both Danforth and Woodrow Wilson fellowships, which paid for my entire graduate education, plus living expenses.

Civil Rights, Poverty, and an Unjust War

During college, I had not ventured far from the conservative values of my upbringing. Because I was so focused on my studies, I was pretty much unaware of the Civil Rights Movement and the social upheaval that was going on around me. I spent the summer after graduation on the Stanford campus where I took a class in the German language. My best friend and I rented rooms in a fraternity. One of the guys with whom we hashed—served food in the dining hall to the other girls in exchange for our board—was staying there too. He decided to make it his summer project to convert me from conservative to liberal, a journey he himself had made. He plied me with information and managed to convince me that caring about civil rights and poverty and opposing the war in Vietnam followed from the Christian value of loving your neighbor as yourself and the American value of freedom and justice for all. Before I left Stanford to go back east for graduate school, I had become deeply committed to ending discrimination, poverty, and the war in Vietnam. Needless to say, my parents were horrified.

And Then There Was Yale

When I left Stanford for Yale with the intention to study and later teach Old Testament, and to discuss religion and values with my students, as the Danforth Fellowship specified, I brought my religious and value commitments with me. I believed in the loving and punishing, but ultimately merciful, God of the Old Testament who I understood to be kind of like a really good version of my father and my professors. I was a Christian, but had no ethnic, family, or other strong ties to my Protestant denomination. Presbyterianism was not the religion of my grandparents or cousins; I had experienced class discrimination within my church, and my family no longer went to church because my father refused to listen to sermons about civil rights. I remembered my grandmother's devotion when I learned of the new Catholicism of Vatican II. I was open to the idea of faith healing that my other grandmother had so deeply believed in and sensed that I owed my good health in part to her influence. I was deeply moved by the writings of Jewish theologian Martin Buber, and also by hearing Abraham Joshua Heschel give a series of lectures at Stanford during my senior year. I felt a deep sense of spiritual communion in nature, particularly in my grandmother's garden with the peacocks, flowers, and fruit trees, and in the Pacific Ocean. I loved to float into a state of trance on calm days, and to feel the exhilaration of being part of the ocean's power when the waves were high and I dove under them at the last minute. I was still seeking to understand why there was so much death in my life. I was newly committed to working for social justice and to ending the war in Vietnam and considered this a religious as well as a moral commitment. The dean of the Stanford Chapel, B. Davie Napier, who had relocated from Yale, told me that I would have a hard time at Yale because the Yale professors didn't like women. I remember brushing this warning off, saying, "I am as smart as any man and surely they will recognize my intelligence." More than thirty years later, I met B. Davie again, and we had a good laugh.

I was accepted into the Old Testament program in the religious studies department at Yale. My Old Testament professor at Stanford had been one of the first to practice a method of interpreting the Bible that analyzed the literary conventions of Hebrew poetry and narrative as a way of uncovering the meaning of the texts. This approach is common today but it was not then. At my first meeting with the professor I had come all the way across the country to study with, I got my initial taste of the reality behind B. Davie Napier's warning. Bright-eyed and bushy-tailed and all of twenty-one years old, I told the professor that I had used literary methods to explore nature imagery in the prophets in my senior thesis and said that I hoped to continue this kind of work in graduate school. When I finished, the man I had chosen to become my new mentor replied, "Well, Miss Christ, then why didn't you go into comparative literature?" This was the first, but not the last, time I was simply erased at Yale.

When I met the other students in Old Testament, I found myself among a group of married men with devoted wives who were helping to support their husbands' studies by working as secretaries, and who copyedited, proofread, and typed their husbands' manuscripts. These male graduate students had all completed divinity degrees before beginning graduate school, so they were quite a bit older than I was. There was only one other woman in the religious studies program, Margaret Farley, a Roman Catholic sister, still in partial habit and ten years older than I was, who did not socialize with the other students. There were a few male students who had also come into the religious studies program without a divinity degree, but they were in the minority and none of them were in Old Testament. I had entered a culture defined by men of another generation—who were not baby boomers and who were not as concerned as I was about social issues—and I was effectively the only woman among them. I would learn that both professors and students imagined California to be a strange place—the summer of love, of which I had not been part, had just concluded. For them, the West Coast was not the kind of place a scholar should come from.

At that time, graduate students socialized primarily with other graduate students. Although my colleagues and I were in the newly formed religious studies department, there were still strong links with the Divinity School. Most of our classes were at the Divinity School; we used the Divinity School library as much as the larger Yale library; we ate lunch in the Divinity School dining hall; and we celebrated the week's end at the sometimes drunken Friday afternoon sherry hour hosted by the Divinity School for faculty and students. Theoretically, the Divinity School professed religion and the religious studies department studied it objectively, but in practice, these divisions were blurred. Almost all of the students in the religious studies program already had degrees making them eligible for the Christian ministry or priesthood. While Stanford had accepted women undergraduates from its inception, Yale was very much a gentleman's club. The architecture of the main campus is medieval; imposing oil portraits of men in academic robes hang on cold stone or dark wood-paneled walls; the arm-chairs and couches are leather; and in my day, men in suits sat on them smoking cigars and pipes. The faculty had very little experience teaching women. There were no women undergraduates and only a small number of women graduate students. Although I never had a woman professor at Stanford and can remember having been assigned to read only one book by a woman—Hannah Arendt's *Eichman in Jerusalem* in my freshman year—I was not consciously aware of having been discriminated against. Male professors recognized my mind and encouraged me to break what was still the pattern for Stanford women students of getting married right after graduation or pursuing grade school or high school teaching degrees.

Not feeling there was anyone I could talk to in the Old Testament program, I found that there were at least a few students not married, closer to my age, and, like me, having trouble adjusting to Yale, in the theology program. Two of them were Roman Catholic, and we, along with two Protestant male divinity students, had many long late-night conversations in which we tried to figure out what was wrong with the way theology was being taught at Yale. Because I could speak with these students, I changed my area of study to theology part-way into my first semester. I did not have as extensive or the same kind of background in theology as most of the other students, and I did not understand the abstract conversations they were having with the professors in the classroom. For example, when a student asked if a certain theologian was making "an ontological or merely an aesthetic statement," I did not know what this meant. By the next year, I was beginning to grasp that the professors and the other students were debating the orthodoxy of theological statements by testing them against lines in the sand they perceived to have been drawn by favored theologians like Karl Barth and Martin Luther. In the meantime, I was flailing. At the end of my first year, the Director of Graduate Studies wrote to the director of the Danforth Foundation that he had serious reservations as to "whether I had a theological mind" that could grasp the subtleties of theological questions. I was put on probation by the Danforth Foundation, which was quite humiliating, and a senior professor was asked to assess my capacity to study theology at the end of the summer.

The professor assigned to this task determined that I did have a theological mind and was making progress toward filling in the gaps in my knowledge, and so I was able to keep my fellowship and continue my studies. However, my theological comments and questions continued to be ignored in the classroom and at social gatherings. When I spoke of my interest in Martin Buber, I was told that he was "only a poet" and that his ideas about having an I-Thou relationship with a tree made no sense. If I countered that maybe theology needed more poetry in order to connect it to real life, the conversation continued as if I had said nothing. A new Director of Graduate Studies later told me that it was his opinion that, after I caught up with the other students, I surpassed most of them. He said that, because I was asking a different level of questions than they were, they still thought of me as ignorant. This was a comfort, but a small one, as it did not change the day-to-day reality, which was that I was being ignored and silenced.

Women and Theology Don't Mix

During the time I was at Yale, my skirts were short, as was the fashion of the day, and I rode around on a red Vespa motor scooter. Most of the faculty and student wives dressed and acted in ways that would not call attention to themselves or their sexuality. I was also over six feet tall. When I walked into a room, I was consciously and unconsciously perceived as a threat to a world that these men had simply assumed was theirs. Their response was to categorize me as a sexual being (I was once introduced as "our department bunny") and to erase my mind. I was to discover that the male graduate students were making bets in the dining hall about "where she will sit today." One of my friends frequently fell down and feigned to worship me when I passed him in the hallways. I had never received so much attention from men before and it was flattering.

At the same time, I was told by these men that of course "no one expected me to finish my degree" and that even if I did, "all of the jobs should go to men who have families to support." The generic male, as in "when a man finishes his PhD," was the common language of both faculty and students. If I protested, I was reminded that I probably would not finish my degree anyway. I dated two of the other students in my first year, fell in love with one of them, and lost my virginity to the other. They both dumped me. I was being told in every way possible that I could not be a woman and a theologian. There was such a disconnect between the way I was perceived and the way I perceived myself that I came close to suffering a mental breakdown.

I found a clue to what was going on in a most unexpected place. While reading the assigned passages from medieval theologian Saint Thomas Aquinas's *Summa Theologica*, I decided to see what the great man had to say about women. I discovered that he agreed with the philosopher Aristotle that women were defective males and that our defect was a lesser rational capacity.[7] With respect to each other,

---

7. Thomas of Aquinas, *Summa Theologica*, trans. Fathers of the English Dominican Province (Cincinnati: Benziger Publishers, 1947), question 92.

woman was body, and man was mind. Thus, the revered theologian opined, man was to rule over woman as a man's mind rules over his body. I was both angry and excited to discover that theology itself was the key to understanding what I was experiencing. If the men with whom I was studying accepted the view that, in relation to me, they were mind and I was body, then everything fell into place. When I tried to explain to the men who were ignoring my mind why they were doing it, they erased me again. "No one thinks that way anymore," they replied. With that simple statement, they killed three birds with one stone. They excused the history of male dominance in theology; they refused to look at their current attitudes; and they made me feel stupid.

When I discovered that Karl Barth had said a version of the same thing in the twentieth century,[8] I was told, "No one reads that part of his work because it isn't important." Two years later, I wrote a class paper in which I argued that Barth's view of the man-woman relationship is important. Barth used the same model of hierarchical domination combined with love—sometimes described as love patriarchalism—to explain the "man-woman" and the "God-man" relationship. The relation of man and woman is one of love, but man is to have "initiative, precedence, and authority." In relation to each other, man will be *A* and woman will be *B*. Barth used exactly the same words to describe the relation of God to man. I argued that if we criticized Barth's understanding of the man-woman relationship, we ought to think about criticizing his understanding of the God-human relationship as well.[9] My paper demonstrated beyond a doubt that I could think systematically. The professor (the same one who had earlier concluded that I did have a theological mind) glanced at my paper and flicked it aside.

8. Karl Barth, *Church Dogmatics III*, ed. G. W. Bromily and T. F. Torrance, trans. J. W. Edwards, O. Bussey, and H. Knight (New York: T & T Clark, Ltd., 1958).
9. The original typescript of this paper, written in 1970, is in the Alverno College Library Archives and can be viewed online at https://feminismandreligion.files.wordpress.com/2015/07/barths-theology-and-the-man-woman-relationship-by-carol-p-christ-1971.pdf; a version of it distributed as "A Question for Investigation: Karl Barth's View of Women" by the Conference of Women Theologians, Alverno College, 1971 is also in the Alverno College Library Archives and can be viewed online at https://feminismandreligion.files.wordpress.com/2015/07/a-question-for-investigation-christ.pdf.

Roman Catholic Years

While I was at Yale, I regularly attended the Roman Catholic folk mass on Sunday evenings at the Yale Roman Catholic chapel. This mass was attended by a motley group of graduate students who understood that, though we were at Yale, we certainly were not part of the white American Protestant elite of one thousand male leaders that Yale professed to turn out every year. I first went to the mass with a boyfriend, but after we broke up, I stayed in the community. The mass was part of the movement to open the church to the world. The priest faced us, the bread and wine were real, and we hugged each other after taking communion. A common meal with wine followed the service. I loved the Easter drama. I experienced it as an enactment of God loving the world so much that He was willing to share its suffering and to redeem it from death—set within nature's drama of the celebration of rebirth and renewal in spring. One of the priests, who was also an older male graduate student in our program, knew that I was not a baptized Catholic, and he loved to joke that while many baptized Catholics did not "practice" (go to church regularly), I was a "practicing Catholic." After *Humanae Vitae* prohibited the use of contraception among Catholics, Father Bob delivered a sermon telling us that we should follow our consciences. This was the time of post–Vatican II optimism when we really believed that the Church would change. I liked the ritual of the Roman Catholic mass, and it felt good to be part of a Church that was far larger and more diverse than the Presbyterian churches I had known or, for that matter, the Yale Chapel ministered to by the flamboyant political activist and white male elitist William Sloane Coffin Jr. Being a practicing Catholic connected me to my paternal grandmother and to half of my family, including relatives on Long Island with whom I celebrated Thanksgiving and Easter.

Questions That Could Not Be Asked

I was voicing my newfound political convictions every chance I could. I wore a button with a drawing of a starving baby in Biafra on my raincoat. I asked the faculty what they were doing to end racism, poverty, and an unjust war. I attended graduate student meetings to discuss the politics of the New Left, and I took the bus with other students to Washington to take part in demonstrations. I supported Eugene McCarthy's antiwar bid for the presidency. When Yale went on strike in support of Black Panther Bobby Seale's assertion that he could not get a fair trial, and against the war in Vietnam, I was in the thick of it. Like others of my generation, I really did believe that the world could change. My desire to change the world was not something that came and went depending on what else was going on in my life. It was an ever-present reality that colored everything. I felt the bombing of Vietnamese villages and the horror of rats crawling across beds in ghetto apartments in the United States, almost as if these things were happening to me—and I also felt responsible for the fact that they were happening to others. I believed that we could end racism, poverty, and war in my lifetime. I was disillusioned to discover that most of the Yale faculty was not as outraged about injustice or the war as I was. For the most part, my professors believed that theology and politics should be kept separate.

Protestant Neo-orthodoxy reigned at the Divinity School and in the Department of Religion. Karl Barth's assertion that man could not save himself or know anything about God apart from revelation was the unspoken standard by which other theologies were judged. As I had studied theology with a Roman Catholic theologian who, like his mentor Aquinas, had a great respect for the human mind and for human beings' capacity to act morally, Barth's view was foreign to me. However, as everyone else seemed to revere Barth, I tried to adopt his way of thinking. When Barth died in the first semester of my second year of study, I played Mozart's *Requiem* for a whole day in honor of Barth's love for Mozart,[10] and then put Barthianism behind me. However, my failure to grasp the Barthian standpoint in the beginning

10. Barth's statement, "It may be that when the angels go about their task praising God, they play only Bach. I am sure, however, that when they are together *en famille* they play Mozart," was fondly repeated in the classroom. See Barth, *Wolfgang Amadeus Mozart* (Eugene, OR: Wipf & Stock, reprint 2003).

and my rejection of it shortly thereafter probably contributed to the long-lasting perception of many of the faculty and students that I just did not "get" theology. Indeed it was reported to me that, when the faculty read my comprehensive exams at the end of my fourth year, they expressed astonishment that "she really can think theologically."

During my graduate study, I did not find a mentor or become attracted to any particular theological school. Buber remained the only theologian I really loved, and his idea that life is based in relationship felt true to me. Charles Hartshorne spoke on campus while I was there, and I read and deeply appreciated his *The Divine Relativity*.[11] I intuitively understood that God is the most relational of all relational beings. This would have been the perfect time for someone to point me in the direction of process relational metaphysics, but no one did. I was also attracted to Tillich's notion that God is the "Ground of Being," and especially to his books *The Dynamics of Faith* and *The Courage to Be*,[12] but no one encouraged me to focus on Tillich either. So I floundered, yet kept trying to find ways to articulate my sense that the theologies we were studying were overly abstract and disembodied. I was drawn to theology and literature as a way of bridging the gap between religion and life, but Yale did not have that specialization.

Because I was being treated as a body but not a mind and was often told that I was too emotional, I sensed that issues concerning body and mind and mind and feeling also needed to be addressed, but I had not a clue where to begin. I was part of the sexual revolution too, and it raised questions about the relation of spirituality and sexuality that I wanted to think about. I had been taught that it was the will of God that sex should occur only within marriage. I was reading and hearing and acting on the idea that love was free and that expressing sexuality inside or outside of marriage was a good thing—perhaps even a holy act. Needless to say, nothing we were reading in class helped me to understand the choices I was making.

11. Charles Hartshorne, *The Divine Relativity: A Social Conception of God* (New Haven: Yale University Press, 1948).
12. Paul Tillich, *The Dynamics of Faith* (New York: Harper & Row, 1957); *The Courage to Be* (New York: Harper & Row, 1962).

During the summer following my second year at Yale, I read Elie Wiesel's *The Gates of the Forest*,[13] which someone had recommended as a book in theology and literature. Elie Wiesel was not well-known, and I had not heard of him. I was totally unprepared to enter into his world. I had heard about the concentration camps and had read Anne Frank's *The Diary of a Young Girl*,[14] but I had not faced the reality that was the Holocaust, nor had I connected what happened to the Jews to my belief in the God of the Old Testament. Reading *The Gates of the Forest* challenged my theology to the core. I believed God was powerful, loving, and good, and I believed that He had a special relationship with the Jews. For me, Christianity did not change the covenant; it only added new people to it. Wiesel's story affected me deeply, because, like his character Gregor, I believed that God would never abandon His chosen people. Yet it seemed that He had. Wiesel's anger at God seemed perfectly justified, and his questioning of God followed a pattern established in the Old Testament that felt right to me. Wiesel also wrote about how the performance of the Christian Easter story in annual passion plays provoked violence against the Jews for killing Christ. I loved the Easter rituals, and I knew that the Jews were blamed in most of them—including the Roman Catholic mass I attended. Both my belief in God and my religious community were called into question.

Something in Wiesel's story also provoked a profound release of all the emotions that had built up in me during my first two years at Yale. Wiesel's character Gregor was haunted by the laughter of a man called Gavriel—a laughter that arose from the absurdity of trying to understand the Holocaust, a laughter that refused to be defeated by overwhelming sadness. During the days when I was reading *The Gates of the Forest* for the first time, Gavriel's laughter overtook me. I laughed at everything that had made me cry during my first two years at Yale and gained power over my suffering. When I tried to speak to my professors about the theological questions Wiesel had raised for me,

---

13. Elie Wiesel, *The Gates of the Forest*, trans. Frances Frenaye (New York: Avon Books, 1966).
14. Anne Frank, *The Diary of a Young Girl*, trans. B. M. Mooyaart (New York: Bantam Books, 1952).

I was silenced again. "I would have thought the crucifixion of Christ answered that," was the answer I received in a tone that indicated "no further discussion necessary." For me the question was by no means resolved, and I became increasingly sensitive to anti-Judaism in worship and theology.

Feminism

Feminism came into my life in the spring of 1969, at the end of my second year of graduate school. Several other women had entered the Yale graduate program in religious studies the previous fall. I met some of them right away and began to feel less alone. Judith Plaskow had entered that year too, but we did not have any of the same classes, and as she was soon engaged and about to get married, she did not socialize much with the other students. We did not get to know each other well until the next year. I was still the only woman in most of my classes, and I was still not being heard. The Director of Graduate Studies, who remained perplexed by me and my questions, suggested that his wife Violet Lindbeck, who was ABD (all but dissertation) in the ethics program, might be able to help me. Vi, who taught at a local junior college, had been in the graduate program at Yale more than fifteen years earlier. She had not finished her dissertation because her advisor had not approved what she had to say about the ethics of women's equality. Vi was the first avowed feminist I had ever met. She gave me xeroxed copies of several of the earliest second-wave feminist articles and urged me to read them. They were a lifeline. These articles helped me begin to see that it was not me, but Yale, that was crazy! A year or so later, Vi, Judith, and I initiated a series of lectures at the Divinity School on Women in Church and Theology. I remember reading out a very long list of Rosemary Radford Ruether's accomplishments before she spoke, because I wanted to make sure that she was taken seriously as a scholar.

In the fall of that year, Judith and I joined the Yale Women's Alliance, a group of graduate student women from different departments who met together to share our experiences and to empower each other.

Though we felt isolated in our separate departments, we were the first group of the baby boomers to enter graduate school, and this was probably the first time in the history of Yale that there were enough women enrolled in doctoral programs at one time to form a group. The women in the other departments told stories of being silenced that were similar to my own. I remember listening to an intelligent and very beautiful woman with long black hair named Barbara Packer tell her story, and thinking, I know she is not crazy, I know she is not stupid. I began to feel that it might really be true that I was not crazy or stupid either.

Shortly thereafter, radical feminist Naomi Weisstein spoke at the Law School. I went to hear her lecture with Judith and her new husband Robert. I cannot remember what Weisstein said, but I do know that her words were electrifying and that Judith and I felt like the ground had opened beneath our feet. Later that year, Judith and I participated in picketing Morry's, a male-only club for Yalies, and I took part in a guerilla theater skit in the dining halls urging the newly admitted undergraduate women to "drop the mop." The next year, Judith and I examined our lives and spoke of feelings we never even knew we had in a consciousness-raising group. In my final years at Yale, I would help to found the Academic and Professional Women's Ad-Hoc Affirmative Action Committee that brought the US Department of Health, Education, and Welfare to Yale in the spring of 1972 to investigate charges of sex discrimination. At the close of the investigation, we were told by one of the inspectors that Yale would be found guilty. Over the summer, the top ten universities convinced the government that they should be excluded from affirmative action investigations because their hiring was highly specialized, and the charges were dropped.[15]

In our first year as feminists, Judith and I invited the graduate student women in the religious studies department, who now totaled ten including us, to tea. We did this with some trepidation, because

15. The "Model Affirmative Action Plan" that Caroline Whitbeck and I wrote as part of this effort was distributed by WEAL (Women's Equity Action League) for many years afterwards.

most of the other women had told us they had no interest in feminism. Surprisingly, the one issue we all agreed upon was the insult conveyed by the lack of a women's bathroom in the stacks of the Divinity School Library. The next day, a group of us marched through the library, locked ourselves in the men's bathroom, and put plastic flowers in the urinals. By the end of the day, the dean of the Divinity School liberated the bathroom with a white flag of peace and installed a revolving sign to indicate whether it was in use by men or women.[16] The women in the department bonded after that, and we worked together to improve our lot. As Judith and I became known as feminists, we also became the targets of jokes, comments, winks, chortles, and guffaws that dismissed feminism.

When Judith and I began to speak with each other, the walls came tumbling down. We called each other almost every day to deconstruct the experiences of being silenced that were still occurring regularly. Our mantras were, "What you said made sense," and "No, you are not stupid or crazy." And yes, we had to keep saying that to each other because we were still being made to feel that we were stupid and crazy by the faculty and the other students. When we talked about theology, Judith and I discovered that we shared a great deal beyond the fact of being women in a male-dominated PhD program. We both felt connected to the Hebrew Bible. We both loved Buber. We both found Wiesel's writing powerful and felt the problem of evil as raised by the Holocaust was one of the most important theological questions of our time. We both felt that theology should not be separated from the real problems of people's lives or from political issues like racism, poverty, and war. We both were interested in theology and literature as a way to bring concreteness into what seemed to be a very abstract study of theology. We also sensed that we were about to embark on a very long conversation about theology and women. There would be no turning back.

Like other women without role models, Judith and I sought

---

16. I published a tongue-in-cheek account of this action called "The Liberation of the Shit Room" in *Pulling Our Own Strings: Feminist Humor and Satire*, ed. Gloria Kaufmann and Mary K. Blakeley (Bloomington, IN: Indiana University Press, 1980).

validation of our thoughts and feelings in literature. This was more difficult then than it is now because, in the absence of a women's movement, very few women had been able to write about the deepest questions of their lives. Doris Lessing's Martha Quest stories, *Children of Violence*, spoke to us. *The Four-Gated City*, the last book of the series, became a kind of touchstone.[17] Like Martha Quest, we were seeking to find ways to live as women outside the conventional roles of lover, wife, and mother. Like Martha, we had sensed connection to a power greater than ourselves while alone in nature. Like Lynda, the visionary madwoman, we often felt that we were banging our heads against a wall, not only because we felt caged in, but also because we could feel truth pressing toward us from the other side. Like Martha, we knew that we were "children of violence," and we were seeking ways to end its cycles. Like Martha, we often fell victim to the internalized violence of the "self-hater." For a number of years, whenever one of us was trying to articulate something that was bubbling up from inside, as soon as we put it into words, we would suddenly remember that "Martha said that." We understood that Lessing had anticipated our feelings because she was exploring the social and historical forces that had created the "currents" and "energies" that were shaping our lives.

Religion, Story, and Theology

Though I never found a mentor at Yale, I did find two mentors outside of it. I was lucky that my Stanford professor Michael Novak—at that time he was still liberal theologically and politically—had accepted a position at Old Westbury College on Long Island, New York. He invited me to be his research assistant during one of my graduate school summers to help him on a book called *Ascent of the Mountain, Flight of the Dove*[18] in which he attempted to redefine religious studies as personal and social and deeply connected to the stories we tell about our lives. Michael was quite clear in conversations with me that this book was a response to the abstract and disembodied way he had experienced

17. Doris Lessing, *The Four-Gated City* (New York: Bantam Books, 1970).
18. Michael Novak, *Ascent of the Mountain, Flight of the Dove* (New York: Harper & Row, 1971).

theology in his graduate days at Harvard. He understood the problems I was having at Yale, and he valued my opinions. Toward the end of the summer, he urged me to borrow his family's car and drive into New York City to take part in the historic "Women's Strike for Equality" march in celebration of the fiftieth anniversary of the passage of the women's suffrage amendment. The experience of working with Michael helped to begin to restore my badly damaged confidence in myself.

My work with Michael Novak on the relation of story and religion enabled me to articulate what was wrong with a study of religion that ignored the questions that arise in the stories of people's lives—the study of religion as I knew it at Yale. At about the same time, Stephen Crites wrote a groundbreaking essay called "The Narrative Quality of Experience"[19] that made a similar point. I met Crites through connections the Danforth Foundation fostered, and he also took me under his wing. I would draw on the theories of Novak and Crites about the relation of stories and theology when I wrote my dissertation "Elie Wiesel's Stories: Still the Dialogue"[20] and again when I wrote my first book *Diving Deep and Surfacing*.[21] The embodied theological method of this book also owes a debt to the conversation about religion and stories. It was very important for me to have the support of these two men at a very difficult time in my life.

If I had to sum up my years of study at Yale in a few words, I would say that, while the theology professors and most of the other students were discussing Neo-orthodoxy and its variations, I had come expecting a broader conversation that included Vatican II and Judaism, and other religions as well. I was looking to discuss the meaning of life, while my colleagues were content to probe the orthodoxy of doctrines. I thought that nature must have a place in the divine plan, but they were convinced that it did not. I liked the way Buber wrote evocatively

19. Stephen Crites, "The Narrative Quality of Experience," *Journal of the American Academy of Religion* 39, no. 3 (September 1971): 291–311.
20. Carol P. Christ, "Elie Wiesel's Stories: Still the Dialogue" (PhD diss., Yale University, 1974). Available from ProQuest (University Microfilms).
21. Carol P. Christ, *Diving Deep and Surfacing: Women Writers on Spiritual Quest* (Boston: Beacon Press, 1995, [1980, 1990]).

or poetically and thought other theologians should do the same, while they thought Buber was confused and confusing and that theology was just fine the way it was. I was asking why the body and feeling had been excluded from theology, while they thought it was a good thing that they had been.

One way or another, I did learn to think theologically and systematically while I was at Yale, skills I built upon when I later wrote my own feminist systematic thealogy. I probably have Julian N. Hartt to thank for that. Although he too was influenced by Neo-orthodoxy, he was one of the few members of the faculty who did not think that the sun rose and set over the *Church Dogmatics* of Karl Barth. He had a wide ranging intellect that included interests in theology and literature. In his introductory course in systematic theology, Hartt introduced the three *C*'s of systematic thinking: coherence, comprehensiveness, and consistency.[22] A theological worldview must "cohere" with the world as we know it, incorporating knowledge gained through other disciplines, including science, and making sense of our own experiences and those of others. A "comprehensive" theology must be able to interpret or illumine a wide range of knowledge and experiences—in principle everything imaginable. The ideas in a "consistent" theology must hold together from chapter to chapter. For example, a theologian cannot say that human beings are completely free in one chapter and that they are entirely a product of social conditioning in another: these insights must be brought together in a theory that human freedom is real, but not unlimited. Hartt explained systematic thinking in a memorable way when he consoled students who were baffled by Tillich's obscure language. "Don't worry," he said, "Tillich runs the same team through in different colors in every chapter. If you didn't get it this time, you will get it the next." The "team" that can be recognized in every chapter is a set of basic insights

---

22. This is how I remembered the three *C*'s when I wrote about them in this chapter. In *Rebirth of the Goddess*, xv, I remembered them as clarity, coherence, and consistency. Thinking back, I am pretty sure the third *C* was comprehensiveness, not clarity. Theologians have not regularly criticized their obscure language systems. In our final chapter, Judith and I add clarity as the fourth *C*.

that are used to discuss every particular topic: the team is the "system" in "systematic" theology.

Feminist Theology

Judith and I took our comprehensive exams at the same time. Due to student organizing that I had spearheaded, the format of the exams had been changed to allow more weight to be given to the individual interests of the students. Judith and I decided to propose to write our history of Christian doctrine exam on the "History of Christian Attitudes toward Women." The professor in charge of this exam was well-known to be a grandiose egotist, narcissist, and a dyed-in-the-wool patriarch, but still we were not prepared for his response. We had barely opened our mouths to share the bibliography we had compiled when he slammed his fist on his desk and bellowed, "Not for me, you're not!" And that quite simply was the end of that. We were so angry that we decided to review the proposals of the other students and to choose the easiest one in order to get the exam over with as soon as possible. The easiest one turned out to be "Interpretations of the Adam and Eve Story in Genesis as a Foundation for the Doctrine of Original Sin." We did not realize it at the time, but this topic is in fact a major foundation of theological attitudes toward women. In choosing it, we beat the old man at his own game! We also provided a firm base for our subsequent work in feminist theology.

I was one of twenty women invited to the first Conference of Women Theologians, held at Alverno College in the summer of 1971. This was a historic meeting that marked the beginning of a conversation about women and religion that continues to this day. Most of us had not yet discussed this topic in a group of women. Some of us were eager to do so, while others were not so sure there was anything to discuss. At one of our sessions, we debated Mary Daly's recently published "After the Death of God the Father."[23] Several of the women stated vehemently

23. Mary Daly, "After the Death of God the Father," originally published in *Commonweal* (March 12, 1971) and reprinted in Carol P. Christ and Judith Plaskow, eds., *Womanspirit Rising* (San Francisco: Harper & Row, 1979), 53–62.

that God language was not important. I was the most enthusiastic advocate of Daly's insight that when God is male, the male is God. This conference, where I met feminist foremothers Valerie Saiving and Nelle Morton, sister theologian Rita Gross, and reconnected with Sallie McFague, gave me confidence that asking questions about women and theology was really important. I had two papers in the packet distributed after the conference, my essay on Karl Barth, and a second coauthored with Emma Trout, called "Alternative Images of God: Communal Theology" on female language for God.[24]

At the Alverno Conference, I proposed that we found a women's caucus in religious studies—as had been done in other fields. Because I was one of the few women at the conference who had attended the meetings of the American Academy of Religion, I was asked to take charge of this. My first task was to call the executive director of the AAR, Harry Buck. Harry greeted our proposal with enthusiasm, and not only offered us space at the next annual meeting, but also offered to send me a list of all the members whose names were not obviously male, so that I could contact them.[25] When I arrived at the hotel for the AAR meeting in Atlanta in the fall of 1971, I was waylaid by a man who asked me if we were intending to propose a woman for president of the AAR. That thought had not crossed my mind, but when the forty or so women who answered my letter met together, it quickly became part of our plans. We packed the poorly attended AAR business meeting and elected Christine Downing president.[26] We also passed proposals to establish a Working Group on Women and Religion at the next annual meeting and to establish a Task Force on the Status of Women. I was elected cochair of the Women's Caucus with Sallie McFague and

24. For the Barth essay see n. 9. The essay I wrote with Emma Trout can be found in the Alverno College Library Archives and viewed online at https://feminismandreligion.files.wordpress.com/2015/07/alternative-images-of-god-carol-p-christ-emma-trout-1971.pdf; in it we argued that God must be addressed using female as well as male images, including Mother as well as Father; it was a foreshadowing of work to come.
25. Harry Buck became an enthusiastic proponent of the study of women and religion, going on to found the periodical *Anima*, which published early work by many young feminists in religon (myself included) who went on to become major voices in the field.
26. The AAR rules were changed immediately to a mail ballot in order to prevent grassroots nominations from the floor from ever happening again.

Elisabeth Schüssler Fiorenza. The task force established a Registry of Women in Religious Studies and sent it to departments of religion so that they would know they could hire women; it also proposed an open listing of positions in the field. This was the beginning of the end of "the old boy system" of hiring by word of mouth.

Beginning My Dissertation and Leaving Yale

After finishing my exams, I began thinking about my dissertation topic. I wanted to do something in theology and literature, because I was interested in the idea that theological questions could be expressed in a more personally meaningful way through story. I began discussing possible topics with Julian Hartt. Though he did not see (or perhaps saw but did not feel the need to change) structures that prevented women from pursuing careers in the field of religion and in society at large, Hartt was more open-minded that his colleagues. He recognized a bright mind even when it was found in a woman's body, and he had already directed Sallie McFague's PhD dissertation in theology and literature.[27] He was probably the only member of the faculty who would have agreed to supervise our unconventional dissertations. Because I had been so profoundly moved by *The Four-Gated City,* I asked Hartt if I could write about women's spiritual quest in Doris Lessing. He said no. I next proposed Elie Wiesel's Holocaust theology as expressed in *Night, Dawn, The Accident, The Town beyond the Wall,* and *The Gates of the Forest*, the memoir and four novels he had published at that time. Hartt said yes, and my dissertation topic was decided. For the next three years, I would be struggling to reconcile God and the Holocaust. My own faith was on the line with this topic because I did not know if I could continue to believe in a God who had failed to save His own special people. Like Wiesel, I was often paralyzed by the enormity of the subject and, for years, felt that even to begin writing would somehow betray the victims.

While I was working on my dissertation, I accepted a position as

---

27. Julian Hartt's daughter told me that her father belatedly became a feminist more than three decades later, a few years before his death (email communication).

assistant professor of religion at Columbia University in the City of New York. As I prepared to leave Yale, I had begun to question many of the convictions that had brought me to the study of religion and theology. While I had entered Yale with a firm belief in the God of the Old Testament whose covenant was renewed in Christianity, I was not at all sure that I still believed in Him. I had stopped attending the folk mass regularly because I literally could not stomach the male language for God and the congregation: it made me feel like throwing up. Exodus and the prophets had shaped my faith, and I had studied them intensively in the original Hebrew. As my commitment to ending war grew, I could not help but notice that the very parts of the Bible I most loved portrayed God as a man of war who stretched out a mighty arm to free His people from the Egyptians in Exodus, and in the prophets to punish them for not attending to the poor. I began to cringe whenever I heard God described as a warrior. My own country was engaged in what I felt was an unjust war, and God Himself seemed to be part of the problem. I knew that other Americans felt they were fighting this war with God on their side. Unlike many of my contemporaries, I would never be able to divorce what would come to be called the liberating actions of God from the violence with which He achieved his ends. I also could no longer participate fully in the Easter drama because I did not want to be part of a liturgy that blamed the Jews for killing Christ. The Holocaust had raised the question of whether God had abandoned the covenant. I asked again and again: How could a powerful and good God allow six million of His own people to be killed? If God had a mighty arm, there could have been no better time for Him to have used it. I had not received answers from God to any of my questions. In addition, I was still looking for ways to bring connection to nature into theological discussions and to address the relation of body and mind, mind and feeling, sexuality and spirituality. I was beginning to suspect that the question of women and women's experience would increasingly become the lens through which I would view absolutely everything.

When I left Yale, I would have called myself a Christian because

Christianity was still the larger context in which I was asking questions about God. But I had no interest in seeking out a worshiping community, because worship itself threw salt on my wounds. I remained profoundly committed to the study of religion, to the pursuit of truth, and to answering all of the questions I had raised. I had suffered what must accurately be called profound and repeated psychological abuse during my five years at Yale. There would be a long road of healing ahead. I had also experienced the joy and exhilaration of a community of women hearing each other into speech.[28] I was ready to leave Yale and begin a new chapter in my life.

---

28. Nelle Morton, *The Journey Is Home* (Boston: Beacon, 1985), 17, 29, and passim.

2

Stirrings

Judith Plaskow

I am certain that I was born a theologian. Did God call me to be one? That formulation does not fit with my concept of God. But my early interest in theological questions set me apart from my family and from most other Jews in the suburban Long Island community in which I grew up. They seemed to assume or ignore the existence of God rather than discuss or reflect upon it. I have a very sharp memory from when I was seven of being at the children's service at our Reform temple on Yom Kippur and being deeply moved by both the words and music of a particular hymn:[1]

> Lord, what offering shall we bring to the altar when we bow?
> Hearts, the pure unsullied spring, whence the kind affections flow.

---

1. In my individual chapters, I try to avoid using male or female pronouns when referring to divinity, because for me divinity is not personal and therefore has no gender. However, when I quote from the Bible, traditional texts, or the liturgy, I do not change traditional language or the capitalization conventions found in the texts I cite.

Willing hands to lead the blind, heal the wounded, feed the poor,
Love embracing all mankind, charity with liberal store.
Teach us oh thou heavenly king how to show our grateful mind.
This accepted offering bring love to thee and all mankind.[2]

These lyrics still echo powerfully in my head sixty years later, and they capture both the particular picture of God and the inseparable connection between God and ethics that was so meaningful to me as a girl. Although my parents did not expect me to return to the temple for the afternoon High Holiday service—my attendance at the children's service was enough to justify my staying out of school—I promised God that I would come back. When I got home, a neighbor from across the street invited me to play with her, and I said that I couldn't because I had to go back to temple. When she pressed me, I replied that I had promised. Promised who? she asked. I told her that I had promised God, but I can still feel my awkwardness and sense of embarrassment in doing so. I could not have explained the feeling, but I know I had the distinct impression that it was peculiar to make a promise to God and equally peculiar to talk about it.

I have few memories of my preadolescent musings about God. I went to Hebrew school for twelve years, twice a week between fifth and eighth grades, and I know that I was looking for something that it rarely provided and that I could not have defined. By the time I was in ninth grade, I was the only student who was still attending of my own free will, and although it was basically a waste of time, I kept hoping that I would learn something substantive. In the fifth through seventh grades, I had one wonderful teacher, Louis Brasz, who had a powerful influence on me. At least one year, we studied Bible with him, and he was the only one who spoke to us seriously and with respect about many important topics. To me, he radiated integrity and spiritual depth. He had been a colonel in the army during World War II and may even have been involved in liberating the concentration camps. It was from him that I first learned about the Holocaust. I don't

---

2. I think I am conflating two hymns with the same lovely melody, one from the 1952 Reform *Children's Service for Rosh Hashanah* and one I learned somewhat later but cannot track down.

remember what he said, just that he talked to us with real passion but also with care not to overwhelm and frighten us. He also encouraged us to imagine ourselves into various biblical narratives. He gave us a homework assignment, for example, to write about how it felt to be part of Joshua's army circling Jericho. When I adopted the perspective of a terrified young recruit, he commented that my interpretation was not borne out by the text, but he also acknowledged my effort and thoughtfulness. As I think about it, he provided me with my first experience of doing midrash, though he never taught us that word.

My father grew up in an Orthodox Jewish home, my mother in a Conservative one; but, when I was three years old and we moved from Brooklyn to Long Island, they chose to affiliate with a Reform temple. In addition to attending Hebrew school, I occasionally went to synagogue on Friday nights with my family. Our classical Reform congregation used the Union Prayer Book, which was deeply meaningful to me at the time. Although as a young adult I would come to reject it as merely a series of excerpts from the traditional prayer book, there was something about the purity of its image of the Lord God Father and King that I found deeply appealing. Our rabbi was a thoughtful orator who frequently addressed topics of current ethical concern. When, wearing a long black robe (white on the High Holidays), he raised his arms each week for the priestly benediction at the end of the service, he definitely seemed like God to me. At the same time, I thoroughly disliked him on a personal level (perhaps an important influence on my conception of God!). When I was being picked on by my seventh-grade Hebrew teacher, he took the teacher's side without listening to me, and I felt that he never "got" or cared to get the fact that my interest in religion was deeper than that of my classmates. Years later, he would say under my marriage canopy that he had always hoped that a rabbi would come out of the congregation and now, at last, he had a *rebbetzin* (rabbi's wife)—without the slightest awareness that I had wanted to be a rabbi. In fact, he was opposed to the ordination of women because it was "against tradition," even though our congregation's practices violated Jewish tradition in a dozen different ways.

One thought about God stands out for me during my preadolescence. I must have been about nine years old when, as I was lying in bed one night, it suddenly occurred to me that God might be a woman. I remember thinking, "We don't know what God is; there's no reason God couldn't be a woman." I felt overcome by a kind of giddy exuberance as I hugged the thought to myself. I lay awake for fifteen or twenty minutes just turning the revelation over in my mind. I don't recall playing with the thought any time but that night. It was only when I began to think about female God-language as a graduate student that the incident came back to me. I suspect the idea was too incompatible with all I had absorbed from my surroundings for me to have been able to hang onto it for more than a moment.

Adolescent Questioning

In my junior high and high school years, I began to think about God and other theological questions in a more sustained and focused way. When I was twelve, one of my closest friends and I began reading and talking about the Holocaust. We devoured the diary of Anne Frank, spent hours discussing it, and also read a number of other books that we seem to have picked up haphazardly.[3] This reading inducted me into the mystery of human evil. The issue of God's involvement in the Holocaust troubled me, but my more urgent questions were how human beings could be capable of such evil and whether Jews could have been Nazis. I pondered whether there was something in the German character that led to the Holocaust or whether it was simply historical accident that Jews had been the victims and not the perpetrators. I felt a deep sense of relief that I did not need to know the answer to that question. It was a moral privilege to be a victim, I thought, a conviction that was very central to my Jewish identity for many years. My sense of relief was not wedded to a sense of moral superiority, however, because I did not

---

3. Anne Frank, *Anne Frank: The Diary of a Young Girl*, trans. B. M. Mooyaart (New York: Pocket Books, 1952).

know whether Jews would have refrained from acting similarly if given the opportunity. This uncertainty was possibly the first expression of the theme of ambiguity that has been so central to my work. For me, it was never a simple matter of us and them, the good guys and the bad guys. Rather, reading about the Holocaust made me aware of what human beings are capable of.

Significantly, at the same time I became obsessed with the Holocaust, I was also learning about the Civil Rights Movement. I was ten when Governor Faubus mobilized the Alabama National Guard to prevent the integration of Central High School in Little Rock. One of the most vivid memories of my childhood is of my father pointing to Faubus's picture on the front page of *Newsday* and telling me that Faubus's resistance was shameful because everyone is equal regardless of the color of their skin. I had seldom heard my father speak with such passion, and I felt that he was treating me as person rather than a child and passing on something of great importance to him. I followed the developments of the Civil Rights Movement in the papers and on television, and I also devoured the novels of Howard Fast, which dealt with both American slavery and a range of freedom struggles around the world. This reading reinforced what I was learning about the Holocaust in that it made clear the many ways throughout history that some groups of human beings have oppressed others. In seventh grade, I won second place in the grade-wide speech contest for a speech comparing segregation in the South with apartheid in South Africa. One phrase from the speech sticks in my mind: "We must hold hands with you, South Africa; we must work together. . . . " Thus, again, evil for me was never just about "them;" I always saw it as something that was close to home.

As a twelve-year-old, I felt out of sync with my peers because I thought a lot about topics deemed too serious for young people. By the time I was in high school, my interest in the Civil Rights Movement was widely shared, but I continued to keep my religious questions to myself. I have memories of walking down the street debating the existence of God in my mind or thinking about the origin of evil and

God's connection to it. One Friday evening, I went with a friend to the Ethical Culture Center (a center for humanist faith) and heard a lecture on the inadequacies of Anselm's and Aquinas's proofs for the existence of God. I found it enthralling, way beyond anything I had ever heard in temple—much to my mother's annoyance. The lecture gave me food for thought for a long time. Sometime in ninth or tenth grade, I began to think about becoming a rabbi. Of course, there were no women who were rabbis at the time, and I had no idea whether the Reform rabbinical school would even accept woman. I decided that, since I wasn't completely certain that there was a God, it wasn't appropriate for me to apply. It might be acceptable for a man to have some doubts and still be a rabbi, but not for a woman. I do not know where I got this idea, but I had an instinctive sense that a pathbreaker would have to have more impeccable credentials than those who could take access for granted.

I left high school for college with a deep interest in theological questions and also in social justice. In line with the classical Reform perspective of the time, I had been taught that Judaism was ethical monotheism, an understanding that made deep personal sense to me. I might not have been certain whether I believed in God, but I definitely knew that, if there was a God, then God was One, a Lord and Father who watched over us and who demanded concern for others. At the same time, rather contradictorily, I was reluctant to attribute my concern for justice to my Jewish upbringing. In the summer of 1963, I went with a good friend and her family to the March on Washington for Jobs and Freedom. It was an amazing day that remains vivid in my memory: getting up at 4:00 in the morning and walking to my friend's house in the predawn darkness; marching down the Washington, DC streets in step with tens of thousands of others; listening to the amazing words of Martin Luther King Jr., which, in the moment he was speaking, seemed to make real the dream he was talking about. When we got back, my rabbi wanted me to give a talk to the Hebrew school about how I had gone to Washington because I was a Jew. I indignantly refused, arguing that I had gone to Washington as a human being and a concerned

American. Probably it was just my way of acting out against what I experienced as the rabbi's imperiousness and lack of interest in my experience because in retrospect, it seems entirely clear to me that my going to Washington was a perfect enactment of my conception of Judaism.

The Emergence of a Vocation

Perhaps because I rarely shared my interest in religious questions with others, no one suggested to me that I should look for a college with a religious studies department, and so I went to a school—Clark University—without one. It was in college that I first encountered the works of Elie Wiesel. Reading *Night,* and then over time, his early novels—*The Accident, Dawn, The Town beyond the Wall,* and *The Gates of the Forest*—brought together the two themes of God's existence and the mystery of evil that I had spent so much time contemplating in high school.[4] Wiesel's anger at a God from whom he was unable to disconnect shaped my own understanding for many years. I loved the integrity and deep irony of his story in *The Gates of the Forest* of three rabbis in Auschwitz who put God on trial for the Holocaust and find him guilty, only for them to be chosen for extermination the next day.[5] I can no longer reconstruct exactly when I read each book or when certain constellations of ideas began to come together for me, but the notion of holding God accountable for Jewish suffering resonated deeply with a theme that I had always loved in the Jewish tradition: the idea that the covenant entails mutual obligations and that, just as God can hold the Jewish people responsible for their sins, so God is also bound by God's covenantal promises. In the mid-1970s, I gave a *d'var Torah* (talk on the Torah) on the second day of Rosh Hashanah on the story of the binding of Isaac in which I argued that God's command to Abraham to sacrifice his son illustrated "the amoral sovereignty of

4. Elie Wiesel, *Night,* trans. Stella Rodway (New York: Bantam Books, 1960); *Dawn,* trans. Frances Frenaye (New York: Avon Books, 1960); *The Accident,* trans. Anne Borchardt (New York: Hill & Wang, 1962); *The Town beyond the Wall,* trans. Stephen Becker (New York; Avon, 1964); *The Gates of the Forest,* trans. Frances Frenaye (New York: Avon, 1966).
5. Wiesel, *Gates,* 195.

God"—an important theme in Jewish tradition, from Isaiah's "I form light and create darkness, I make weal and create woe" (45:7) to Wiesel's sad, angry, and ironic tales. Though this was some years after college, it expressed an understanding of God that had been percolating in me for a long time—since my first encounter with Wiesel. My favorite line from Albert Camus's *The Plague*, another novel that spoke to me deeply during my college years, also captured this understanding. Explaining his response to the plague to a comrade in struggle, the protagonist Dr. Rieux says, "Since the order of the world is shaped by death, mightn't it be better for God if we refuse to believe in him and struggle with all our might against death, without lifting our eyes to heaven where he sits in silence?"[6]

While my theological development in college was being nurtured by my reading, my Jewish experiences were fairly minimal. Clark had no Hillel rabbi, though the lively and interesting Orthodox rabbi in Worcester occasionally came to campus and invited students to attend his synagogue. My closest friend and I went to a Conservative synagogue for the High Holidays our first year, but the services were boring and, despite our reluctance to attend a congregation where we had to sit behind a *mechitzah* (barrier separating women and men), we went to the Orthodox synagogue for Yom Kippur our sophomore year. At the end of the N'eilah (concluding) service, I had an epiphany that was to shape the rest of my life. At the climactic moment in the service when the congregation recites the central affirmation of Judaism, "Hear O Israel, the Lord our God, the Lord is one," followed by "Praised be His glorious sovereignty throughout all time," repeated three times and "The Lord alone is God," repeated seven times, it suddenly occurred to me that, although I could not be a rabbi, I could get a doctorate in religious studies. Given the context, this was clearly a religious and career decision merging in a blaze of clarity that left me excited, tingling and absolutely certain that I had found my path. I find it interesting in retrospect that, while I had agonized about whether I could be a woman and a rabbi, it never crossed my mind that my being

6. Albert Camus, *The Plague*, trans. Stuart Gilbert (New York: The Modern Library, 1948), 117–18.

a woman was any barrier to getting a doctorate in religious studies. As I was to discover, my femaleness would be the defining aspect of my graduate school experience, though obviously it would not prevent me from earning my degree. But then, I also could have been a Reform rabbi and, had I gone to rabbinical school straight from college, I would have been the second woman to be ordained, not the first.

Study Abroad

I started college with the intention of spending my junior year abroad, and I especially wanted to go to England to study Shakespeare. I come from a family with a deep love of Shakespeare that was passed on to me, and, until my senior year, I was an English major. The professor at Clark who taught Shakespeare had a reputation as a tedious fool, and I had no intention of taking with him what I thought of as the most important course in my major. In the end, I did not go to England but to Scotland, to the University of Edinburgh, for what turned out to be one of the most wonderful and important years of my life. Students at the university took only three intensive year-long courses, and I took an excellent Shakespeare course plus the first- and second-year courses in biblical studies. I got an overview of biblical criticism in first ordinary (the first-year course) at the same time that I was reading selected biblical books in depth in second ordinary. It was an incredibly rich and exciting year intellectually and personally. There were only a dozen students in second ordinary, and we met in the biblical studies library next to the professor's office. The male students were all headed to divinity school and ministry in the (Presbyterian) Church of Scotland, and we used to study together in the library and break for tea in the middle of the afternoon. Our teacher often joined us, and so I came to know both him and my fellow students quite well.

There were several aspects of this experience that were formative for me. I had grown up in a synagogue in which the rabbi had contempt for Orthodoxy. If a congregant had covered his head during services, he would have been asked to remove his kippah (head covering traditionally worn in synagogue by Jewish men). Anyone who was to the religious right of the rabbi, he thought of as a benighted fool. When my mother told him (a few years later) that I was going to marry a man who was Sabbath observant, he suggested that she take me to a psychiatrist. Now, suddenly, I was interacting regularly with committed, "orthodox" Christians whom I both liked and admired and who spoke forthrightly about the importance of faith in their lives. My friendship with them forced me to reexamine my attitude toward religious orthodoxy and to reflect on the thinness of the version of Judaism with which I had grown up. Several times in the course of the year, I attended Presbyterian services and found the hymn singing stirring and the centrality of the word and the absence of iconography consonant with the Protestantized "high Reform" Judaism in which I had grown up.

I discovered fairly quickly that my professor—David Stalker—often "adopted" a visiting American female student, and I was it for that year.[7] At the beginning of the semester, I asked him what Bible to buy for his courses, and he offered to meet me at the bookstore to look over the possibilities. I had never had a professor willing to help me in this way, and he became an important mentor to me—indeed, the only real faculty mentor I ever had in all my years of education. If I lacked the background necessary to understand what we were doing in second ordinary, he was available to explain. When I commented that I wished I could read the Bible in Hebrew, he began giving me weekly lessons in biblical Hebrew and we eventually read the Joseph stories together. He invited me to go with him when he preached at a rural church one Sunday, and I had a wonderful Scottish country Sunday dinner with people who read the sermons of Paul Tillich for pleasure and found them deeply nourishing.

Edinburgh was my first taste of the Christian academic environment that would be my home for virtually my entire career. Being Jewish was completely anomalous in Scotland; it was not among the replies people expected to hear when they asked me my religion. I began to

---

7. In our age of heightened awareness of sexual harassment and misconduct, I am aware that this sounds peculiar, but I experienced it as entirely innocent at the time.

understand what I was protected from by my New York upbringing: that Jews are a tiny people in the world. I was very aware of my Jewishness; yet, as my ability to feel comfortable in church indicates, I found that I could function in a Christian universe and fairly easily translate the issues it raised into my own terms. I had a "feel" for the Christian tradition and, without in any way seeing it as my own, I could comfortably walk in and out of it. It was in Edinburgh that I began to get a sense that the theological questions that so interested me were more generic than specifically Jewish and that I could come at them in a variety of ways.

Of all the biblical books I studied in the course of that year, the one that most engaged me was the book of Job, which remains my favorite book in the Bible. I had first encountered *Job* when I was reading Thornton Wilder's *The Bridge of St. Luis Rey* in high school, and my English teacher asked me to read *Job* and talk about its connection to Wilder.[8] I remember distinctly coming into class completely puzzled about what God's answer to Job had to do with the rest of the book and expecting that the teacher would explain what I had obviously missed. When I had the opportunity to study the book in Edinburgh, I realized that my confusion actually masked an important insight: God's speeches *don't* have anything to do with the question Job was asking.[9] Job, like Elie Wiesel, was a man profoundly connected to God through his overpowering anger. Job undergoes a moral education in the course of the book, moving from raging about his own personal undeserved suffering to recognizing larger patterns of injustice in the world and the absence of any link between people's behavior and reward and punishment. God overwhelms Job with his might when God answers him out of the whirlwind but completely ignores the issue of justice that Job so eloquently raises. I saw God as a great bully saying, in effect, it's my game; if you don't like it, take your marbles and go home. My

---

8. Thornton Wilder, *The Bridge of San Luis Rey* (New York: Avon, 1955).
9. Many scholars feel that God's speeches do not respond to the rest of the book because they are a later pious interpolation. Although I do not disagree, I also think it is important to understand the book as a narrative whole, as it has come down to us. That is the approach I take here and in chapter 8.

immersion in the book of Job fed my fascination with the problem of evil as well as my understanding of God as responsible for evil along with good.

In the summer after my junior year, I joined my best friend from Clark for a month in Israel. This was my first visit, and it was just after the Six Day War, an extraordinary moment to be there. A profound sense of optimism pervaded the country. "Now we have land we can return in exchange for peace" was on everyone's lips. Coming from the year in Scotland in which I had developed a new respect for serious religious commitment and practice, in Israel, I was able to try on a new relationship to Judaism. My month there marked the first time I ever observed a traditional Sabbath. I ate Friday night dinners with friends, sat around and sang songs, went for walks on Saturday and soaked in the atmosphere of a largely quiet Jerusalem. On Tisha B'Av (the fast day commemorating the destruction of the Temple), I joined the throngs walking to the Kotel (Western Wall of the Temple), which did not yet have a barrier preventing women from praying there alongside men, and I shared in the extraordinary jubilation and also contradiction of mourning the destruction of the Temple while standing at its outer wall. Sometime during that month, I went to synagogue at the Reform seminary in Jerusalem and found that Reform Judaism no longer spoke to me. It is difficult for me to explain that realization other than to say that I wanted a Judaism that was more thoroughly grounded in historical Jewish belief and practice. My Reform upbringing remained important to me in that it enabled me to affirm liberal Judaism as normative and to understand the necessity of picking and choosing from tradition. But my year in Edinburgh, and perhaps studying *Job*, had taught me that faith is powerful and complex in ways not captured by a vision of Judaism as ethical monotheism. I wanted a richer and deeper way to be a Jew.

Transitions

When I returned to Clark for my senior year, I changed my major to philosophy to prepare for graduate school in religion. I took a course on the philosophy of science, for which I read Thomas Kuhn's *The Structure of Scientific Revolutions*[10] and learned, in the professor's words, that "we have facts only within frames." I copied the phrase over and over at the top of my notes, absorbing it with great excitement and feeling it shift my way of looking at the world. I fell in love with existentialism and applied to graduate school intending to study existential philosophical theology. In the spring, I had an excellent seminar on Heidegger's *Being and Time* and—my interest piqued by my time in Scotland—did a directed readings course on part of Paul Tillich's *Systematic Theology*.[11] I wrote a paper comparing Heidegger's and Tillich's ontologies, a topic I thought I would pursue in graduate school. When I got into the University of Chicago, Columbia, and Yale, I spent a month agonizing about whether to go to Yale or Columbia. My immersion in existentialism added enormous weight to the decision as I was painfully aware that each choice we make cuts off numerous others. I was pretty sure I would be happier at Columbia (probably a correct perception), but I could not turn down the prestige of Yale. When a faculty member I spoke with at Columbia said to me, "You got into Yale; why would you come here?" the choice of Yale seemed inevitable.

The summer between college and graduate school, I took theological German at Union Theological Seminary, and also registered for a course on Jewish theology at the Jewish Theological Seminary (JTS) across the street. I had hoped to enroll in an introduction to rabbinic literature as well, but dismissed the possibility because it partially overlapped with the hours of my course at Union. At a party on the first night of the JTS Summer Institute, however, I met Robert, the instructor of the rabbinics course, a seminary graduate who was about to go to Brown to get a doctorate in Jewish studies, and, as it turned out, my future husband. He was happy to have me sit in on his class as far as I was able, and so I transitioned to Yale with a summer of Jewish

10. Thomas Kuhn, *The Structure of Scientific Revolutions* (Chicago: University of Chicago Press, 1962).
11. Martin Heidegger, *Being and Time*, trans. John Macquarrie and Edward Robinson (San Francisco: Harper & Row, 1962); Paul Tillich, *Systematic Theology*, 3 vols (Chicago: University of Chicago Press, 1951–63).

study that interested and absorbed me far more than theological German.

Yale and Its Discontents

Yale. What can I say about it? It is striking to me that, in contrast to the vividness of my memories of college and even high school, my time at Yale is very much a blur. I had not been a religion major in college, and virtually everyone in the graduate program in religious studies came in with an MDiv (or BD, as it was called at the time); I think Carol, one male student, and I were the only ones who entered with just a BA degree. People threw around names such as Barth, Bultmann, and Bonhoeffer that were entirely unfamiliar to me, and I felt completely overwhelmed and had no idea what was expected of me. An advanced graduate student tried to direct me into foundational courses, but I chose my classes foolishly and ended up feeling like an idiot who would never be able to keep up. I had come to graduate school ready for a profound intellectual and spiritual adventure, eager to immerse myself in the literature and questions that I cared about most deeply, and, perhaps, even to find a concept of God that I could truly affirm. What I found was that, as opposed to my peers in college, who had delved into ideas with great energy, eagerly exploring the implications of what we read, my fellow graduate students had no interest in talking about whether particular theologies worked or were meaningful. They simply wanted to prove that they were not only smarter than everyone else in the class but also than the theologians we were studying. Quite a few years after I graduated from Yale, I was in New Haven for a bat mitzvah and walked around downtown between the ceremony and the evening party. I found myself feeling spacey and slightly ill and wondered whether I was coming down with something. Then I realized that I was simply feeling what I had felt the entire time I was at Yale. This feeling provides the context for everything else I say.

I know that, in reality, I must have learned a great deal in graduate school because I came into the program knowing virtually nothing about theology or religious studies and, in three years, managed to acquit myself reasonably well on my comprehensives and go on to write an important dissertation. But what I remember is not moments of illumination or exciting conversation but anxiety and numbness. I felt that my fellow graduate students managed to take ideas that were potentially important and exciting and bludgeon them until they were lifeless. My first semester, I took a class on theological hermeneutics with Hans Frei, and I had no more idea at the end of the semester than I did the first day what the title of the course meant. I recall one of the students in the class giving a presentation on Schleiermacher in which he talked about "asymptotic parabolas." I hadn't the faintest idea what he was talking about. (Of course, I realize in retrospect that he probably didn't either!) Robert and I were becoming seriously involved by that point, and I spent a lot of the class writing my future married name on the top of my notes and wondering if I should drop out and become a housewife. Second semester, I took courses on Heidegger, Tillich, and Kierkegaard and was delighted to be focusing on thinkers whom I had come to Yale to study. But while I certainly felt less at sea concentrating on three individuals, none of the courses addressed the existential questions that I had come to graduate school to explore. Interestingly, I took Heidegger in the philosophy department with the faculty member who had been the teacher of my professor at Clark. Although I could see that he was brilliant and had far more depth of understanding of *Being and Time*, there was none of the energy and excitement in his class that had characterized my Heidegger course in college. The one course I took my first year that allowed me to raise religious questions was a Divinity School seminar on the book of Job. But here, I found myself in an equally uncomfortable position: while I wanted to raise critical questions about my favorite book, the other students wanted to focus on the I-Thou relationship that God supposedly established with Job. When we read and critiqued each other's final papers, I was faulted for having so many footnotes that I couldn't possibly appreciate the book's religious meaning. But for me, there was no division between the intellectual and the spiritual. Deeper intellectual understanding was not only a path to deeper religious understanding, but the process of intense intellectual exchange itself had an important spiritual dimension.

Central to my alienation from and sense of disorientation at Yale, and more significant than my lack of preparation, was my being a woman and a Jew. I went to speak to Judah Goldin (the only faculty member teaching Jewish studies) the week I arrived in New Haven to discuss whether I could take one of his courses. His first words to me—just before he announced that there was no such thing as Jewish theology—were, "Oh, I didn't know that Yale was now admitting women to the undergraduate college." Mustering my best twenty-one-year-old sense of dignity, I informed him that I was a graduate student. His comment, however, put me on notice that my femaleness would be an issue at every moment and in every class I took. Since Carol and I were the only two female doctoral students in modern theology, I was frequently the only woman or one of very few women in any class. It is difficult to describe the sense of constant surveillance to which we were subjected. On one occasion in our theological hermeneutics class, when the room was very warm, Hans Frei turned to me and asked my permission to remove his jacket. This meant-to-be-gallant gesture singled me out and highlighted my "only woman" status. On another occasion when I was struggling with Schubert Ogden's *The Reality of God*,[12] a book that I found challenging both intellectually and personally, a fellow graduate student literally patted me on the head and said, "Don't worry your little head about it." More generally, there was a pervasive male-club atmosphere about the graduate classroom. Almost all the men smoked pipes, and when a male student was asked a question, he would take a pinch of tobacco, put it in his pipe and tamp it down, and then lean back, take a puff and respond, giving himself a good three minutes to reflect before answering. After we became feminists, Carol and I used to joke that we should take out our make-up cases and apply a little lipstick while thinking about a question. It would have been an exact analogy, though clearly not

---

12. Schubert Ogden, *The Reality of God: And Other Essays* (New York: Harper & Row, 1966). Ironically, I found this book so challenging because it was my first encounter with liberal theology.

one that would have been acceptable in the graduate school culture. Also, after we became feminists, we were constantly badgered and subjected to a steady stream of belittling remarks. Whenever we came to a door, for example, a couple of the men would say, "Should we open it? They'll be mad at us if we open it." Though the legal concepts of sexual harassment and a hostile work environment had not yet been developed, that was exactly what we experienced.

I certainly was not teased in the same way about being a Jew—though my Kierkegaard professor, Paul Holmer, not knowing who I was, once made an anti-Semitic comment in class—but my being other as a Jew was initially a lot clearer to me than my otherness as a woman. I went to Yale because I wanted to study *theology*, and at the time, there was nowhere to go to study Jewish theology. I didn't realize that, even if I applied to a graduate program as opposed to a divinity school, the course of study would still be shaped entirely by the Protestant divinity school curriculum. I found that my fellow students expected me to know things as a Jew that I had never learned and that, in the Yale department, I had no way to learn. They would ask me what Heschel or Buber said about a topic as if I came out of the womb familiar with the works of these thinkers. In fact, I struggled mightily in many of my courses to connect whatever issue we were studying with Jewish material. In my course on Kierkegaard, for example, I compared his conception of the teleological suspension of the ethical with rabbinic midrash on the binding of Isaac. For theological hermeneutics, I investigated whether there was any parallel within Jewish thought to the quest for the historical Jesus. Ultimately, I wrote my systematic theology exam on the issue of the historicity of revelation in four modern Jewish thinkers. In preparation for that exam, I read the galley proofs of Assyriology professor William Hallo's long-awaited translation of Franz Rosenzweig's *The Star of Redemption*. Widely recognized as one of the most profound works of Jewish theology in the twentieth century, the book was not at that point available in English.[13] I remember sitting on a high stool in the Assyriology library incredibly excited to have access to such amazing material and, at the same time, very lonely, because there was no one with whom to discuss it. I felt myself a stranger in a very strange land.

In many ways, my real life during my Yale years took place outside the classroom. My relationship with Robert quickly became serious, and we spent many weekends together either in Providence or New Haven. He was a Conservative rabbi (although he never had a congregation) and an observant Jew. I began to take on greater observance, an interest and commitment that stemmed partly from my involvement with Robert but also from my year in Edinburgh and my month in Israel. I began attending traditional Sabbath morning services at Yale Hillel, sitting at the back of the chapel at a service led by male undergraduates. I learned to prepare Sabbath meals before sundown and not to turn on lights or travel. After Robert and I married, I started to keep a kosher home. So at the same time I was immersed in a totally Christian environment at school, I was becoming a more serious Jew and learning more about Judaism, both through conversations with Robert and through study and practice. My life was filled with inconsistencies that were sometimes creative and sometimes frustrating and painful. The first serious argument Robert and I had was about whether to shelve the New Testament with the Bible or the history of Christianity. Needless to say, it was I who took the former position. Having begun my Bible studies in Edinburgh, and studying Protestant theology at Yale, it made perfect sense to me to think of the New Testament as the Bible. Although I gave in to Robert because he cared more than I did, my inability to understand why he was so upset points to the contradictions with which I was living.

An Emerging Feminist

These contradictions were greatly magnified when I became a feminist in the fall of my second year of graduate school. This was the year that Yale admitted women as undergraduates and increased the entering class to 1250 students so that the College could still graduate "one

---

13. Franz Rosenzweig, *The Star of Redemption*, trans. William W. Hallo (New York: Holt, Rinehart, and Winston, 1971).

thousand male leaders." The university prepared for the education of women by putting full-length mirrors in the bathrooms and adding a gynecologist to the health center staff. Three female graduate students in the social sciences called a meeting to discuss how it was that we had been at Yale for eighty years and no one had noticed. The energy of the gathering was high, and we decided to keep meeting and to call ourselves the Yale Women's Alliance. We engaged in both consciousness raising and activism, exploring from many angles the contradictions we experienced between our hopes and plans for our lives and the expectations of us as women. We talked about our relationships with our mothers and our fathers, our lovers, husbands, and children. We shared what it was like to be girls headed for graduate school at a time when that was an unusual choice for a woman. One of the most powerful moments in the group for me was realizing that we had all been told that we were "too smart for girls" and advised to downplay our intelligence if we wanted to catch a man. So many of the issues that I and the others had thought were our own personal problems we could now see were products of our socialization as women. We were living "the personal is the political" before it became a slogan, in that we repeatedly made connections between issues in our own lives and broader social structures. It was an incredibly heady, exciting, and difficult journey as we "heard each other into speech,"[14] not avoiding the painful places in our lives. I remember one evening when a woman with children kept asking, "But if I am not a mother, who am I?" She was facing what Mary Daly was to describe as the "experience of nothingness" that comes with stripping away patriarchal definitions of self.[15]

In the spring semester, the Yale Women's Alliance cosponsored a feminist conference with the women's group at the Law School and brought in Kate Millet and Naomi Weisstein as speakers. Weisstein was a feminist psychologist who had written an important article entitled "Kinder, Küche, Kirke as Scientific Law."[16] Her talk described in vivid

---

14. Nelle Morton, *The Journey Is Home* (Boston: Beacon, 1985), 17, 29, and passim.
15. Mary Daly, *Beyond God the Father: Toward a Philosophy of Women's Liberation* (Boston: Beacon, 1973), 23–24.

and meticulous detail the experience of being a female graduate student at Harvard—the pipe-smoking arrogance, the efforts to outdo each other—and every word she uttered applied to Yale. Her central message and refrain was that change is possible but "you cannot do it on your own." At one point she said, "Women grow up wanting to be doctors and lawyers and ministers and end up being doctors' wives and lawyers' wives and minister' wives." I was a girl who had grown up wanting to be a rabbi and who was now married to one, and I felt as if she had punched me in the stomach. All fall, I had been moving closer and closer to defining myself as a feminist, but this was the moment at which my conversion—and it was a conversion—was complete. I walked the streets with Carol afterward not wanting to go home and cried all night that I had wasted my life. (I was about to turn twenty-three!)

My growing feminist commitments immensely complicated my relationship with Judaism. I became a feminist precisely at the moment when I was first learning my way around the traditional prayer book and sitting at the back of the Yale chapel, segregated from the men and not being counted in the minyan (quorum required for a full prayer service, traditionally ten men). One Sabbath morning, as Robert and I were standing outside chatting with a friend, an undergraduate came out and asked him to please come in because they needed him for a minyan. That was a revelatory moment for me as I realized that my presence was irrelevant to the purpose for which we were gathered. Although I did attend services that day, I shortly afterward resolved never to enter a synagogue where I was not counted in the minyan. It was a resolution I kept, and that, for many years, made it difficult for me to find a place to pray communally. I began to speak about the status of women in Judaism, giving talks in a number of places with the title, "Can a Woman Be a Jew?" I contended, only partly facetiously, that Judaism is like color blindness: women pass it on but rarely contract it themselves.

16. Naomi Weisstein, "Kinder, Küche, Kirke as Scientific Law: Psychology Constructs the Female," in *Sisterhood Is Powerful: An Anthology of Writings from the Women's Liberation Movement*, ed. Robin Morgan (New York: Vintage, 1970), 205–20.

I brought my new feminist awareness not just to Judaism but also to my studies. Carol and I had both attended the initial meeting of the Yale Women's Alliance, but we had gone independently. We were not friends during my first year in the program. She was a year ahead of me and seemed to me both older and more sophisticated; she was already critical of the graduate program in theology while I was struggling to find my way in. Our involvement in the Yale Women's Alliance changed all that, however, and we quickly became fast friends. It was immensely important in shaping our career trajectories that Carol and I became feminists together, because it meant that we each had a colleague to encourage our questions and legitimate our new understandings of theology and ourselves. We began to *notice* that in none of our courses had we ever been assigned a book or article written by a woman—a fact that we had simply taken for granted B.F. (before feminism!). We began to *notice* the horrible things that almost all the theologians we were reading had to say about women. In a student-led seminar on leading twentieth-century (male) theologians, Carol wrote a paper connecting Karl Barth's statement that women are ontologically subordinate to men to deeper patterns in his thought.[17] I don't think I immediately grasped the full significance of Carol's argument. In fact, I remember feeling pride that the other woman in the class had written such a smart paper but also discomfort that she had made the professor and the other students angry. But over time, I came to realize the importance of her claim that misogynistic comments are not just verbal asides or personal opinions that can be bracketed off and forgotten. Her insistence that they are thoroughly intertwined with theological understandings of God and humanity ultimately led me to a far-reaching theological critique of Judaism.

Needless to say, such insights were not exactly welcomed by our fellow students. Our becoming feminists greatly increased the teasing

17. The original typescript of this paper written in 1970 is in the Alverno College Library Archives and can be viewed online at http://feminismandreligion.com/2015/07/27/barth-and-woman-at-yale-by-carol-p-christ/; a version of it distributed as "A Question for Investigation: Karl Barth's View of Women" by the Conference of Women Theologians, Alverno College, 1971 is also in the Alverno College Library Archives and can be viewed online at https://feminismandreligion.files.wordpress.com/2015/07/a-question-for-investigation-christ.pdf.

and hostility to which we were subjected. "Come on, *girls*," someone would say each time we pointed out a passage in some theologian that was demeaning to women, "Barth [or Bonhoeffer or Luther or whoever] isn't talking about women; he's talking about creation" or salvation or some other vital subject from which it was important not to be distracted. Conscious of the need for solidarity in the face of this harassment, we decided to try to organize the other women in the department. We were 10 percent of religious studies graduate students at our peak (ten out of one hundred), and we met together a couple of times to discuss issues of common concern. Our conversations enabled us to form a chorus that could add "or a woman" whenever the department chair talked about hiring a "man" in biblical studies or some other field. We presented a solid front and refused to move when Judah Goldin turned to the women sitting together at a departmental lecture and asked one of us to get a glass of water for the speaker. Our most significant joint action was taking over the single restroom (for men of course) in the Yale Divinity School library. Up until the fall of 1970, women studying in the library had to leave the building in order to find a women's toilet. This daily inconvenience was symbolic of the general marginalization of women at Yale and the fact that the university took little note of either women's minds or bodies. The *New Haven Register* came to interview us during our sit-in, and the bathroom remained unisex until the library was renovated years later. This is a day that has gone down in Divinity School lore.

As graduate students in theology, Carol and I had to take four comprehensive exams—in philosophical, systematic, and historical theology and a special exam on a topic of our choice. Given our growing interest in the status of women in the Jewish and Christian traditions, we decided to focus our historical theology exam on the history of attitudes toward women. We were quite aware that Jaroslav Pelikan, who oversaw the exam, would not necessarily be happy with that topic, and so we spent a couple of months gathering sources to demonstrate that there was no lack of material. When we went into his office armed with our findings and told him what we wanted to write on, he slammed his fist on the table and said, "Not for me you're not; women are not a doctrine." He simply would not discuss the matter further. He said we could either choose a different topic or write on several fundamental texts in the history of theology. At that point, furious, humiliated, and interested in doing as little work as possible, we took a look at his list of texts. One of them was Augustine's *On the Trinity*, and despite my general affection for Augustine, I found that text so impenetrable that I decided I would rather not get my doctorate than slog my way through it! It is interesting to me in retrospect that my ability to enter sympathetically into the Christian tradition has always come to an abrupt halt at the doorway of Trinitarianism. Sin, grace, and salvation are all subjects I have written about with no problem. But I not only have no interest in the Trinity but I find the topic both intellectually and religiously repellant. When I study other Christian teachings, I can assume a fundamental continuity between Jewish and Christian understandings of God. But Trinitarianism confronts me with the disturbing otherness of the Christian concept of God. I can only suppose that my feeling of distaste originates in my childhood understanding of Judaism as ethical monotheism and my lifelong commitment to the notion of the Oneness of God, a notion that—all theological arguments to the contrary—Trinitarianism seems to me to violate.

We ended up writing our historical theology exam on the doctrine of original sin, a decision that meant that three of my four comprehensives were related to the problem of evil. I did my philosophical theology exam on the problem of evil in analytic philosophy and my special exam on Holocaust theology. I no longer have a copy of my philosophical theology paper, but I remember ending it by allying myself with Ivan Karamazov's desire to "give back his ticket" in protest against a world in which innocent children have to suffer.[18] Ivan's rebellion against an unjust world order, like Wiesel's anger at a God who could not be disconnected from the Holocaust, and

---

18. Fyodor Dostoyevsky, *The Brothers Karamavov*, trans. Constance Garnett (New York: The Modern Library, n.d.), 254.

Rieux's refusal to believe in a God who remained silent in the face of the plague, spoke to me very deeply. I finished my graduate education still believing in a God with whom it was appropriate to be angry. As the classical formulation of the problem of evil put it, either God *could* not prevent evil or God *would* not, and the notion of God's absolute goodness was much less compelling to me than the idea of God's power.

It was several years before I consciously relinquished this understanding of God, but my feminism in a quiet way was beginning to undermine it. Through the Yale Women's Alliance and another consciousness-raising group that Carol and I joined the following year, I experienced a new kind of agency, a sense of participation in a larger social and even cosmic project, a conviction that women working together could remake the world. One of my deepest experiences of the power of women's bonding took place at a summer Kent Fellowship Conference in Santa Fe, New Mexico at the end of my second year at Yale. The Danforth Foundation, which funded both Robert's and my graduate educations, took the literal meaning of "fellowship" very seriously and required all fellows to attend at least two conferences in the course of our graduate careers. This particular conference was especially rich and interesting and culminated for me with a women's meeting called for the second-to-last night. Many of the women who attended had become involved in feminism during the preceding year, and we began to share our new experiences and insights as well as our anger at the absence of attention to women's issues at the conference. At some point in our discussion, Margaret Farley, a nun in ethics in the Yale graduate program, began to talk about what being a woman meant to her. She wove a spell with the power of her words as she took a series of ideas that had been used to restrict women—being receptive, giving birth—and reinterpreted them metaphorically as a way of being in and contributing to the world. It was an extraordinary moment of connection among all those in the room, and afterward, several of us took a box of crayons and wrote all across a piece of mural paper that covered a whole hallway, "Sisterhood is powerful." Two years later, when I wrote "The Coming of Lilith" at the conference of

Women Exploring Theology at Grailville, it was this meeting that was in my mind when we spoke about consciousness raising as a religious experience.[19] It was also at this conference that I met and became friends with Martha, who, many years later, would become my life partner.

I had come to the meeting in Santa Fe debating whether to drop out of graduate school when I finished my comprehensives. I found the atmosphere at Yale poisonous, and that was even before the experience with Jaroslav Pelikan, which was the nadir of my time there. I felt that theology was idle speculation and that I wanted to do something "real" in the world, like becoming a nurse. In Santa Fe, I experienced a precious moment of absolute clarity that I would still be me whether or not I completed my doctorate. In fact, I did take a leave of absence after my exams, intending never to return, but I decided not to drop out officially until I had lived with my decision for a while. When I completed my exams, Robert and I moved to Montreal where he took his first teaching job at Sir George Williams University (now Concordia). I taught as an adjunct, and my discovery that I loved teaching, coupled with the perspective that distance from Yale gave me, made it possible for me to go back and write my dissertation.

The Feminist Momentum Builds

I had come to Yale planning to write a thesis in existential philosophical theology, but the courses I took on existential thinkers cured me of my enthusiasm in that they were as lifeless as all the other classes I took at Yale. I then thought about writing on some aspect of the problem of evil. This made more sense in terms of my long-term interests, but I was afraid of spending years immersed in a subject that was bound to be both disturbing and depressing. Meanwhile, as Carol and I had searched for material that could support our growing interest in women in religion, we had found the foundational article

---

19. Judith Plaskow, "The Coming of Lilith: Toward a Feminist Theology," in *Womanspirit Rising: A Feminist Reader in Religion,* ed. Carol P. Christ and Judith Plaskow (San Francisco: Harper & Row, 1979), 198–209.

in feminist theology written by Valerie Saiving (Goldstein) in 1960. In "The Human Situation: A Feminine View," Saiving had argued that the theologies of Reinhold Niebuhr and Anders Nygren were written from the perspective of male experience and that this distorted their views of the human situation.[20] I was tremendously excited by Saiving's essay, but I thought her view of women's experience was too essentialist—the term did not exist at the time, but perfectly captures my critique—and failed to give sufficient weight to female socialization. I decided to write a dissertation critiquing the theologies of Reinhold Niebuhr and Paul Tillich from the perspective of women's experience. I briefly considered writing about two Jewish theologians, but I felt that theology was not sufficiently central to Judaism for such a topic to have an impact on Jewish thought and practice. I was excited about the thesis because it provided me with the opportunity to create a complicated and subtle definition of women's experience. Niebuhr and Tillich I regarded as add-ons necessary to complete my degree. I went back to Yale for six weeks in the spring determined to carry out my plan whether or not I had the support of the department, and I wrote a thesis proposal and defended it. Although in fact the Director of Graduate Studies and other members of the department tried hard to discourage me, Julian Hartt agreed to be my advisor even though he knew he would be leaving for the University of Virginia. I was on my way to writing one of the first feminist dissertations in religious studies.[21]

Set once more on the path toward a doctorate, in the summer of 1972, I had the privilege of attending the Women Exploring Theology Conference at Grailville. I had not been invited to the conference, which was essentially a Christian event. But Carol had been asked and was unable to attend because she was in the midst of moving to New York, and she suggested that the organizers allow me to participate

---

20. Valerie Saiving (Goldstein), "The Human Situation: A Feminine View," *The Journal of Religion* 40/2 (April 1960): 100–112; reprinted in Christ and Plaskow, *Womanspirit Rising*, 25–42.
21. Judith Plaskow, "Sex, Sin and Grace: Women's Experience and the Theologies of Reinhold Niebuhr and Paul Tillich," (PhD diss., Yale University, 1975); published under the same title (Lanham, MD: University Press of America, 1980).

in her stead. The conference was an amazing event at which sixty women came together not just to express our pain and anger at our marginalization within our various communities, but also to initiate new modes of thinking and acting as religiously committed women. It was a life-changing experience for me, a week during which I made formative friendships and witnessed the power of women working together to transform our respective traditions.

The center of the conference consisted of morning groups organized around particular themes that met throughout our time together. I was part of a small subgroup of the Bible and theology group that decided to focus on consciousness raising as a religious experience. The four of us in the group spent an extraordinary week both immersing ourselves in and analyzing our prior experiences of consciousness raising and re-creating those experiences through the power of our conversations. At the end of the week, we discussed using the rabbinic story of Lilith as a vehicle for communicating both our process and our insights into the religious dimension of consciousness-raising. I'm not even sure how I knew about Lilith, a figure the rabbis describe as Adam's rebellious first wife. But when I went back to my room to try to compose a story, "The Coming of Lilith"—a feminist retelling of the rabbinic legend—came pouring through me. When all the groups reported out on the last evening, there was a sense of tremendous excitement and jubilation as group after group offered new paradigms and images for thinking about God, self, sexuality, singleness and community, politics and tradition. My Lilith story ended with Eve and Lilith meeting, talking together many times, and returning to the garden, eager not only to transform their world but sensing that their connection would mean changes in the very nature of God. Independently, the group on singleness and community had decided that traditional names for God were no longer adequate and had made a list of words that meant God to them: changing, creating, extending me beyond myself, enabling, connecting, challenging, loving, nurturing, confronting, and numerous others. Their nonobjectifying process words expressed through many -ing endings captured the energy of my Lilith story and of the conference as a whole and conveyed a sense of what Mary Daly would call "God the Verb" in her *Beyond God the Father* published a year later.[22]

I was standing that summer at the cusp of an important change. I was about to immerse myself in literature by and about women to try to convey the doubleness of women's experiences as both socially constructed by the long history of expectations and stereotypes surrounding women and, at the same time, also the products of individual agency. I was writing a thesis that allowed me to sidestep the question of the nature of God in favor of women's experience, and in fact I was not yet intellectually or emotionally ready to surrender my belief in a personal God who needed to be held accountable for the evil in the world. But something was bubbling "up from down under."[23] Initially unperceived by me, the edifice of my prior beliefs was giving way—not with a mighty crash but quietly, hardly noticeably, before the power of an alternative understanding.

22. Reflections of the various groups are assembled in an unpublished packet, "Women Exploring Theology at Grailville" (New York: Church Women United, 1972). My Lilith story was first published (under the name Judith Plaskow Goldenberg) as the epilogue to Rosemary Radford Ruether, ed., *Religion and Sexism: Images of Woman in the Jewish and Christian Traditions* (New York: Simon and Schuster, 1974), 341–43. Mary Daly, *Beyond God the Father: Toward a Philosophy of Women's Liberation* (Boston: Beacon, 1973), 33–34.
23. Nelle Morton, "The Dilemma of Celebration," in Christ and Plaskow, *Womanspirit Rising*, 165.

3

God in the History of Theology

Carol P. Christ and Judith Plaskow

The views of divinity we question in this book can be situated in the larger context of the history of theology. Understanding this context is important because, even when it is not consciously understood, its assumptions shape the ways people think about divinity and divine power. In this chapter, we examine the conflict between the God of the Bible and the God of Greek philosophy, the theological consensus that developed to resolve it, and the challenges that were posed in the twentieth century to the assumptions of traditional theologies. As this history forms the backdrop of our theological explorations as well, we also consider how we encountered and responded to these larger trends in the course of our theological studies.

Reconciling the God of the Bible with the God of Philosophy

While we began graduate school with our childhood understandings of the biblical God largely intact, at Yale we learned that theology developed in order to reconcile the conflicting understandings of God found in the Bible and in Greek philosophy. In the Bible, especially the Hebrew Bible or Old Testament, God is a character in the story of his people.[1] This God walks in the garden of Eden, speaks to Adam and Eve and later to Moses and the prophets. He chooses a special people and enters into a covenant with them. This God gets angry and punishes his people when they fail to live up to their side of the covenantal bargain, but in the end, his heart overflows with redeeming love. In the New Testament as interpreted by Christians, God becomes incarnate in the person of Jesus, suffers on the cross in order to redeem humanity, dies, and is resurrected. In both the Hebrew and Christian Bibles, God is imagined to have a body and to feel, to love and to suffer, analogous to the way humans do.

In contrast, the ancient Greek philosophers, including Pythagoras, Plato, and Aristotle, thought of God as a transcendent rational principle that is the source of order in the world. Plato described this highest principle as "absolute, existing alone with itself, unique, eternal, and all other beautiful things partaking of it, yet in such a manner that, while they come into being and pass away, it neither undergoes any increase or diminution nor suffers any change."[2] Aristotle described God as the "unmoved mover."[3] The God of the Greek philosophers was Being Itself, understood as the abstract and impersonal metaphysical (not physical) Ground of Being. This God does not have a body or feelings. The theological concept of "aseity" affirms that transcendent divinity is entirely self-moved and thus cannot be moved or influenced by the joy or suffering of other beings. Nor is this God seen, heard, or felt in the body. The God of the philosophers is contemplated in the rational mind, for example, by one who understands the principles of mathematics and geometry that

---

1. In this jointly written chapter, when we refer to the God of the Bible and classical Jewish and Christian texts that clearly image God as male, we will use the traditional male pronouns, but not capitalize them.
2. Plato, *The Symposium*, trans. Walter Hamilton (Baltimore: Penguin, 1951), 93–94.
3. In book 12, part 7 of Aristotle, *Metaphysics*, trans. W. D. Ross (Stilwell, KS: Digireads.com Publishing, 2006).

structure the world or the relation of mathematics to the principles of musical harmony that were thought to produce the harmony of the spheres, the regular movements of the stars and the planets. Jews and early Christians came into contact with Greek philosophy through the works of Plotinus and the Neoplatonists who synthesized Greek philosophy with Egyptian and Jewish wisdom traditions. Neoplatonists taught that Being is One, infinite, and transcendent of the world. Unlike the phenomenal world, the source of being cannot be understood through analogy to anything that exists; in this sense, it is in principle unknowable. The negative way of the philosophers assumes that God is *not* earth, air, sky, or water; God does *not* love and judge as human beings love and judge; God is *not* like anything we can imagine or know. The medieval and modern mystical path known as the *via negativa* builds on this insight: mystics deny their connections to everything physical and mental in order to experience an unknowable deity. As we note in chapter 6, many feminist theologians appeal to the idea that divinity is unknowable to relativize traditional male imagery for God.

The Greek philosophers were among the first to articulate the distinction between the transcendent God of philosophy and the anthropomorphic deities of popular religion and myth that were pictured as having human bodies, human faces, human voices, and human passions. For the Greek philosophers, theirs was the true understanding of the nature of divinity. They dismissed the deities of Greek myth and ritual as falsehood or reinterpreted them allegorically as imaginative representations of higher rational truths. The Greek philosophers considered "anthropomorphic" images or concepts of God, which understood God as having human-like form or human-like thoughts and feelings, to be the product of a "lower" order of thinking in contrast to their own "higher" thought.

When Jewish and Christian theologians encountered Greek philosophy, they, in turn, had to consider the relationship between the philosophical concept of God and the God of the Bible. Unlike Plato, who had rejected the Goddesses and Gods of Greek myth, they were unwilling simply to turn their backs on the God of the Bible. Instead, they hoped to be able to reconcile the love, judgment, and suffering of the biblical God with the transcendent rational principle of Greek philosophy. Theologians adapted earlier methods of allegorical interpretation of Greek myths to the Bible in order to explain (or explain away) the contradictions between the Bible and philosophy. The result was a picture of God that represented an uneasy compromise between the principles of transcendent reason and the loving and judging God of faith and piety. The twelfth-century Jewish philosopher, Moses Maimonides, was certain that the truths revealed in the Torah must be compatible with the truths uncovered by science and philosophy. He therefore undertook to harmonize Aristotle's views of the absolute unity and incorporeality of God with the words of Torah. The long first section of his magnum opus, *Guide for the Perplexed*, carefully examines passages in the Torah that seem to imply that God has a body or feelings and reinterprets each of them. Every mention of God "seeing," for example, refers to intellectual apprehension, not to the seeing of the eye. When the Bible calls God "merciful," it does not mean that God is influenced by feelings of mercy but that he performs *acts* similar to those performed by humans who are moved by pity. Maimonides offers similar explanations for dozens of different biblical anthropomorphisms.[4] The thirteenth-century Christian Aristotelian, Thomas Aquinas, who knew Maimonides's work and agreed with its general principles, stated that philosophy could take human beings only part way to God. Reason could apprehend the "unmoved mover," the transcendent rational source of the order in the world, but, Aquinas said, it must be complemented by faith. Faith adds that God as the rational source of the world also created it, judges it, loves it, and will redeem it from sin. For Aquinas, God as Creator, Judge, and Redeemer was not arbitrary and not influenced by passions. Rather, the God who creates, judges, and redeems the world is transcendent,

4. Moses Maimonides, *The Guide for the Perplexed*, trans. M. Friedlander (New York: Dover Publications, 1956), 17, 76, and the whole of part 1.

64

rational, and dispassionate. Thomas, like Maimonides, interpreted the Bible metaphorically, explaining away its depictions of God's passions.[5]

Theological Conundrums

Until recently, almost all theologians agreed that God must be understood to be essentially, or totally, transcendent of the world. God could not have a body nor could God speak in a voice like that of humans. God could not have passions or desires. God's aseity meant that God could not love or suffer as human beings love and suffer, nor could God be moved by any particular love or particular suffering. What the love, judgment, or saving power of God could possibly mean in that case was a theological conundrum.[6] God was also nearly universally understood to be omnipotent and omniscient. God's omnipotent power was absolute and could never be compromised, deflected, or influenced by any other power. The notion of God's omnipotence seemed to rule out any free will on the part of human beings. This was the "free-will problem" theologians tried to explain in various ways. The notion that God is both omnipotent and good raised the theological "problem of evil." Why would an all-good God who was powerful enough to prevent great evil *not* prevent it? This question led theologians to offer various "theodicies": efforts to reconcile God's goodness and power with the existence of evil in the world. God's omniscient knowledge of the world was also understood as absolute, not limited by standpoint or influenced by passions, but rather the transcendent dispassionate rationalism of an unmoved mover. The God of the philosophers is difficult to reconcile with the God of the Bible who cares for a particular people and who, for Christians, suffers in a particular body on the cross. This was a problem theologians could not adequately resolve. Thus, they often concluded that the nature of God was "unknowable" and that the precise character of his relation

---

5. Thomas of Aquinas, *Summa Theologica,* trans. Fathers of the English Dominican Province (Cincinnati: Benziger Publishers, 1947).
6. This conundrum has been largely unexplored. Charles Hartshorne named the notion that God cannot feel the feelings of the world as one of "the mistakes" of "classical theism" in *The Divine Relativity* (New Haven: Yale University Press, 1948).

to the world was "a mystery" or "a paradox." This was one answer (or nonanswer) to the question of how to relate the God of the philosophers to the God of the Bible.

Cracks in the Theological Edifice

The uneasy compromise between these two views of God held the theological enterprise together for most of its two-thousand-year history. Some theologians put the God of philosophy first, others the God of the Bible, but nonetheless, most viewed them as the same God. This synthesis started to fall apart in the twentieth century when the brutality of the First and Second World Wars began to undermine theologians' confidence in both poles of their understanding of God: the powers of reason were challenged by the horrors of wars in which terrible new weapons had been created by human reason; and many could no longer find a judging and redeeming God among the dead on the battlefields and in the concentration camps. Though we did not begin our graduate studies with an understanding of the conflicting forces the theologians we read were struggling with and against, we came to understand that all theologians must deal with the conflicts between anthropomorphic and classical philosophical views of God. We also began to recognize that the unleashing of evil, destruction, and death in the First and Second World Wars had created a crisis in theology that threatened its very foundations.

The Neo-orthodox Response

One response to these challenges was Neo-orthodoxy. Neo-orthodoxy dominated Protestant theology in Europe and America during the mid-twentieth century and structured our theological education at Yale, which was a bastion of Neo-orthodoxy. A reaction to the perceived "impotence" of German humanism and the German churches in the face of Hitler, Protestant Neo-orthodoxy asserted "the commanding power of God" over against reason and culture. Among its leading advocates were Swiss-German theologian Karl Barth; German New

Testament scholar Rudolf Bultmann; German theologian Paul Tillich, who began teaching in the United States in 1933; German theologian Dietrich Bonhoeffer, who was executed for his resistance to Hitler; and American-born thinkers Reinhold and H. Richard Niebuhr, whose parents were German immigrants and whose father was a German Evangelical pastor.[7] For all of them, although in different ways, the "Word of God" was a dynamic force that imploded into history challenging individuals and communities to radically restructure their lives, to turn away from egotism, and to obey the God of the Bible whose self-giving love was the antithesis of humanity's sinful "idolatry," defined as worshiping anything less than God—including self, nation, or wealth. One prong of the Neo-orthodox critique of idolatry was moral: Neo-orthodox theologians insisted that "man" could not create a just and moral world apart from the judgment and grace of God. Nazi Germany seemed to them proof of what happens when Godless human beings try to create an ideal society. The other prong of the Neo-orthodox critique of idolatry focused on reason: Neo-orthodox theologians insisted that "man" could not understand "himself," the world, or God apart from revelation. Since they stressed that human reason can never comprehend God, Neo-orthodox theologians rejected in principle all attempts to reconcile the God of philosophers with the God of revelation. In this regard, Neo-orthodoxy responded to the uneasy compromise between philosophy and the Bible by rejecting (or claiming to reject) philosophical knowledge of God.

There was an unacknowledged masculine edge to Neo-orthodox theologies that presented God as a powerful and dominant other in contrast to the weakness of "man" and the human cultures "man" creates. In the divine drama as portrayed by Neo-orthodoxy, a dominating God "breaks in" and demonstrates the powerlessness or "impotence" of "man" in the face of "the power of God." The idea that God really is in charge appealed to men who were struggling to

---

7. We are using a broad definition of Neo-orthodoxy to refer to the theological consensus we encountered at Yale. Scholars with other concerns debate definitions of Neo-orthodoxy and differ on which theologians should be counted as Neo-orthodox.

comprehend the depth of human evil and destructiveness unleashed during World War II. Neither of us was able to embrace Neo-orthodox theology, but we did not at first have the tools to critique it. The class paper we have mentioned in which Carol identified the model of love fused with domination that structures Barth's understanding of man's relation to woman and his understanding of God's relation to man was the first time either of us spelled out our sense that Neo-orthodox theologies were based on culturally stereotypical notions of male power as domination and control.[8]

Other Theological Voices

There were other voices in mid-twentieth century theology, including Roman Catholic and Jewish voices. A few courses on Roman Catholic theology were offered at Yale while we were there, and Carol took several of them. But as Catholic ideas about the importance of human reason in theology challenged the central claims of Neo-orthodoxy, Roman Catholic theologies never became part of the main conversation. The student-run course on Jewish theology we created offered different ways of approaching theological questions, but as it was not a part of the regular curriculum, it too had no impact on the issues that were being raised in our other classes. Process theologian Charles Hartshorne gave a series of public lectures while we were at Yale, but his insistence that reason must inform theology, and his concept of the divine relativity, were simply ignored.

Yet other voices were emerging that would eventually undermine the Neo-orthodox theological consensus. Gabriel Vahanian's radical

---

8. The original typescript of this paper written in 1970 is in the Alverno College Library Archives and can be viewed online at https://feminismandreligion.files.wordpress.com/2015/07/barths-theology-and-the-man-woman-relationship-by-carol-p-christ-1971.pdf; a version of it distributed as "A Question for Investigation: Karl Barth's View of Women" by the Conference of Women Theologians, Alverno College, 1971 is also in the Alverno College Library Archives and can be viewed online at https://feminismandreligion.files.wordpress.com/2015/07/a-question-for-investigation-christ.pdf. Kate Sonderegger works hard to redeem Barth for feminists, but does not contest the fundamentally hierarchical nature of Barth's view of the relationship between man and woman; she also notes that Barth's view of revelation is antithetical to the notion that "theology begins in experience." "Barth and Feminism," *The Cambridge Companion to Karl Barth*, ed. John Webster (Cambridge: Cambridge University Press, 2006), 258–73.

book titled *The Death of God* launched "the death of God movement" before we began our studies.[9] The God who was said to be "dead" in modern culture was variously identified with the transcendent God of philosophers and the commanding God of the Bible, both of whom were imagined to be in control of the world. In *After Auschwitz,* rabbi and theological "bad boy" Richard Rubenstein argued that the Holocaust had made belief in an omnipotent God who entered into a covenant with the Jewish people impossible for Jews.[10] We heard Rubenstein speak and were deeply moved by his argument that the traditional notion of God had died at Auschwitz. Carol would pursue this subject further in her dissertation on Elie Wiesel, while for Judith, Rubenstein gave voice to questions she had been asking since childhood. In the years after we left Yale, as we discuss in the chapters that follow, we each found that the omnipotent God of the philosophers and the biblical God who acts in history had died for us as well, in light of the Holocaust and other evils in our world.

The emergence of the Civil Rights and Black Power movements along with other movements for social justice also had a major impact on theology. Martin Luther King Jr. spoke of a God who demanded reconciliation and rectification of the evils of racism and poverty and who was a palpable presence in struggles against injustice.[11] James Cone's *Black Theology and Black Power* articulated a theology of black liberation rooted in the saving power of God who freed the Jews from slavery in Egypt and would continue to free black Americans from the ongoing effects of slavery in the United States.[12] Roman Catholic Gustavo Gutierrez's *A Theology of Liberation* argued that theology must be grounded in the struggles of the poor in Latin America; for him, God was a "liberator" who had a "preferential option for the poor."[13]

---

9. Gabriel Vahanian, *The Death of God: The Culture of Our Post-Christian Era* (New York: G. Braziller, 1961).
10. Richard L. Rubenstein, *After Auschwitz: Essays in Contemporary Judaism* (Indianapolis: Bobbs-Merrill, 1966), esp. chap. 2.
11. Martin Luther King Jr., *Testament of Hope: The Essential Writings and Speeches of Martin Luther King, Jr.,* ed. James M. Washington (San Francisco: Harper One, 1991).
12. James Cone, *Black Theology and Black Power* (New York: Seabury, 1969).
13. Gustavo Gutierrez, *A Theology of Liberation: History, Politics, and Salvation,* trans. Sister Caridad Inda and John Eagleson (Maryknoll, NY: Orbis, 1973).

Because Carol became profoundly opposed to all wars, she was mystified by liberation theology's failure to criticize the warrior God of exodus and the prophets. Though Judith saw liberation theology as clearly Christian, she found that it resonated with central themes in her understanding of Judaism, especially the exodus from Egypt and prophetic concern for the widow and the poor.

The counterculture and humanistic psychology also influenced theology in our graduate years. Their emphasis on the connection between mind and body was leading to fresh theological explorations of embodiment, to reexamination of Christian and Jewish attitudes toward the body, and to the development of spiritualities rooted in the body. Sam Keen's *To a Dancing God* was among the books that gave voice to our own emerging critique of what we and other feminists would later call antifemale and antibody theologies.[14] At conferences organized by the Danforth Foundation and the Society for Values in Higher Education, we took part in body exercises inspired by the Esalen Institute, where new ideas about the relation of body, mind, spirit, and politics were emerging. In the years that followed, we each undertook individual therapy that helped us to explore the relations of our own minds and bodies. At the same time, we were beginning to realize that most Western theologies had identified women with the body and men with the mind, thus justifying men's rule over women using the analogy of the mind ruling the body. For us, body theologies became feminist theologies.

Feminist Theology Emerges

Feminism was welling up from under during those years too. We became feminists early in graduate school but did not discover feminist theology until we were preparing for our comprehensive exams. As Judith was later to write, feminism placed a question mark over absolutely everything for us: the maleness of God, the male authorship of the Bible, and the male perspectives from which virtually all

---

14. Sam Keen, *To a Dancing God* (New York: Harper & Row, 1970).

theologies had been written. Three key essays set the stage for future work in the field, including our own. We have already mentioned these essays, but it is important to address the challenges they posed to traditional theology, and our own responses to them, in more detail here.

Valerie Saiving (Goldstein's) groundbreaking essay "The Human Situation: A Feminine View"[15] argued that the Neo-orthodox identification of sin with prideful self-assertion was based on masculine or male experience and ignored the female or feminine sin of self-negation. Men, Saiving suggested, need to undergo a complex and challenging process of differentiation from the mother by repeatedly proving their masculinity, while women grow to be women naturally, through the physical maturation of their bodies. The temptations of women thus have a different character than those of men and are better captured by terms such as triviality, distractibility, and dependence on others rather than pride. Judith challenged Saiving's understanding of what constitutes "masculine" or "male" and "feminine" or "female" experience in her dissertation, insisting that the experiences of women are not the same in all times and places, but are rooted in specific situations, cultures, and histories.[16] Nonetheless, the notion that the experience of the theologian matters and that gender matters in the construction of theology came to us as a revelation. Both of us have continued to assert that theology must be rooted in human experience, including the particular experiences of women in differing cultural situations.

The lecture Rosemary Radford Ruether delivered when we brought her to Yale Divinity School was later published as "Motherearth and the Megamachine."[17] In it, Ruether explained that classical Greek

15. Valerie Saiving (Goldstein), "The Human Situation: A Feminine View," *The Journal of Religion* 40, no. 2 (April, 1960): 100–112; reprinted in Carol Christ and Judith Plaskow, eds., *Womanspirit Rising: A Feminist Reader in Religion* (San Francisco: Harper & Row, 1979), 25–41.
16. Judith Plaskow, "Sex, Sin and Grace: Women's Experience and the Theologies of Reinhold Niebuhr and Paul Tillich" (PhD diss., Yale University, 1975); published under the same title (Lanham, MD: University Press of America, 1980), 9–11, 29–34.
17. Rosemary Radford Ruether, "Motherearth and the Megamachine: A Theology of Liberation in a Feminine, Somatic, and Ecological Perspective," *Christianity and Crisis* (April 12, 1972); reprinted in Christ and Plaskow, *Womanspirit Rising*, 43–52.

thought, which became the foundation of Western theology, had separated mind from body, creating a set of oppositions that included rational and irrational, soul and body, spirit and nature, male and female. In each case, women were identified with the despised and subordinated side of the polarizations. "Man" was rational, spiritual, and able to transcend the body and nature, while "woman" was defined by her connections to the body and nature, and had a lesser rational capacity than man. These dualisms were encapsulated in the traditional opposition between "transcendence" and "immanence." "Transcendence" refers to pure thought or pure spirit imagined to exist alone without dependence on the body, nature, or relationships with anything other than itself. "Immanence" refers to views in which the self and the world are understood through the body, nature, and relationships of interdependence. God has generally been understood to transcend the world, and men have been seen as capable of transcendence through rational thinking, while women have been understood to be trapped in immanence, mired in the body and nature. Ruether argued that women's liberation would require the transformation of classical dualisms and a reintegration of the separated.[18]

Ruether's analysis provided support for our conviction that mind and body are connected and that the experiences of the body must become a resource for theology. It validated Carol's insight that traditional theological ideas about the relation of women to men and the relation of body to mind are connected and confirmed her conviction that theologians must reexamine traditional ideas about the relation of God and human beings to nature. For Judith, Ruether's talk shed light on the messages she had received about being too smart for a girl and encouraged her to explore the history of attitudes toward the body in Jewish, Christian, and feminist thought. Our recognition of the need to transform all of the classical dualisms in a new understanding of the relation of reason and feeling, mind and body, humanity and

18. Ibid.

nature, transcendence and immanence, would be central to all of our future work.

In "After the Death of God the Father,"[19] Mary Daly argued that the God who had been proclaimed "dead" by male theologians was the male God modeled on images of male power and authority. The traditional picture of God, Daly said, glorified the qualities of "hyper-rationality, 'objectivity,' aggressivity, the possession of dominating and manipulative attitudes toward persons and environment, and the tendency to construct boundaries between the self (and those identified with the self) and others."[20] Daly drew a strong connection between this understanding of God and the subordination and oppression of women, for "if God in 'his' heaven is a father ruling 'his' people, then it is in the 'nature' of things and according to divine plan and the order of the universe that society be male dominated."[21] Daly did not believe "the real" God was dead; rather, she predicted that, with the liberation of women, new and more authentic images and conceptions of God would emerge. This essay supported and clarified our nascent sense that a male God created by male theologians supported male domination and our conviction that the insights of women's liberation had the power to change the world. In time, we would reject the image of God as a dominating male other and the conceptions of God that followed from such images, including notions of God's transcendence, omnipotence, and omniscience, and we would develop new understandings of God rooted in our experiences as feminists.

These essays raised questions that we, along with many others, are still pondering today. How should we understand and evaluate theological traditions that were created almost exclusively by men? How would theologies written by women and informed by our experiences be different? Should we continue to participate in

---

19. Mary Daly, "After the Death of God the Father: Women's Liberation and the Transformation of Christian Consciousness," *Commonweal* (March 12, 1971); reprinted in Christ and Plaskow, *Womanspirit Rising*, 53–62.
20. Ibid., 55.
21. Ibid., 54.

traditions that subordinated women and defined God as a dominating male other? Can traditions change, and are there limits to the changes that are possible? We truly had no idea where our questions would take us, but we knew we would follow them wherever they might lead.

4

———

From God to Goddess

Carol P. Christ

Leaving Yale for Columbia was like emerging from a dark tunnel into a brightly lit room. At Columbia, where the graduate study of religion had not yet fully separated from Union Seminary, I became part of the kind of open-minded religious and theological discussion I had hoped to find at Yale. The religion department was dominated by Joseph Blau, a kindly liberal Jewish scholar. Christian process theologian Daniel Day Williams and Jewish folklorist Theodor Gaster were among the old guard. Black liberation theologian James Cone was challenging us to make racial justice a central concern; Tom Driver was suggesting that we could think theologically through the body; scholar of Gnosticism Elaine Pagels was asking us to reconfigure Christian origins; biblical scholar Morton Smith was alleging that monotheism was not the only view in ancient Hebrew religion; and, like me, ethicist Beverly Harrison was questioning everything from a feminist perspective. The religion department was teaching the Native American narrative *Black Elk Speaks*—a book that connected spirit and nature in ways that would profoundly shape my own journey—in the introductory course.[1] Not encouraged even to speak about Martin Buber at Yale, I was now able to teach a whole course on his work. As one of still only a few female members of the Columbia faculty, I became friends with leading feminist thinkers and professors of English Catherine Simpson and Caroline Heilbrun. As a feminist pioneer, I was invited to join small academic gatherings on the Holocaust, the future of higher education, and theology. I began to be asked to speak at other universities on feminism and religion. I was hired in part because I was a feminist, and I was asked to teach a course on women and religion. For the first time in many years, my questions were heard and my point of view respected.

Deepening My Questions

Although I had read and reread Elie Wiesel's books, and ideas were swirling in my mind about God and the Holocaust, I had not really begun to write my dissertation. Wiesel spoke of the failure of words in the face of great evil. I too felt paralyzed. Would my words be up to the task I had chosen for myself, or would I betray the millions whose lives had been lost? If even Wiesel feared to write, how could I dare put pen to paper? Every time I thought about writing, I was confronted with Elie Wiesel's question: Where was God? In part because I could not answer it for myself, I could not begin my dissertation.

One of the courses I taught at Columbia was Western Civilization, and the first book on the reading list was the *Iliad* by Homer. As I had been actively opposing the Vietnam War for five years, I found it very difficult to teach this book as the fountain of wisdom from which culture began. My office mate saw "Achilles's metaphysical dilemma," as he called it, of whether to seek glory on the battlefield or to live a

---

1. *Black Elk Speaks: Being the Life Story of a Holy Man of the Ogala Sioux*, as told through John G. Niehardt (New York: Pocket Books, 1972 [1961]). When I began to create earth-based Goddess rituals, this book was a resource, both confirming and relativizing ideas and images derived from Wiccan traditions.

happy but unremembered life at home, as the crucial decision every "man" must make. I, on the other hand, could only see dead bodies falling to the ground in a senseless war. Moreover, as I kept pointing out in vain to my office mate, Achilles's metaphysical dilemma was sparked by the fact that he and Agamemnon were fighting over who had the right to rape a beautiful "spear captive"—a scholarly euphemism for women as the spoils of war. Though the atmosphere at Columbia was far more open than it had been at Yale, there were still questions that could not be asked. I had majored in humanities at Stanford in the belief that the ideas in the major works of literature and philosophy of Western culture were not only true, but also that they could illumine our lives. I now began to wonder if the great books were deeply flawed. The questions I was asking about the *Iliad* were questions I was also asking about the Bible. I would come to similar conclusions: both were shaped around patriarchy and war.

Another question that could not be asked was whether the God of the exodus and the prophets, called the liberating God by the increasingly popular liberation theology movement, was a "Man of War" (Exod. 15:3). Liberation theology accepted biblical theology's assertion that God acts in history, and its touchstones were the liberating acts of God in Exodus, the preaching of the prophets, and Jesus' concern for the poor. Liberation theology made the astonishing assertion that wherever the liberation of the oppressed was occurring in our own times, there was God. As I profoundly desired the liberation of the oppressed and marched against poverty and racism, I was sympathetic to liberation theology's goals. Moreover, feminist theologians, led by Rosemary Radford Ruether, were claiming the God of liberation theology as the liberator of women.[2] However, I could not understand God's liberating activity as an abstract principle. When I heard Exodus and the prophets invoked, I remembered the texts from which the theological notion of God as liberator of the oppressed was

2. Rosemary Radford Ruether, *Liberation Theology: Human Hope Confronts Christian History and American Power* (New York: Paulist Press, 1972). Also see Carol P. Christ, "A Spirituality for Women" and "Yahweh as Holy Warrior," in her *Laughter of Aphrodite: Reflections on a Journey to the Goddess* (San Francisco: Harper & Row, 1987), 57–72 and 73–81.

extracted. I knew that Exodus 15 celebrated God as a warrior who threw the horses and horsemen of the Egyptians into the sea. When others spoke of the prophetic principle of justice, I knew that the God of the prophets who cared about the poor and widow was also one who said He would "slay their beloved children" (Hosea 9:16) and "dash their infants in pieces" (Isa. 13:16). The God of the prophets was a violent God who could turn His vengeance against the enemy or His own people. I found it dishonest to ignore the violent aspects of the biblical story of God as liberator of the oppressed. But more importantly, I was attuned to the power of symbols to shape consciousness and actions. I felt that the liberation traditions of the Bible would reinforce the notion of going to war with God on our side—which was exactly what many Americans thought we were doing in Vietnam. Even though I still considered myself Christian, I could not adapt the paradigm of God as a liberator to a feminist context.

Teaching Women and Religion

In preparation for my Women and Religion class, I discovered the biblical heroine Miriam, who is the probable author of the ancient victory song in Exodus 15. Yet as I taught about Miriam, I recognized that the words attributed to her celebrate a warrior God. Bringing Miriam to the fore did not solve the problems I was having with the biblical God—but rather reinforced them. Raphael Patai's *The Hebrew Goddess,* also on my reading list, dealt another blow to the prophetic principle of justice touted by liberation theologians.[3] Patai taught me to read the prophets with different eyes. I saw that the prophets' rant against idols was directed against those among the Hebrew people who continued to worship Goddesses such as Asherah in the temple and on "the tops of the mountains . . . upon the hills, under oak, poplar, and terebrinth" (Hosea 4:13)—in other words, in nature. Realizing this, I began to hear the common characterization of sinfulness as "idolatry" differently. Patai's assertion that the prophets' view had been a

3. Raphael Patai, *The Hebrew Goddess* (New York: KTAV Publishing House, 1967), third enlarged edition (Detroit: Wayne State University Press, 1990).

minority view within Hebrew religion gave me hope that the Hebrew Goddess could be restored as one of the images for God in Judaism and Christianity. But while Christian women have recovered Sophia, female Divine Wisdom, they have shown little interest in the Hebrew Goddess. Though some Jewish women have begun to reclaim the Hebrew Goddess, they are likely to speak of Her as Shekhinah, the female Divine Presence. The Hebrew Goddess raises questions about the so-called triumph of Judaism and Christianity over paganism and idolatry that neither community seems eager to face.

Therapy

One of the most important things New York gave me was therapy. I tended to think of therapy as something only crazy people needed. Yet, in New York, everyone seemed to be talking about it. A friend encouraged me to give therapy a chance. When I first met Lenore Hecht, whose combination of gestalt and bio-energetic therapies would change my life, I was afraid of losing myself. "I do not want you to tell me that I cannot be a feminist or that I am crazy," I remember telling her. She assured me that she would do neither, suggesting that, like many others, I could benefit from exploring certain aspects of my life. Although I did not want to think that I might be crazy, I did believe that my problems were entirely unique. I doubted that anyone else could understand what it was like to be a woman in a six-foot-tall body or that anyone in New York would know what it was like to grow up in the suburbs of Los Angeles.

What I discovered in therapy—both group and individual—was that others shared my problems in varying degrees. For example, when I was asked why I had not spoken in the therapy group for the first six weeks, I said, "Because I am afraid no one will understand me." Immediately, one of the other women replied, "That is exactly how I felt when I first entered the group." When, in those same years, I began to write, I found that women (and sometimes men) whose life stories might have seemed very different from mine thanked me for expressing their feelings and thoughts. In therapy, I learned that I was very disconnected from my body and its feelings, even though I thought that, as a Californian, I was more in touch with my body than many of my academic colleagues. One of the first things Lenore Hecht asked me to do was to breathe from my belly. I believe it was more than a year before I could. I had retreated so far into my head that breath simply would not come down from my throat and my lungs. Another insight came during a session when I couldn't think of anything to say. Lenore pointed to my clenched fists and asked me what I was angry about. At first, I had no idea. But as she probed, I came to see that our bodies often hold feelings we try to deny with our minds. Over several years, I started to become more in touch with my feelings. This was good for me, but it was not necessarily appreciated in the academic world. In time, I would incorporate the insights I gained in therapy into my attempts to transform the separation of mind and body, reason and feeling in Western dualistic traditions.

Sprinting to the Finish Line While Changing Course

At the end of my first year of teaching, I was told by my department chair that, if I had not completed my dissertation by the end of my second year, I would not be rehired. As I loved my job and did not want to lose it, I realized that I would have to overcome the paralysis that had prevented me from writing my dissertation. As Judith was also writing her dissertation, we agreed that I would take a summer rental in Montreal where she lived, so that we could support each other. However, I continued to procrastinate. This was part of a writing pattern that began in college and would continue for many years after I finished my dissertation. I loved thinking and reading, but was afraid to start writing. What stopped me? Was it feelings of inadequacy? Did I fear how others would judge what I wrote? Was it because I knew there were no easy answers? Did I enjoy thinking about problems more than I did resolving them? Probably it was a combination of these things, alongside the fact that I had no female role models for becoming a theologian or a writer. In any case, I would continue to procrastinate and then complete academic papers and lectures at the last minute on airplanes and in hotel rooms for years to come. I am often thankful for the dictum "publish or perish" because without it I might never have written at all. One of the benefits of my procrastination process was that, due to exhaustion and pent-up energy, I was able to tap into an unconscious source and then words would flow out of me. These words were not always well-organized (that would come afterward), but they often felt inspired. I was able to write things that I had not previously been able to think, say, or understand. Despite the obvious drawbacks of my "method," it made writing a process of discovery—when I finally got down to it. The fact that I often discover what I am feeling and thinking through the writing process means that many of my "aha" moments are more tied to the essays and books I agreed to write than is case for someone like Judith who (as she and I have often discussed) usually has a clear idea of what she will say before she begins to write. At some point after I left academia, I became able to tap the unconscious source of my own knowing more easily.

Ensconced in Montreal, I spent the first two months of the summer obsessively watching the Watergate scandal unfold on television. In August, I accepted another friend's invitation to spend a month writing in an isolated cabin on Lake Champlain. As there was no television, and as my friend was writing in the next room, I wrote several chapters of my thesis at a mad pace. I returned to Montreal having written as much in a month as Judith had during the whole summer. Judith did not think that was fair.

During my final weeks in Montreal, I began working on the paper I had promised to present at the American Academy of Religion on women's spiritual quest in Doris Lessing's *The Four-Gated City*,[4] the book that Judith and I turned to when we felt most alone. In the book, Lessing's heroine begins to develop "prophetic powers" by "tuning in" to "currents and forces of energy," first in nature and then in the social world. Like Lessing's Martha Quest, I was staying up late and sleeping little. I began to feel that I too was tuning into currents and forces

4. Doris Lessing, *The Four-Gated City* (New York: Bantam Books, 1970). My essay was published as "Explorations with Doris Lessing in Quest of the Four-Gated City," in *Women and Religion*, ed. Judith Plaskow and Joan Arnold Romero, rev. ed. (AAR & Scholars Press, 1974), 31–61.

of energy. I took courage from Lessing's statement that Martha knew that "if she was feeling something, in this particular way, with the authenticity, the irresistibility of the growing point, then she was not alone, others were feeling the same."[5] Lessing explained that this is so because individuals share a common social and historical world. She said that all of those born in the twentieth century "are children of violence," shaped by wars and the memory of wars. Similarly, women born in the twentieth and twenty-first centuries almost anywhere in the world are shaped by patriarchal institutions, though these affect individuals and groups of women in different ways. I found that when I presented my first feminist paper at the AAR, written from "the growing place in myself," others thanked me for articulating what they did not know they were thinking or feeling until I put it into words. I did not know it at the time, but I was beginning *Diving Deep and Surfacing: Women Writers on Spiritual Quest*, a book that was in its own way revelatory, both for me and for my readers.[6] I was also exploring the topic of my original dissertation idea, which had been rejected.

During the next school year, I taught in the daytime and worked late into the nights on my electric typewriter, writing and rewriting the chapters of my dissertation, while smoking and drinking gallons of Tab diet cola. Though I was stressed about the deadline, I enjoyed the insights that came to me in the night. When I complained to my therapist that I was worried about not finishing on time, she said that I was like a racehorse that falls behind and then spurts to the finish line ahead of all the others. "I think you learned that you would not be rewarded for being smarter than the others," she said, "so you hold back. But," she continued, "you always know you can finish the race."

One of the reasons I was drawn to Wiesel, as I have said, is because, on my first reading of his book, I "tuned in" to the laughter of Gavriel and used it to distance myself from my own suffering. In the process of writing about Wiesel, I went back and forth between his questions and my own. Sometimes I was the young boy in the concentration camps

---

5. Lessing, *The Four-Gated City*, 512.
6. Carol P. Christ, *Diving Deep and Surfacing: Women Writers on Spiritual Quest* (Boston: Beacon Press, 1980).

who watched his father die and wondered why God had abandoned him. Sometimes I was with those who were humiliated while God watched. Sometimes I wondered if I would have been one of the good citizens who stood by while their neighbors were loaded onto cattle cars. Sometimes I was a young American woman who had never suffered as Wiesel had, asking how God could have abandoned His chosen people and how I could believe in Him after that. Sometimes, I felt I was like the last rabbi who tried to intervene with God, saying, "I am unable to light the fire and I do not even know the prayer; I cannot even find the place in the forest. All I can do is tell the story, and this must be sufficient."[7] In the words of the mystics, I went through my own dark night, confronting the evil in the world and my inability to explain it. Yet I felt that it was important to continue this journey with God.

Most of all, I shared Wiesel's anger at God. As my own theology was biblical and informed by Buber's stories of the Hasidim, I knew that Moses, the prophets, and later the rabbis spoke to God and that some of them even accused God of forgetting His people. I loved the raw anger born of faith and bewilderment in Wiesel's early books, especially *The Gates of the Forest*. Wiesel wrote his own questions into these books while he was still struggling with them, and there always seemed to be an answer lurking just beyond words. I loved Gavriel's response to the main character's questions about God: "It's so simple. Your uncertainties are what interest me."[8] It has always seemed to me that after he wrote *The Gates of the Forest*, Wiesel found a kind of solace in Jewish tradition that lessened the intensity of the questioning of God that made his early books so powerful.

I was also fascinated by the fact that Wiesel chose to write theology in the form of stories. Gavriel echoed the words of the rabbi at the edge of the forest when he told Wiesel's character, "You must go on with your story."[9] God revealed Himself in the Bible in stories. The rabbis told stories. And in telling stories, Wiesel found a way back to life and

---

7. Elie Wiesel, *The Gates of the Forest,* trans. Frances Frenaye (New York: Avon Books), 6–9.
8. Ibid., 208.
9. Ibid.

perhaps to God. On the last page of *Gates*, Wiesel's character was able to pray. "He prayed for the soul of his father and also for that of God."[10] "And so they renewed the ancient dialogue whose words come to us in the night, tinged with hatred, with remorse, and most of all with infinite yearning."[11]

At the end of my dissertation, I invoked the kabbalistic idea found in Wiesel's writing that the prayers or moral goodness of human beings could have the power to turn God back, to reclaim the attention of a God who has lost interest in the world, or perhaps even to redeem a God who is no longer good. I had not resolved the problem of evil in my dissertation, but in invoking these ideas, I was moving toward the conclusion that the solution to it would be found in abandoning the idea of God's omnipotence. As the title and subtitle of my dissertation, "Elie Wiesel's Stories: Still the Dialogue,"[12] suggested, I also affirmed the storied nature of theology and the importance of continuing to journey with God. In the part of this story that was not included in the dissertation—my own questioning of God—my story with God took a new turn.

I did indeed finish my thesis and submitted it "under the wire" on the last day I could. That day was a Monday, and I was still correcting typos on the manuscript on Saturday night. Then I discovered that no copy centers were open on Sundays in the entire city of New York. I tried copying my thesis at a friend's place of work, but the computer overheated. Finally, I called Naomi Goldenberg, who was still at Yale, took a bus to New Haven, and handed my dissertation to her. In the morning, she had it copied and bound and submitted it for me. That call was the beginning of a friendship that was to be crucial in my spiritual journey. Naomi became a good friend. She questioned my continuing ties to Christianity, and it was through her that I was introduced to the Goddess of women's spirituality.

After I finished my dissertation, I gathered up my courage and sent

---

10. Ibid., 223.
11. Elie Wiesel, *The Town beyond the Wall,* trans. Steven Becker (New York: Avon Books, 1970), 190.
12. Carol P. Christ, "Elie Wiesel's Stories: Still the Dialogue" (PhD diss., Yale University, 1974). Available through Proquest (University Microfilms).

it to Elie Wiesel. He invited me to his apartment in New York where he told me that I had understood his books as no one else had up to that time, expressing his surprise that a young American woman who was not even Jewish had entered so deeply into his work. He urged me to publish my dissertation, but after a single rejection, I set it aside. In those days it would never even have crossed my mind to ask Elie Wiesel for his help in finding a publisher, and I did not know how to go about finding one myself. Had feminism not been a part of my journey (and perhaps if I had not become friends with Naomi), I might have continued on the path of a biblically inspired dialogical theology in which human beings find God in stories and in which stories may have the power to redeem God. Who knows, like two of the other women who were at Yale in religious studies with Judith and me, I might even have converted to Judaism. But by the time I finished my dissertation, I was already on another spiritual path. My struggles with God about the Holocaust and my deep immersion in Wiesel's dialogical theology led to a crucial and unexpected turning point in my journey.

Expressing My Anger at God

Late one night when I was writing about Wiesel's anger at God, my own anger and my own questions for God welled up. I lay down on my bed as the words poured out of me. I asked God how He could have allowed Himself to be portrayed as a man, as God of the Fathers, as a Man of War, as King of the Universe. I asked why He never sent a female prophet or savior to set the record straight. I asked how He could let women be raped and beaten, be told they are less than men and unworthy, again and again, century after century. I continued and continued. I do not remember exactly what I said, but I do remember that in the silence that followed, I heard these words in my own mind: "In God is a woman like yourself. She shares your suffering. She too has had Her power of naming stolen from Her."[13]

13. See Carol P. Christ, "Women's Liberation and the Liberation of God," originally published in *The Jewish Woman: New Perspectives*, ed. Elizabeth Koltun (New York: Schocken Books, 1970) and reprinted in Christ, *Laughter of Aphrodite*, 20–26.

Although I had been aware of Goddesses in the history of religions and even in the Bible, I do not think I had imagined God as a woman or felt Her presence in my life until that moment. I have been seeking to know and understand Her ever since. This does not mean I think that God really is female and not male. But I do believe that female imagery for God is necessary. It is profoundly healing for women brought up without Goddess and God imaged as She: for us, speaking of Her has the power to transform the way we think about divinity.

This revelation led me to seek images of Goddess and God-She in the history of religions. I was not drawn to the Greek or Hindu Goddesses. I was no more interested in warrior Goddesses than I had been in warrior Gods. Yet Athena, Devi Mahatmya, and Kali/Durga were portrayed as warriors. Other Goddesses were dependent on Gods. They were not for me. I kept rereading *The Hebrew Goddess* and hoping that some of my friends would join my quest for a female God rooted in biblical traditions. But they did not seem interested. Instead, I turned to fiction and poetry written by women, hoping that there I would find my own questions articulated and maybe even answered. I would soon include Margaret Atwood's *Surfacing*, Denise Levertov's and Adrienne Rich's poetry, Kate Chopin's *The Awakening*, and Ntozake Shange's *for colored girls*, along with Doris Lessing, on my Women and Religion reading lists.

Exiting the Church and Creating a Community of Women

In the summer of 1974, the first Episcopal women priests were irregularly ordained. While I found this exciting, I also wondered why these women wanted so badly to be ordained in a church that didn't want them. I did not understand their loyalty to tradition because I had never called any Protestant denomination home. Though I do not recall having attended a single church service in New York City until then, I decided to attend a service of celebration for some of the women priests held at Riverside Church. I sat in the back of a crowded church. When the women priests processed in singing the (patriarchal) hymn, "A Mighty Fortress Is Our God," and a black male cleric welcomed them using traditional male language for God, I slipped out the door. Symbolically, that was my exit from the church.[14] I felt estranged from the women priests who seemed to find it was more important to be included in patriarchal traditions than to change them. As I was aware of the social structure of denominationalism,[15] I wondered why the women priests wanted to stay in an upper-class church, where—as my previous experience with a Presbyterian church suggested—the likes of someone like me might not ever be welcomed. I now understand that, in contrast to me, these women had strong family or other ties to their denomination.

If the celebration of women priests marked my exit from the church, thinking about Mary Daly's *Beyond God the Father*, which was published as I was completing my dissertation, led to my exodus from Christian and Jewish theology. I had hoped that biblical traditions could change, in part because I had found nothing to replace them. I was already unable to worship using the patriarchal and militaristic language of domination found in the Bible, in liturgies, and in theology. Mary Daly suggested that patriarchal conceptions, which she called "the Unholy Trinity" of rape, genocide, and war, were so fundamental to biblical traditions that they could not be changed.[16] Naomi Goldenberg insisted in our frequent conversations on the subject that Christianity was fundamentally patriarchal, while asking if I really believed that God became a man or that a savior was necessary to redeem humanity. At some point, perhaps a year or so after I finished my dissertation, I realized that I really did not believe in the doctrines of incarnation, original sin, or salvation through Christ. I was also coming to the conclusion that the God of the Old Testament, who I still did believe in, probably could not be stripped of the patriarchal and warlike language

---

14. In November 1971, Mary Daly delivered the sermon at Harvard Memorial Church, which she ended with a call for the "exodus" of women from the patriarchal church. At that time, Daly left open the question of whether or not the "exodus community" was leaving the church or calling for its transformation. See Barbara Flanagan, "Mary Daly Leads Exodus after Historic Sermon," *The Heights* (Boston College), November 22, 1971, p. 11 http://newspapers.bc.edu/cgi-bin/bostonsh?a=d&d=bcheights19711122.2.4#. My "exodus" was far less dramatic than Daly's.
15. H. Richard Niebuhr, *The Social Sources of Denominationalism* (n.p.: Kessinger reprint, 2004 [1929]).
16. Mary Daly, *Beyond God the Father: Toward a Philosophy of Women's Liberation* (Boston: Beacon Press, 1973), 114–22.

through which He had always been known. Had it been only the male language that needed to be changed, I might have believed that was possible. But the imagery of violence, domination, and war through which God was portrayed made it clear that something even more fundamental was at stake. Biblical traditions, like the Western tradition as a whole, were deeply flawed by war. I did not think they could be reformed.

That same fall, Anne Barstow and I founded the New York Feminist Scholars in Religion, which brought feminist scholars together for discussions once a month. This group came to include many women who would become leaders in feminist theology and spirituality—besides Anne and me, Judith Plaskow, Naomi Goldenberg, Beverly Harrison, Nelle Morton, Elisabeth Schüssler Fiorenza, Lynn Gottlieb, Elaine Pagels, Ellen Umansky, Karen McCarthy Brown, and others. Our group soon became a new spiritual home for many of us. Together we read each other's work and carried on lively discussions about the implications of feminism for the future of religions. My classes too began to take on a kind of sacred character as we sought and found a language that could carry us beyond God the Father. As Nelle Morton would write, "We literally heard one another down to a word that was *our* word and that word was ourselves."[17]

Finding the Goddess

The next summer, I left New York to begin an early sabbatical year in Berkeley, California, where I went to live with a man I thought I would marry. I loved living in New York in so many ways. As I walked its streets, I felt I was stepping into the footfalls of many ancestors. I loved New York's ethnic diversity. For the first time in my life, I felt that even I, a six-foot-tall blonde, could simply blend into the background. While I loved the ethnically diverse and intellectual milieu into which I had been thrown, I had also sensed a kind of disdain for all things Californian in my New York colleagues. I suspected that I would never

17. Nelle Morton, "The Dilemma of Celebration," in *Womanspirit Rising: A Feminist Reader in Religion*, ed. Carol P. Christ and Judith Plaskow (San Francisco: Harper & Row, 1979), 165.

really be accepted as a New York intellectual unless I gave up whatever I had brought with me from California. One of those things was my love for nature, epitomized by the crashing waves of the sea and the peacocks in my grandmother's garden. Class may also have been involved in my sense that I was not really a New York intellectual. I was interested to see how I would feel living in California again after an absence of eight years.

Shortly after I arrived back in California, a friend of mine from graduate school, Kit Havice, introduced me to A Woman's Place bookstore in Oakland, where I found copies of the first issue of *WomanSpirit* magazine and Marija Gimbutas's recently published *The Gods and Goddesses of Old Europe*.[18] Kit also encouraged me to attend a series of workshops with womanspirit pioneer Hallie Austen Iglehart, then writing under the name Hallie Mountainwing, at her home in the Berkeley hills. These workshops included discussions and demonstrations of hands-on healing and herbal remedies, but my strongest memory of them is that Hallie told us to trust ourselves and our intuitions and that she served delicious herbal tea made from peppermint, lemon grass, and licorice root. I met Charlene Spretnak, who would also become one of the leaders of the women's spirituality movement, at Hallie's workshops.

During the winter, the man I loved went off on a personal journey to Asia, making it clear that I was not welcome. I fell into a deep depression (this was neither the first nor the last time disappointment in love left me hanging), and it was all I could do to hold myself together. One night I decided to see if cutting my wrists would hurt. When I discovered that the very tiny trial cut I made didn't, I had the presence of mind to call my friend Kit, who picked me up and invited me to stay in her spare room over the weekend. Shortly after that, Naomi, who was also suffering from being left behind by a man she

---

18. Marija Gimbutas, *The Gods and Goddesses of Old Europe* (Berkeley: University of California Press, 1974); the book was republished in an updated edition using the title Gimbutas had originally chosen (which the publisher had rejected as too provocative), *The Goddesses and Gods of Old Europe*, in 1982.

loved, came to stay with me. We were supposed to be supporting each other's writing, but we never got very far with that.

Naomi decided that we should take one of the many free university courses advertised in alternative newspapers in order to get our minds off our problems. The course she chose was "Witchcraft." It was taught by a then unknown young woman called Starhawk. On the first night of the workshop, Starhawk introduced us to the Goddess, describing Her as the energy of the life force in nature. She also created a simple ritual in which we learned to raise energy. The Goddess and ritual were the two elements that had been missing for me in Hallie's workshops. Goddess was the female God revealed to me after I expressed my anger at God. As the energy of the life force, Goddess connected me to my grandmothers and to my childhood and adult experiences of the spirit in nature. As the power of birth, death, and renewal, the Goddess could help me understand the relationship of life and death that had haunted me since my teenage years. Though Mara Keller, who had come to the class with us, and Naomi questioned aspects of what we had heard on the way home, I was silent. I knew that I had found Her.

My love affair ended in anger and tears, and I returned to New York with my newfound love of the Goddess. That fall, Merlin Stone's *When God Was a Woman* was published in the United States. I remember lying on my bed in New York City reading this book with nothing less than astonishment. Whereas Starhawk had given me a name and an experience of Goddess ritual, Stone unfolded a Goddess history I had not known despite having earned a PhD in the field of religion. To this day Stone's words, "In the beginning . . . God was a woman. Do you remember?"[19] make my skin tingle. Years of further study have convinced me of the accuracy of most of Stone's major assertions. She spoke of Indo-European invasions of previously peaceful egalitarian matrilineal Goddess-centered societies. She was the one who saw that the Genesis story of Eve and the snake was a "tale with a point of view" intent on discrediting the Tree of Life, the Mother of All the Living, the Sacred Snake, and the Fruit of the Tree of Life.

---

19. Merlin Stone, *When God Was a Woman* (New York: Dial Press, 1976), 1.

During that same fall, I saw Ntozake Shange's *for colored girls who have considered suicide/when the rainbow is enuf* off-Broadway with a feminist friend from graduate school. We were mesmerized. The women in the play seemed to be speaking of our lives, even though the stories were very much rooted in black women's experiences. "Somebody almost walked off with all of my stuff" could have been our refrain. Chills went up and down our spines as the woman in red rose from her despair to sing, "I found god in myself/and I loved her/I loved her fiercely."[20] For me Shange's play was a sacramental drama. I returned to see it again and again with friends and students. I began teaching it as soon as the first edition of the book came out. In class, my students and I would read our favorite passages out loud and discuss them. One of the chapters in the book I would write, *Diving Deep and Surfacing*, was the first literary analysis of Shange's work. I was thrilled when pioneer black feminist literary critic Mary Helen Washington told me she carried a copy of my book around with her and read my chapter on Shange when she felt discouraged.

Around that time, Anne Barstow presented her research on the Goddess of Çatal Hüyük[21] to the New York Feminist Scholars on the same night I spoke of the Goddess I found while in California. Neither Anne nor I were prepared for the response we received. What we said touched a deep chord among the women present, but the loudest voices were those that insisted that what we were talking about was "idolatry" and that there could be "no ethics in Goddess religion" because ethics must stem from a transcendent source outside of nature. While I had expected that the other feminist scholars in religion would rejoice in the Goddess, most of them clung tightly to their traditions of origin. I began to feel less accepted than I once had in the new home I had helped to create for myself. The same reaction would follow when Naomi and I began to speak of the Goddess to other feminist scholars at the American Academy of Religion.

20. Ntozake Shange, *for colored girls who have considered suicide/when the rainbow is enuf* (New York: Macmillian, 1976), 63.
21. Anne Barstow, "The Uses of Archaeology for Women's History: James Mellaart's Work on the Neolithic Goddess at Catal Huyuk," *Feminist Studies* 4, no. 3 (October 1978): 7–18.

Finding My Voice

At this time I naively believed that the academy would reward the search for truth that I had embarked upon. However, I began to discover that the directions in which my work was taking me were not to be easily understood or respected in the field. Since I had been told when I took the job at Columbia that junior faculty were rarely promoted, I decided to try to find a job in California. The one I found was in women's studies at San Jose State. As I was eager to get back into the thick of things in the emerging women's spirituality and Goddess movements that were flowering on the West Coast and to live closer to nature by moving out of the city, I did not realize that, in the academy, scholars are often judged not by the quality of their work but by the status of their academic position—and that moving from a prestigious university to a state university would make it more difficult for me to move "back up" the academic ladder.

I did get into the thick of things in the Goddess movement in California. My career also flourished during my years at San Jose State. The anthology Judith and I coedited, *Womanspirit Rising*, a collection of the essays we were using in our classes, made quite a splash and eventually sold over one hundred thousand copies, defining the field of women and religion for some time, and raising issues that have yet to be fully addressed in the field of religion as a whole. I was invited to speak an average of three times a month at universities and churches. I published not one but two books and many articles and reviews. I won not one but two National Endowment for the Humanities Fellowships. I served on major committees in the American Academy of Religion. At the same time, I was saddled with a very heavy teaching load and had decided to take on large numbers of students in order to demonstrate the need for a second full-time faculty member in our small women's studies program. Many of the students who came to my office hours told me stories they had not voiced before of incest, rape, and beating. Listening to these stories day after day was emotionally and psychically exhausting, even though I felt honored that my students had trusted me with their stories.

My first year in California, Naomi and I introduced the Goddess to feminist scholars at the American Academy of Religion in San Francisco, choosing the venue of a closed seminar because we were afraid to speak about the Goddess in an open forum in the academy. For this meeting, I wrote what has since become the most widely published work of my career, "Why Women Need the Goddess."[22] At the conference, Judith and I found a publisher for *Womanspirit Rising*, and I introduced Starhawk to our editors John Loudin and Marie Cantlon, who signed her to a contract for her first book. This marked the beginning of a decade and a half when Harper San Francisco became known for its line of books on feminism and religion, women's spirituality, and the Goddess. I was both helping to create and being swept along in an enormous current of energy.

Writing "Why Women Need the Goddess" was like giving birth, and Naomi, who was writing her talk in the next room, was my midwife. I remember reading sentences and paragraphs to Naomi, asking, "Can I say that?" and "Dare I say that?" Her answer was always yes: she heard me into the speech that in its own small way would change the world. In "Why Women Need the Goddess," I discussed the psychological and political implications of the newly emerging symbol of Goddess. I showed how Goddess symbolism legitimates and celebrates women's power, bodies, wills, and bonds with each other. I argued that, in a patriarchal culture that has had only male symbols for God, the Goddess symbol has both psychological and political consequences. In transforming women's views of themselves, the Goddess symbol could lead to the transformation of the world. In this essay, I bracketed theological questions about the nature of Goddess. However, in stating that Goddess affirmed both the female body and women's will, I was suggesting that the Goddess symbol had the power to transform

---

22. Carol P. Christ, "Why Women Need the Goddess" was first published in *Heresies* (Spring, 1978) and is the last chapter in Christ and Plaskow, *Womanspirit Rising*, 273–87. A partial list of the places it has been reprinted can be found in the bibliography at the end of this book.

Western dualisms of mind and body, reason and feeling, spirit and nature—a theme that would become central in my future work.

In the spring of 1978, I helped to organize a weekend seminar at the University of California in Santa Cruz with Charlene, Hallie, and Carolyn Schaeffer called "The Great Goddess Re-emerging." I delivered "Why Women Need the Goddess" as the keynote address to an electrified audience of over five hundred cheering women and a few men. I understood that by moving through my fears and speaking the truths of my life, I was empowering other women to join me in what had begun as a lonely journey. The essay was published in *The Great Goddess Issue* of *Heresies*, a widely read feminist journal, as the final essay of *Womanspirit Rising*, and in Charlene Spretnak's *The Politics of Women's Spirituality*.[23] It has since been republished many times and has introduced hundreds of thousands of women to the Goddess.

That same spring, I taught my first course on Goddesses and Gods, beginning my own intensive study of Goddess history. One of the most powerful aspects of the course for me and for my students was the slides—hundreds of images of Goddesses from many cultures. In conscious and unconscious ways, the images of Goddesses reshaped our sense of female power and the female body. With Karen Voss and E. Carmen Torres, two returning students in the class, I cofounded a Goddess ritual group that combined our creativity with insights from *Black Elk Speaks* and used books by Z. Budapest, and Starhawk as "cookbooks" for our own rituals.[24] This group continued for more than ten years, even after I moved from San Jose to Berkeley, and then to Greece. Unlike Christianity, Goddess practice does not require adherence to a set of theological beliefs. As most of us in the ritual group had come from Christian or Jewish backgrounds, we tended to think of Goddess as a personal power who cared about the universe, but we also saw Her as the powers of birth, death, and regeneration in

---

23. Charlene Spretnak, *The Politics of Women's Spirituality* (New York: Doubleday, 1982), 71–86.
24. Z. Budapest *The Feminist Book of Lights and Shadows,* ed. Helen Beardwoman (n.p.) and Z. Budapest, *The Holy Book of Women's Mysteries, Part 1* (Los Angeles: Susan B. Anthony Coven No. 1, 1979); Starhawk, *The Spiral Dance: A Rebirth of the Ancient Religion of the Great Goddess* (San Francisco: HarperSanFrancisco, 1979).

nature. As we celebrated seasonal holidays and full moons, we learned to find the Goddess in darkness as well as light. We understood that in reclaiming the Goddess, we were honoring our female bodies and much-maligned female body wisdom, women's intuition, and women's traditions of healing with our hands. These years of practice helped the Goddess take root in my mind and body. Though our group did not engage in political action, we understood that, besides healing ourselves as women, we were undertaking a sacred commitment to heal the world. Inspired by antinuclear activist Helen Caldicott, Goddess sisters Karen Voss, Mara Keller, and I created an antiwar, antinuclear slide show called *Genesis/Genocide.* As I had argued in "Why Women Need the Goddess," our emerging spirituality had political implications.

My First Book

In my early years at San Jose State, I realized that the essays I had written on women's spiritual quest in Doris Lessing and Margaret Atwood, combined with the insights I had been gaining in teaching Kate Chopin, Ntozake Shange, and Adrienne Rich, formed the nucleus of a book. The book I would write, *Diving Deep and Surfacing: Women Writers on Spiritual Quest,* begins with these words: "Women's stories have not been told. . . . If women's stories are not told, the depths of women's souls will not be known."[25] My first book, like my dissertation, was situated in the field of religion and literature and drew upon the theories of Stephen Crites and Michael Novak about religion and stories. I was still suspicious of theology because I felt it often was not grounded in experience and had become overly abstract. Yet I worried that the theology and literature approach found Christian themes like sacrifice or incarnation in works of secular literature. I was hesitant to read Christian or even Goddess themes into the works that became the subject of the chapters of my book.

It is hard to recall the darkness of the dark night of the soul that

---

25. Christ, *Diving Deep and Surfacing*, 1.

has left its traditional moorings. I was within the mystic's "cloud of unknowing" until I found voices that could help me find a way to a new knowing. Lessing, Atwood, Chopin, Rich, and Shange were among the voices that helped me find the words to express my experience. When I was writing the book, I wondered if anyone other than Judith would respond favorably to it. To my great surprise, like "Why Women Need the Goddess," *Diving Deep and Surfacing* became a minor feminist classic that provided a way out of the wilderness for many other women.[26] Women's responses to my work gave me the strength and courage to continue.

In *Diving Deep*, I said that hearing and telling women's stories would lead to a new revelation of the sacred in women's lives. I spoke of a "new naming of self and world" that would emerge when women spoke the truths of their lives. I highlighted nature mysticism, sexual mysticism, and communal mysticism in women's experiences and suggested that women's new naming of the sacred would strive to unite the spiritual and social quests of women, and would affirm the body and nature, and the power of women's relationships with each other. In the conclusion, I tentatively suggested that finding "god in myself" or discovering Goddess would be part of the new naming. I added that I hoped the telling of women's stories would lead to the transformation of dualistic thinking. "I like to think [of] women's celebration of the body, nature, feeling, and intuition as the first stage in an attempt . . . to move toward a more whole way of thinking . . . [in which] the body, nature, emotion, and intuition will be affirmed, but also reason, freedom, and the spirit will not be left behind."[27] I set the agenda for my subsequent books.

While writing *Diving Deep* was a process in which I was naming myself and the world anew, I was very much aware that this book would be judged by (primarily male) academics when I applied for other jobs or for tenure. Thus I wrote the book in a distanced third-person, seemingly objective, voice. This trope was only partially

---

26. As of this writng, nearly fifty thousand copies have been sold.
27. Christ, *Diving Deep*, 130.

successful, as my connection to the subject matter was evident. I did include a more personal preface in the original edition and addressed the problem of voice in the preface to the second edition and in the afterword to the third edition. The question of voice was one I would struggle with in subsequent years. While I never wavered in my conviction that theologies must be connected to experience and thus to stories, I was not sure how to achieve that connection. Later, I would experiment with writing in a more personal voice and in more poetic prose in some of the essays in *Laughter of Aphrodite.* I often wondered if I should be writing poetry or fiction, rather than theology. I urged my feminist colleagues to experiment more boldly with inserting personal experience into theological discussions. Karen McCarthy Brown and Christine Downing were among the few academic colleagues at the time who explicitly explored their personal relationships to the subjects they wrote about.[28] Our friendships were the matrix in which we found the courage to do so. Yet as I followed my own truth and intuition, I was distancing myself even further from most other academic feminists.

And Then There Was Greece

While at San Jose State, I was asked by my colleague Ellen Boneparth to teach Greek Goddesses in the International Women's Studies Institute summer program that she was organizing in Greece. I said no, because I had only recently gotten married, had just finished my first book, and had no interest in Greek Goddesses or visiting Greece. As Ellen would not take no for an answer, I finally said yes, thinking that the project was a pipe dream in any case. Instead, in the following spring, I packed my bags and headed for six weeks of teaching in Greece—in the village of Molivos, Lesbos, on the island of Sappho, that Ellen had fallen in love with. As with so many other things in my life, chance

---

28. Christine Downing, *The Goddess: Mythological Images of the Feminine* (New York: Crossroad Press, 1981); Karen McCarthy Brown, "Olina and Erzulie: A Woman and a Goddess in Haitian Vodou," *Anima* (Spring, 1979): 110–16; and "Plenty Confidence in Myself: The Initiation of a White Woman Scholar into Haitian Vodou," *Journal of Feminist Studies in Religion* 3, no. 1 (Spring, 1987): 67–76; also see *Mama Lola: A Vodou Priestess in Brooklyn* (Berkeley: University of California Press, 1991).

not choice led me to a place that would change my life. In my first summer in Greece, I came to understand that the myths of the Goddess and their familiar white marble images were edifices erected on top of something far more ancient. As art historian Vincent Scully shows, all of the Greek temples were situated in sacred places in nature.[29] The Greek Goddesses had emerged from Mother Earth. Returned to their source, the Greek Goddesses took on new meaning for me. The cover of my next book, *Laughter of Aphrodite*, illustrates this: the face of the Goddess emerges from the landscape.[30]

Though I taught rather conventionally in my first year in Lesbos, in subsequent years I felt freer to experiment because the students were no longer taking the course for academic credit. I used Christine Downing's *The Goddess*, in which she connects the stories of the Greek Goddesses to her own life, in tandem with *Diving Deep and Surfacing*. My students and I spent part of each class writing on the themes of the experience of nothingness, nature mysticism, sexual mysticism, and the new naming that I discussed in my book, in relation to Downing's stories of the Goddesses. Again my classes took on a sacred character. In the community we created, we were able to name and articulate our deepest knowing. Back home, I experimented with introducing some of the teaching techniques I had discovered in Lesbos into my courses. Even in my larger classes, I insisted that the students arrange the chairs in a circle in order to promote sharing. This simple gesture was perceived as revolutionary. A faculty member whose class followed mine called the dean to complain that he couldn't control his students when the chairs were in a circle! Yet this was but one of the small ways in which I was testing the boundaries of academia.

In a writing exercise on sexual mysticism and Aphrodite in one of my classes in Greece, many of us wrote about unresolved issues in our lives. Like others in our culture, we had been taught that sexuality belongs in marriage and is for the purpose of creating children. We

29. Vincent Scully, *The Earth, the Temple, and the Gods: Greek Sacred Architecture* (New Haven: Yale University Press, 1962, 1969, 1979).
30. I had to fight with my publisher to create this cover, as the original suggestion was a photograph of the Venus de Milo.

had also learned that our female parts "down there" are dirty and our sexuality somehow shameful. Most of us were trying to break free from those ideas, yet we had also found that following the sexual freedom of the counterculture often created other kinds of problems. In graduate school, I began to become proud of my body and my sexuality, refusing to dress or act like a nun or a good Christian girl, but this meant that my colleagues often saw only my body and not the whole intelligent embodied and sexual female human being that I was. Moved by similarities in our stories, Alexis Masters, one of the students in my Greece class who would become a close friend, and I decided to visit the temple of Aphrodite—which we had heard was somewhere in the center of the island of Lesbos—to see what inspiration and healing we might find there. Before we left, we prepared. We bought wine and honey as offerings and bedecked ourselves in golden-toned jewelry and golden shawls we found in a local shop.

In those days, none of the locals even knew where the temple was, and we had quite an adventure finding it. As we would learn, we had to travel winding roads, cross three bridges, and turn left down a dirt road at the heart of the Gulf of Kalloni. The temple, which was next to a farmyard, was in ruins in a swampy area overgrown with weeds and wild flowers next to a spring. A wire fence had fallen down, and we easily scrambled over it. Once inside the sacred precinct we found a carving of a flower in the shape of a vagina on an ancient stone: it seemed to us to be a symbol of the power and beauty of our female sexuality. We were each drawn to remove all of our clothing except our golden jewelry and shawls and to sit separately in meditation next to trees that had grown up at the center of the temple. As the sun caressed our bodies, we seemed to hear the laughter of Aphrodite that Christine Downing and others had described. We felt transformed.[31]

I spent many years trying to understand what had happened to us at the temple of Aphrodite. To this day, the fullness of the experience defies words. We experienced our female bodies in the image of the Goddess and sexuality as sacred. We felt ourselves become part of a

31. See "You Know the Place," in Christ, *Laughter of Aphrodite*, 186–92.

sacred place in nature where others had been before us. In the next years, I would bring other women to the place to share the experience we had. I would speak of myself as a priestess of Aphrodite and that day as my initiation.[32] I understood Aphrodite to be one of the names of the Great Goddess, the life force in my body and in all of nature. I chose to devote myself to the Goddess as Aphrodite because She promised to heal my body, myself, and to help me to integrate spirituality and sexuality. Audre Lorde's "Uses of the Erotic"[33] helped me to understand the power of the Goddess as Aphrodite. Lorde writes that the erotic connection with the world we experience as joy in our bodies can unlock our deepest knowing and the power to change the world. Though Lorde spoke of experiencing the erotic in a variety of ways, reclaiming sexuality as sacred was uppermost in her mind. I knew that affirming the power of the erotic was an aspect of the feminist struggle to overcome the dualism of mind and body, reason and emotion, spirit and nature bequeathed to us by Western culture.

Though I experienced a sense of connection to a power beyond myself in and through sexual experiences both before and after visiting Aphrodite's temple, I found this confusing, because in my life, sexual relationships rarely stood the test of time. Following my erotic feelings often caused me to fall into a deep hole where feelings of abandonment and despair overwhelmed everything else. I now understand that I made the mistake of identifying sexual experiences and the person with whom I shared them with the power of the erotic. When I was still in my twenties, I heard Doris Lessing, who must have been in her early fifties, respond to a question about why sexual relationships were no longer a central theme in her work. Lessing said something like, "Those things just don't seem so important to me anymore." I was horrified, because at the time and for many years afterward "those things" seemed to me to be the most important things. As I have

---

32. "The Initiation of an American Woman Scholar into the Symbols and Rituals of Ancient Goddesses," *Journal of Feminist Studies in Religion* 3, no. 1 (Spring 1987): 57–66.
33. Audre Lorde, "Uses of the Erotic: The Erotic as Power," in *Weaving the Visions: New Patterns in Feminist Spirituality*, ed. Judith Plaskow and Carol P. Christ (San Francisco: Harper & Row, 1989), 208–13.

grown in wisdom and years, I tend to agree with Lessing. I think that when I was younger, I opened to the world intensely through sexuality because I was not open to experiencing the power of the erotic in other ways. Now that the power of the erotic is more everyday and less mysterious, I too have stopped thinking so much about sex. I recognize the power of the erotic in the birds that bathe in the fountain in my garden, in the poppies that flower in the olive groves in spring, in good food shared with friends, in conversations that probe the meaning of life, and in the commitment I share with my friends in the Green Party of Greece to heal the world. These days I no longer feel a special connection to Aphrodite or to any other particular Goddess, and it has been years since I called myself a priestess of Aphrodite. I celebrate the Goddess in nature and in sacred places in nature, and I am drawn to the smaller, more intimate images of the Goddess from Neolithic Europe and ancient Crete.

When I moved back to California, I saw San Jose State as a stepping stone to a job in which I would teach graduate students in the field of religion. But despite the academic recognition I achieved while teaching at San Jose, I began to wonder if that would ever happen. When I left Columbia, I was told dismissively by the female chair of the religion department that she was not interested in creating a position in women and literature. In California, I was invited to teach feminist theology at the Pacific School of Religion by a woman dean. Though the course was successful, I was not asked to teach it again. As my life was busy, I did not think much about that. A few years later, I learned that, even though only one book on my reading list was post-Christian, I had not been rehired because a student had reported that I had said that "Mary Daly might be right." Apparently, all of my credentials in the field of theology were erased by the fact that I had suggested that I might not be a professing Christian.

Moving On

When, a few years later, I delivered the prestigious Antoinette Brown Blackwell Lecture at Vanderbilt Divinity School, I mentioned my desire to teach graduate students to my feminist colleague Sallie McFague. She told me that, even though she considered my work to be first rate, I would never be offered a job teaching graduate students in theology because I was not a Christian. I reluctantly concluded that she was probably right. At the same time, the already punishing working conditions at San Jose State were deteriorating under Governor Ronald Reagan. I had achieved tenure and full professor, but the thought of being the only full-time faculty member in women's studies, teaching four courses and nearly two hundred students a semester, while listening to stories of abuse that burdened my soul, and trying to find time for speaking and writing—for the rest of my academic career—was depressing. As if to add insult to injury, about a month later, the day before I was leaving to teach in Greece, my husband told me that our marriage was over.

Every year when I came back from Greece, I felt renewed and everyone told me I looked radiant. Without grades and structures, I enjoyed my teaching more than I did back home. I loved the fact that in the village where I taught there were almost no cars and no streetlights and an incredible peace and quiet. Still, Greece was the interlude, while teaching and writing in the United States was real life. The combination of the end of my marriage and the dashing of my hopes to find a better job caused me to look at Greece differently. I extended my stay, and I met another visitor who was thinking of changing his life by moving to Greece. Though I had heard others speak of living in Greece, I never imagined this as anything more than a pipe dream. This time I heard it as a real possibility. Well, I thought, if academia won't reward me for all my excellent and very hard work, then maybe I don't need academia. Without a husband to consider, I was free to choose a new life. I began to make plans to take a leave of absence from San Jose and to fantasize a life in which I married a Greek fisherman, lived a more simple life by the sea, and wrote poetry. I calculated that I could pay for this new life in Greece in the era of the drachma with royalties and advances from my books. I spent the next spring and summer in Molivos, Lesbos, where I did live simply, I did write, I did begin to learn Greek, and I did flirt with the many available men and fell in love with one who was not. Decisions about the future were put on hold for a year when I was offered a position as research associate at Harvard Divinity School for the following academic year.

At Harvard, I had wonderful students in my class on Goddesses. Most of them insisted that we continue the journey we had begun in an independent study course the next semester. My public lecture, "Rethinking Theology and Nature,"[34] was greeted with stunning applause by an overflow crowd of students and faculty. Harvard theologian Gordon Kaufman, whose work I both made use of and challenged in my talk, said that he liked the lecture very much.[35] Despite all of that, I learned some things while at Harvard that confirmed my suspicion that there was no place for me in academia. The few women on the Harvard faculty seemed stressed and unhappy. A male Harvard professor died suddenly as the fall semester was beginning, and his colleague told the rest of the faculty that if they offered the position left open to feminist biblical scholar Elisabeth Schüssler Fiorenza, he would commit suicide. This threat was enough to scare the faculty into voting for a less well-known male scholar.[36] Even more disappointing to me, at the seminar for women faculty to discuss my public lecture, the most senior woman faculty member praised my paper as brilliant and powerful for the way it combined passion with deep and profound thinking. "But," she added, "we could never do anything like that at Harvard." For the next hour and a half she and the other women talked about everything under the sun—except my paper. I was devastated. I desperately wanted to be part of a feminist conversation on religion, but the message I received loud and clear that day was that my work was too threatening to the other women for them to feel comfortable discussing it, even in a

---

34. Carol P. Christ, "Rethinking Theology and Nature," in Plaskow and Christ, *Weaving the Visions,* 314–25.
35. Unlike the women at Harvard who were unable to discuss my paper, Kaufman spent over an hour with me debating my ideas, treating me as a valued and valuable colleague.
36. This story was reported to me by a faculty member and was widely known among the students as well. Elisabeth Schüssler Fiorenza was hired a year later to a position created especially for her.

closed room. A few days later, I decided to resign my job at San Jose State and move to Greece.

While at Harvard, I negotiated a two-book contract that included collecting my essays into the book that became *Laughter of Aphrodite: Reflections on a Journey to the Goddess* and a second book, a systematic Goddess theology, eventually published as *Rebirth of the Goddess*.[37] I felt it was too soon to write a systematic theology about the Goddess, and I was not certain that systematic theology was the appropriate medium for writing about the Goddess movement; however, the promise to do so was the condition for publishing my collected essays. *Laughter of Aphrodite* was released at the end of my year at Harvard. The essays in it were written in different voices: one third person, distanced, and analytical; another that told stories; and a third emerging voice in the introductions to the sections of the book and in its final essay, where I was beginning to integrate the two. The book included photographs of Goddess images and of me experiencing the Goddess in ritual spaces. As the rebirth of the Goddess is in part a remaking of our images of embodied femaleness, the images were an important part of the whole. At the time of the publication of *Laughter of Aphrodite*, I felt divided within myself, with one part of me still in academia and one part in the Goddess movement. I was not sure if there was a way to integrate the two parts of myself or the two voices in which I was writing.

Laughter of Aphrodite brought together essays voicing my criticisms of biblical traditions, and charting my journey from God to Goddess. It included my response to Judith's analysis of Christian feminist anti-Judaism—an essay in which I urged Goddess feminists not to blame Jews for the rise of patriarchy or the death of the Goddess.[38] If there had been any lingering doubt in anyone's mind, the book made it clear that I was no longer Christian. Looking back on these essays now, it is easy to forget the tenacity and courage of the young woman who wrote them over the course of a decade and a half, for the most part to be delivered as public lectures. As I documented my struggle with

---

37. Carol P. Christ, *Rebirth of the Goddess: Finding Meaning in Feminist Spirituality* (New York: Addison Wesley: 1997; paperback, New York: Routledge, 1998).
38. "On Not Blaming Jews for the Death of the Goddess," in Christ, *Laughter of Aphrodite*, 88–92.

God and my discovery of the Goddess, I knew that the stakes were very high: I expected that my questioning of biblical religion would not be universally welcomed, and I feared that speaking the truth as I saw it would make it even less likely that I would ever find a permanent job teaching graduate students in my field. In "Finitude, Death, and Reverence for Life," the last chapter of the book, I began to find a voice that integrated my intellect and my deepest nonrational knowledge. In it, I returned to the question that had motivated me to study religion in the first place: *the meaning of death and its place in life.* While once I had asked why God permits suffering and death, I had come to understand that death is part of life. I suggested that we must embrace finite life that ends in death and that our failure to do so has brought us to the point where humanity stands poised to destroy the conditions of life as we know it on planet earth. I traced the root of our culture's denial of finitude and death to the Platonic dualisms that associate women with the body, nature, and finitude, and the rational mind of men with transcendence of the world. I understood this to be a wrong turn that had not only shaped Western culture ever since, but that might lead to its demise. This essay, written in the shadow of the nuclear threat, explored my conviction that "this earth is holy and our true home,"[39] which for me is one of the central insights of Goddess spirituality.

In my public lecture at Harvard, also written in a voice that combines passionate feeling, ethical concern, and deep thinking, I returned to this theme, asserting that "we have lost the sense that this earth is our true home, and we fail to recognize our profound connection with all beings in the web of life." I argued that the absolute metaphysical distinctions between "God, man, and nature" that are assumed in Western philosophies and theologies are one of the roots of the crisis that threatens life on planet earth. I chose Gordon Kaufman as my dialogical partner because I agreed with him that we must construct a theology adequate to the central problem of our time—which is the human potential to destroy the conditions for life as we know it on planet earth. I contrasted Kaufman's claim that human

39. Christ, *Laughter of Aphrodite,* ix.

beings stand apart from nature by virtue of rational self-consciousness with Susan Griffin's assertion that "we are nature" and Paula Gunn Allen's statement that "we are the land." I argued that, rather than assuming that intelligence sets us apart from nature, we might find the roots of our intelligence within nature. I suggested that a philosophy that stressed our human connection with all forms of life might be more useful in facing the challenge of our age than one that sets us apart from nature.

In my Harvard lecture, I left open the question of whether or not the whole of which we are a part is an "impersonal process of life, death, and transformation" or whether "the universe has a center of consciousness that cares for us."[40] In the following years, I would come to discover that my inability to answer this question was one of the reasons I was reluctant, and for a long time unable, to write a thealogy of the Goddess.

---

40. Carol P. Christ, "Rethinking Theology and Nature," in Plaskow and Christ, *Weaving the Visions*, 314, 316, 320, 323–24.

5

Finding a God I Can Believe In

Judith Plaskow

Tracing the development of my mature understanding of God seems a more daunting task than describing the God of my childhood and young adulthood. Perhaps because my early memories are limited, and the simple fact that they remain with me testifies to their significance, it feels relatively straightforward to connect the dots into something resembling a coherent picture. For the recent past—even for the last thirty years—my memories are both more abundant and more tangled. I have artifacts in the form of publications and lecture notes that reflect changes in my thinking without necessarily indicating the steps that led me from one perspective to another. I am aware of how often a new way of seeing took me by surprise, emerging in a moment so full-grown that I know it must have been developing slowly without my knowledge. In the words of poet Marge Piercy,

Connections are made slowly, sometimes they grow underground.
You cannot always tell by looking what is happening.
More than half a tree is spread out in the soil under your feet.[1]

At other times, a particular insight has been like a pebble cast into a pond whose ripples continue to extend out even when I can no longer follow them. My ideas about God are interwoven with the fabric of my life, and it is both more necessary and more difficult to select judiciously the events and experiences that I describe as contributing to my current thinking. In assembling a narrative, moreover, I cannot view my adult beliefs with the mixture of sympathy, indulgence, and distance that I bring to my younger self. Youth no longer serves as an excuse for the gaps and contradictions in my thinking. If having a degree in theology is by itself no guarantee of developing a satisfying conception of God, it should at least allow me to set out what I believe coherently and persuasively. In a way that was less true of me as a child, I am now responsible both for the substance of my ideas and my capacity to defend them.

Desert Wanderings

I mentioned at the end of my first chapter that my adolescent understanding of God was still intact when I left Yale but, largely unbeknownst to me, was being quietly eroded by new ideas and experiences. It remained the case throughout the decade after I became a feminist that my intellectual explorations ran far ahead of my capacity to fully integrate the ideas I was studying and advocating. With the exception of two years in the New York Havurah—an independent, lay-led Jewish community that was completely egalitarian—these were desert years for me religiously even while my mind exploded with new thoughts and insights. In the Reform congregation in which I grew up, Sabbath services were a mix of Hebrew and English and lasted about an hour. Although I was unaware of this at the time, the Union Prayer Book that we used consisted

1. Marge Piercy, "The Seven of Pentacles," in her *To Be of Use* (Garden City, NY: Doubleday, 1969), 90.

of just those carefully selected excerpts from the traditional liturgy that accorded with Reform theology. The service was compact, easily comprehensible, and dominated by the notion of God as Helper, Lord, and King who cared deeply about social justice and demanded that we act justly. Once I became involved with, and then married, Robert, I found myself at three-hour services that, with the exception of the sermon, were entirely in Hebrew. They spoke of a God who raised the dead, distinguished the people Israel from idolatrous nations, and would some day rebuild the temple in Jerusalem and restore animal sacrifices. Thus, on those fairly rare occasions when I went to synagogue, I found myself using a prayer book with which I was unfamiliar in a language I did not understand, saying words I did not believe that had no childhood resonance for me.

I felt equally at sea with regard to developing a substantive scholarly agenda. When I left Yale after my comprehensive exams and began to work on my dissertation, the task that excited and energized me was developing a definition of women's experience that I could use to critique the theologies of Reinhold Niebuhr and Paul Tillich. I tried to set out an understanding of women's experience as situated at the juncture of "male definitions of women and the lived experiences of women within, in relation and in opposition to these definitions."[2] I drew on the work of contemporary female novelists, particularly but not only Doris Lessing's Children of Violence series, in order to create a thick description of the delicate dance required of women between cultural expectations and our own aspirations—aspirations that would always be partly shaped by culture. Evaluating Niebuhr's and Tillich's doctrines of sin and grace in light of this definition was for me the far less interesting part of the thesis, the part I needed to write to get my degree and teach. When I finished my dissertation, I found myself in the extremely awkward position of having been trained to be something I could never be: a Protestant theologian. While other feminist scholars seemed happy to embrace me as an emerging

2. Judith Plaskow, "Sex, Sin, and Grace: Women's Experience and the Theologies of Reinhold Niebuhr and Paul Tillich" (PhD diss., Yale University, 1975); published under the same title (Lanham, MD: University Press of America, 1980), 10–11.

Protestant feminist thinker, I did not see how I could possibly write constructive theology in someone else's tradition.[3] I had no interest in rethinking a tradition that was not mine and in which I did not believe; nor did I feel I had a right to do so. Yet how could I be a Jewish theologian when I had virtually no training in Jewish studies?

Intellectual Explorations

This is where things stood with me on an existential level, at the same time that, on an intellectual level, I was devouring the scanty literature in women and religion and making important contributions to the development of the field. While I was still a graduate student, I cochaired the Women and Religion Group of the American Academy of Religion during its second and third years. I shaped the program, edited the papers into a collection for classroom use, and became part of a bourgeoning community of feminist scholars dedicated to reshaping the study of religion.[4] While writing my dissertation, I was a research associate in women's studies in religion at Harvard Divinity School, the first year of what was to become an important ongoing program. It was a year of great ferment at the Divinity School, and I threw myself into the emerging feminist community, giving lectures on feminism in the introductory theology course and convening an ongoing discussion group on feminist theology. This was the year that students in a required lecture course interrupted the professor with whistles whenever he used male generic language. It was also the year that Emily Culpepper made and showed her groundbreaking and provocative film "Period Piece" for her final MDiv project—a lyric meditation on menstruation that placed it in the context of women's daily lives and ended with a close-up of Emily doing a vaginal self-exam while she was menstruating. This was also the year that saw the publication of Mary Daly's *Beyond God the Father*, a watershed event that was celebrated with a panel at Harvard in which I participated.

---

3. A number of times in the 1970s, I found myself on lists of Protestant feminist theologians.

4. Judith Plaskow and Joan Arnold Romero, *Women and Religion: Papers of the Working Group on Women and Religion*, rev. ed. (Missoula, MT: American Academy of Religion and Scholars Press, 1974).

The following fall, I moved to New York to teach at New York University and started attending the newly established New York Feminist Scholars in Religion, a group that was to provide an important intellectual home for me for over two decades. Started by Carol and Anne Barstow, the group met monthly and brought together many women who were to make significant contributions to feminist studies in religion. The first years of our meetings were especially exciting because we were exploring uncharted territory and mapping out new approaches to theology and other fields. I remember a paper by Naomi Goldenberg on dreams and fantasies as sources of revelation that generated a lively and fascinating discussion about the archetypal significance of various dreams. A presentation by Anne Barstow on James Mellart's work on the Goddess at Çatal Hüyük constituted my introduction to the evidence for prehistoric Goddess worship. I recall finding her paper enormously stimulating and challenging intellectually, but I was also struck that it did not resonate for me emotionally or spiritually. The presentation that spoke to me most deeply was Karen McCarthy Brown's description of attending a Voudou ceremony that involved killing a live chicken and then, afterward, looking up from a room spattered in blood to see a saccharine portrait of Jesus hanging on the wall. For me as for her, the juxtaposition of violence and sentimentality spoke of the necessity for religion to address all aspects of human existence—our capacity for brutality as well as for love and care.

That fall, I also began to teach Women in Western Religion—first at New York University, the following year at Drew Theological School, then at Wichita State University. All the work that Carol and I had done to prepare for our aborted historical theology exam suddenly became useful as I began to explore the history of women's roles and status from the biblical period up to the present. It was exciting to teach pioneering works in an emerging field and to engage students in asking new questions that often led them to reassess their lives. Several times, I asked students to create rituals that expressed their views of what the role of women in religion should be, and I was repeatedly amazed by their boldness and creativity. One ritual in particular stands out in my memory not just as an excellent presentation but as a rare spiritual moment that brought to life ideas central to my thinking and teaching that I had few places to try on. A group of older students in an evening class at Wichita State, two of them married to ministers in town, decided that they wanted to create a Goddess liturgy for their final project. They told me later that, much to their disgust, their first effort sounded like a Presbyterian service with female God-language. Frustrated and unsure what to do next, they sat around one evening, shared some wine and started talking about their lives, their husbands and children, their disappointments and hopes. At the end of the conversation, rather to their astonishment, they developed a liturgy that grew organically out of their time together and evoked the Goddess using their own words. Although I no longer have a copy of what they wrote, I can still picture the class sitting in a circle on the floor in a room lit by candles. For me, it was a rare moment in which the Goddess was present, and the ritual was an extraordinary demonstration of the riches women can unearth when they dig deeply into the truths of their lives.

Immersing myself in feminist study and community was not all excitement and delight, however; it also had its problematic side. As the only Jew in numerous feminist religious contexts, I frequently encountered both Christian ignorance of Judaism and an unexamined Christian triumphalism. When Leonard Swidler's "Jesus Was a Feminist" was published in *Catholic World* and its argument reiterated by numerous Christian feminists, I was disturbed to realize that the case for Jesus' feminism depended on depicting first-century Judaism in unrelievedly negative terms, often using much later Talmudic texts as evidence for the first century.[5] To me, the effort to lay Christian sexism at the feet of Judaism was not simply a sign of ignorance or academic sloppiness but a profound failure of the feminist ethic—in Mary Daly's words, "a failure to lay claim to that part of the psyche that is then projected onto 'the Other.'"[6] Feminist consciousness, I

---

5. Leonard Swidler, "Jesus Was a Feminist," *Catholic World* 212 (January 1971): 177–83.

discovered, was no protection against reproducing patterns of exclusion and domination. In response, I published what is probably my most widely reprinted article—"Christian Feminism and Anti-Judaism," in which I argued that Christian feminists had just given a new twist to old anti-Jewish arguments.[7] But shortly after the article appeared, it was brought home to me that my critique of the inadequacies of Christian feminism applied equally to me. Alice Walker published a piece in *Ms.* Magazine in which she took white feminists to task for their ignorance of black women's literature and their inability to imagine themselves into black women's experience.[8] I recognized myself in every word she wrote. The lesson of my childhood musings on the Holocaust reemerged with renewed urgency and became an ongoing theme in my speaking and writing: there is no us and them, no group that is only oppressed or only oppressor. We all must school ourselves to look beyond the pain and persecution of our own people to appreciate the situations of multiple others.

While I was learning these difficult lessons, there were still only a handful of books in women's studies in religion, and it was often difficult to find the scattered germinal articles needed to teach effectively. Rosemary Ruether's *Religion and Sexism* and Elizabeth Clark and Herbert Richardson's *Women and Religion* were useful texts for historical issues, and Daly's *Beyond God the Father* was the foundational text in theology, but there was as yet no collection that discussed the breadth of feminist constructive thinking in religion.[9] In the summer of 1977, when I was pregnant and visiting New York from Kansas, and Carol was packing her books to move from New York to California,

---

6. Mary Daly, *Beyond God the Father: Toward a Philosophy of Women's Liberation* (Boston: Beacon, 1973), 10.

7. Judith Plaskow, "Christian Feminism and Anti-Judaism," *Cross Currents* 33 (Fall 1978): 306–9; reprinted in Plaskow, *The Coming of Lilith: Essays on Feminism, Judaism, and Sexual Ethics, 1972–2003*, ed. with Donna Berman (Boston: Beacon Press, 2005), 89–93.

8. Alice Walker, "*One* Child of One's Own: A Meaningful Digression within the Work(s)," *Ms.*, August 1979; reprinted in Walker's *In Search of Our Mothers' Gardens* (San Diego: Harcourt, Brace Jovanovich, 1983), 361–83.

9. Rosemary Radford Ruether, *Religion and Sexism: Images of Woman in the Jewish and Christian Traditions* (New York: Simon & Schuster, 1974); Elizabeth Clark and Herbert Richardson, *Women and Religion: A Feminist Sourcebook of Christian Thought* (New York: Harper & Row), 1977; Daly, *Beyond God the Father*.

she and I began to sketch an outline and proposal for *Womanspirit Rising*. We wanted to bring under one cover the most important work being done in feminist theology, history, and ritual and to place it in a framework that would make clear its freshness and significance. In the winter, Carol flew out to Wichita. We worked out the substance of our introductory chapters and divided up writing assignments while I nursed my newborn son.

Looking back at the contents of *Womanspirit Rising* from the distance of more than thirty years reminds me of both what I was reading at that time and my continued ambivalence about my own religious path. Clearly, I was familiar with Rita Gross's critique of male language in the Jewish context and Naomi Janowitz and Maggie Wenig's effort to rewrite the Sabbath prayer book using female God-language. Indeed, I had been teaching Gross's article from the time that she first shared it with me and, using both it and Daly's book, had discussed with my students the problems with imaging God exclusively as male. Soon after Carol moved to California, she introduced me to the work of Starhawk and Z. Budapest. Her own "Why Women Need the Goddess"—which she wrote while we were working on *Womanspirit Rising*—eloquently and compellingly argued for the importance of Goddess language. I continued to straddle what we called the Reformist/ Revolutionary divide, however, standing with one foot firmly in the Jewish tradition and one potentially in the posttraditional camp. My "The Coming of Lilith" essay included in the volume came out of my small group at Grailville in 1972 that had analyzed consciousness raising as a religious experience. In our discussions, the group had been unclear—*I* was unclear—whether we wanted to create a new religion or to think in new ways within the boundaries of our own Jewish or Christian traditions.

Turning Points

While *Womanspirit Rising* was in press, and when my son was only fifteen months old, my mother died of a malignant brain tumor that, ten months earlier, had robbed her of her intellect and personality and left her in a persistent vegetative state for six months. Her funeral was a turning point for me, a crucial moment of recognition that I had truly left behind my earlier understanding of God. My mother was fifty-eight when she died her cruel and lingering death. Her illness and loss could easily have provided me with a splendid new opportunity to be angry at the God who had evaded Job's questions about justice and remained silent during the Holocaust. But quite to my surprise, I found I was angry not at God but at the colossal irrelevance of the Reform funeral service. I simply did not want to hear about God the Lord and King, mercy and judgment. I wanted to be told that people are born and die, that God gives and takes away, that the moon waxes and wanes, that tides move in and out, that nothing really dies, that everything is taken up in our memories and in the ecology of the planet. I associate the shift that I experienced in that moment with Nelle Morton's article "The Goddess as Metaphoric Image," in which she talks about her fear of flying and her irritating tendency to revert to pleading with the powerful male deity in the sky whenever a plane hit turbulence. She describes an occasion on which she told herself she was behaving like a child and decided to see what would happen if she invoked the Goddess. Morton discovered that the Goddess was not mistress of the skies and wind but was *in* the clouds and air currents, and she relaxed her tightened limbs and even enjoyed the rhythm of the plane's movements.[10] This was the God(dess) that I wanted to hear about at my mother's funeral—a God(dess) who *is* the cycles of life and death, who gives birth to myriad life forms as the ocean gives rise to waves, and who sustains us in life and also in sorrow. The transcendent and omnipotent God of my girlhood and young adulthood, who had betrayed his promises to the Jewish people and who could have prevented a brain tumor if he so willed it, had simply vanished. I no longer looked to a God enthroned above me in the sky but God(dess) all around and in me, in the firm ground beneath my feet that allowed me to walk upright. Without my conscious awareness of the steps in

10. Nelle Morton, "The Goddess as Metaphoric Image," in her *The Journey Is Home* (Boston: Beacon, 1985), 157–58.

the process, my feminist insights and commitments had brought me to the place I had longed for in enrolling in graduate school: to an understanding of God that I could gladly embrace.

The recognition that I had somehow come to a new conception and relationship with God did not in itself, however, resolve the matter of where I stood in relation to Judaism. In February of 1973, I had given a paper at a first-ever national Jewish feminist conference entitled "The Jewish Feminist: Conflict in Identities." I described being torn between the deeply androcentric Judaism in which I was raised and the excitement and new possibilities opened up by my experiences of feminist community.[11] At the time I gave the paper, my feminist involvements were far more enlivening and spiritually meaningful than anything I had experienced in relation to Judaism. The publication of Mary Daly's *Beyond God the Father* later that same year and Carol's increasing attraction to Goddess spirituality over the course of the decade provided vivid examples of how it was possible to move beyond patriarchal religion to imagine a more thoroughly feminist spiritual future. When I thought of taking their path, however, I came up against the reality that my Jewish identity was important to me. I valued my outsider's perspective on the world. My engagement with the Holocaust as a young girl had shaped my theology and sense of self. I valued the rhythm of the Jewish year, the Jewish commitment to social justice, and Jewish willingness to wrestle with God and to ask questions about matters of ultimate concern. Even putting aside the fact that the Goddess never really spoke to me deeply, if I identified with the women's spirituality movement, I would always be fundamentally divided: religiously a follower of the Goddess, but ethnically and culturally a Jew.

This conflict, which lasted the better part of a decade, was resolved when I agreed to teach a course on Jewish feminist theology for the first National Havurah Summer Institute in 1980. The institute was essentially a week-long summer camp for grownups in which members

11. Judith Plaskow, "The Jewish Feminist: Conflict in Identities," in *The Jewish Woman: New Perspectives*, ed. Elizabeth Koltun (New York: Schocken Books, 1976), 3–10; reprinted in Plaskow, *The Coming of Lilith*, 35–39 and 31–32.

of havurot—independent, lay-led, generally egalitarian Jewish communities—from all over the country met for study, prayer, conversation, and relaxation. At the time I offered the course, I had already been studying, teaching, and writing about feminist theology for almost ten years, but I had never had the opportunity to do so in a sustained way in a Jewish context. There were three feminist courses offered at the institute and I taught one and took another. I had no idea whether anyone would even be interested in my class, but in fact several people signed up for the institute in order to take it. It was one of the most important and exciting teaching experiences of my life, as exciting as any feminist group I had ever been part of. My students were hungry for a vocabulary to talk about the root issues involved in women's marginalization within Judaism, and as we grappled together with the androcentric nature of Torah and the maleness of God, I felt the separated aspects of my identity come together. The answer to the question I had been struggling with since finishing my thesis was suddenly clear: yes, it was possible to be a Jewish feminist without seeing those identities as in conflict; yes, I was committed to the feminist transformation of Judaism. I left the institute and immediately wrote "The Right Question Is Theological," in which I called for the radical reconstruction of the central Jewish concepts of God, Torah, and Israel.[12] While my first serious article on Jewish theology was entirely critical—I laid out the magnitude of the changes I thought were necessary without the faintest idea of how to achieve them—I was able to formulate the critique because I was no longer facing it alone. I had tasted Jewish feminist community and felt its power to make asking even painful questions seem both urgent and meaningful.

The institute marked the beginning of important changes in my life. Several women present had taken two of the three classes offered on Jewish feminism, and our excitement about studying together led us to think about creating an independent space where we could explore feminist issues more deeply. In the fall, a small group of us met in

12. Judith Plaskow, "The Right Question Is Theological," in *On Being a Jewish Feminist: A Reader*, ed. Susannah Heschel (New York: Schocken Books, 1983), 223–33; reprinted in Plaskow, *The Coming of Lilith*, 56–64.

New York City and began planning a retreat for the following summer. Through my time at Grailville, I knew of the Grail retreat center in Cornwall-on-Hudson, New York. I reserved the space for Memorial Day weekend, and the committee sent a letter to every woman we could think of who was literate in both feminism and Judaism and interested in Jewish feminist spirituality. B'not Esh (Daughters of Fire) was about to be born.

B'not Esh

I have described in a number of contexts the remarkably fertile period of my life that followed on the founding of B'not Esh.[13] Here, I will follow the thread that pertains to my developing understanding of God, up to the point that I wrote *Standing Again at Sinai*. The invitation letter to the first retreat described attention to God and God-language as a central purpose of our meeting. It spoke of "the shared longing . . . for a Judaism—and a Jewish community—which reflects and informs our sense of ourselves as heirs to and shapers of a tradition that celebrates both human and divine femaleness, and encourages exploration of the implications of such cosmic re/visioning for our relationships to one another, and our relationship to God."[14] The letter was not modest in laying out our hopes for the weekend; it compared feminism's challenge to Judaism to the deliberations at Yavneh, the founding moment of rabbinic Judaism. But it also made clear that the outcome of the meeting would depend on the contributions of the participants; the organizers provided only an outline of the retreat that would take on flesh in the course of our time together.

The biggest issue we confronted that first year was the extent of our differences. Every one of us came to Cornwall expecting it to be "home." Every one of us had been made to feel a feminist among Jews

---

13. Judith Plaskow, "Intersections: An Introduction," in my *The Coming of Lilith*, 5–19; "Critique and Transformation: A Jewish Feminist Journey," in *Lifecycles: Jewish Women on Biblical Themes in Contemporary Life*, ed. Rabbi Debra Orenstein and Rabbi Jane Rachel Litman (Woodstock, VT: Jewish Lights, 1997), 94–103.
14. "Beyond Halakha: Jewish Feminist Spirituality" (unpublished letter, March 30, 1981). The letter is reproduced on the website of the Jewish Women's Archive: http://jwa.org/feminism/plaskow-judith. Accessed January 29, 2016.

and a Jew among feminists and longed for a space where she could integrate the separated parts of herself. But what we discovered was that the substance of that integration was different for each of us. I am not certain what I wanted or expected—prayer that was radical and amazing, services I could neither have imagined nor created on my own but that would emerge in community with other Jewish feminists. Certainly, I expected to use female language, but I wanted something beyond that too that would spring from our synergy. Others present, however, dreamed only of the opportunity to pray with other women. For them, that was enough; they had no interest in altering the language or structure of the traditional service. We spent the first part of Sabbath morning sitting and crying in the main foyer because each of our expectations had been disappointed and we could not agree on a plan that would satisfy all of us. Finally, we decided that each of us would bring to the service whatever it was that she most wanted to see happen and we would weave together our various offerings. We went to a beautiful spot by a stream in the woods and stretched our bodies, contemplated photographs, sang, read poetry, heard the Torah and a prophetic reading, listened to one of our members throw a tantrum about the prophetic reading, and wove together a magical service that satisfied none and all of us. Interestingly, my contribution was not a prayer using female God-language but excerpts from Adrienne Rich's extraordinary poem, "Transcendental Etude," that captures the terror and exhilaration of coming to feminist consciousness and ends with the words, "And now the stone foundation, rockshelf further/ forming underneath everything that grows."[15] That image of the rockshelf underlying and supporting everything was the image of God I had longed for at my mother's funeral, the sustaining presence undergirding and upholding all life.

The following year, B'not Esh didn't meet. Our first gathering had been too difficult and painful; we needed time to reflect and recover. But I went to the Women's Spirit Bonding conference at Grailville at

---

15. Adrienne Rich, "Transcendental Etude," in her *The Dream of a Common Language* (New York and London: W. W. Norton, 1978), 77.

which over a hundred women, most Christian but some posttraditional or Jewish, gathered for a week of feminist theologizing. The conference coincided with the Israeli invasion of Lebanon, and a southern Christian woman with a Lebanese husband angrily challenged Israel's right to exist.[16] We engaged in passionate and painful private and public dialogue in which I found it very difficult to separate out her unexamined, everyday Christian anti-Judaism from the important and difficult questions that she raised. In the weeks after the conference, I continued to struggle with the issues we discussed. The Sabra and Shatila massacre that fall, in which the Israeli defense forces stood by as a Lebanese Christian Phalangist militia slaughtered hundreds of Lebanese and Palestinian civilians, shook me very deeply, challenging my understanding of what it meant to be a Jew. A year later, I attended an international feminist conference, this time at Harvard, at which a Palestinian woman took issue with my use of the word *tzedakah* (a Hebrew word meaning righteousness but usually inadequately translated as "charity") to talk about Jewish solidarity with Palestinians. I began to weep. My friends assumed that I felt misunderstood by her criticism, but in fact, I was experiencing the edifice of my Jewish identity crumbling. I had received an answer to my childhood question. Yes, Jews could behave like Nazis; yes, Jews could cooperate with slaughter; yes, Jews could act oppressively when we held power. I felt that, as a people, we had lost the moral privilege of victimhood, and therefore I could no longer see my Jewish identity as a victim identity. How could I be angry at God when *we* were responsible for our misuse of power? I needed to redefine what it meant to me to be Jew.

The publication of Alice Walker's *The Color Purple* that same year was a very different kind of significant event for my conception of God. Within months of the book's appearance, womanist[17] and feminist

16. I should say that that is how I experienced her words at the time. Some of our exchange is published as Mary Bentley Abu-Saba, Judith Plaskow, and Rosemary Radford Ruether, "Women Responding to the Arab-Israeli Conflict," in *Women's Spirit Bonding*, ed. Janet Kalven and Mary I. Buckley (New York: Pilgrim Press, 1984), 221–33.
17. A womanist is a black feminist. The term was coined by Alice Walker, *In Search of Our Mother's Gardens*, xi–xiii.

theologians begin to cite "The God chapter," as we came to call it, as almost a second Bible. In that chapter, Celie, the novel's black, poor, abused heroine announces to her lover Shug that she will no longer write letters to God because he is as "trifling, forgetful, and lowdown" as "all the other mens" she knows. In a brilliant description and deconstruction of the big, old, tall, greybearded and white God who's in the "white folks' white bible," Shug challenges Celie to "git man off your eyeball" and find the God who is "inside you and inside everybody else." Describing with great eloquence the hard work involved in getting rid of the white male God who has infiltrated individual and cultural consciousness, Shug says, "I believe God is everything. . . . Everything that is or ever was or ever will be. And when you can feel that, and be happy to feel that, you found It." "God ain't a he or a she," she explains, "but a It" that is manifest in the world around us—the trees, wildflowers, the color purple in a field, and also in our sexual feelings, "some of the best stuff God did."[18] Both Walker's depiction of the challenge of dislodging an age-old and ubiquitous image and her passionate articulation of an alternative understanding spoke powerfully to the historical moment. After critiquing the traditional picture of God for a decade, feminists were seeking a new understanding that emphasized divine immanence over transcendence. Throughout the 1980s, whenever I spoke about the new images of God emerging from women's experiences, I always read parts of the God chapter from *The Color Purple*.

After a year's hiatus, the committee that had called the first gathering of what was to become B'not Esh tried again. We had learned many lessons from the first year, among them to name some of our differences up front and explore them as part of the program. Slightly more than half the original group returned to the Grail Center at Cornwall, along with many new members who would form the core of an ongoing collective. The weekend was exhausting, sometimes painful and contentious, but also amazing, challenging, and for me life-changing. I had come feeling as if I had hit a wall in my thinking.

---

18. Alice Walker, *The Color Purple* (New York: Harcourt, Brace, Jovanovitch, 1982), 164–68.

I had laid out a systemic critique of Judaism and had no idea how to move beyond it. It was one thing to say that feminism demanded a new understanding of Torah, God, and Israel and quite another to imagine the shape of such a transformation. Like my students with their Presbyterian Goddess service, I thought I had reached a dead end. I cannot fully account for what happened next, but in the midst of an extraordinary session on the connection between sexuality and spirituality, I realized that I was in love with Martha, a member of the group who had been a friend of mine for many years. I spoke the words out loud, and a series of iron bands that I did not know were constricting my chest popped open. Within six months, I had outlined my Jewish feminist theology *Standing Again at Sinai*, and I began to share my ideas with women's groups, synagogues, and universities nationally and in Europe. Meanwhile, the last night of our gathering, we held a ritual in the beautiful prayer room at the retreat house where we met, and one of our members cast a circle in the manner of the Goddess covens described by the feminist witch Starhawk. Though our leader cast the circle in terms that were thoroughly Jewish, connecting the four directions with the four matriarchs, many of us were terrified, shaking. Could we survive if we stepped so far beyond the boundaries of the familiar in Jewish prayer? The energy in the room was unfocused, wild, bouncing off the walls. We began to sing a three-part round that group member Faith Rogow had just written: "Praised be, woman, ARISE." The roof of the prayer room lifted up several inches.

The year following this retreat was a period of great ferment, pain, and exhilaration in my life. Acknowledging that I was in love with another woman precipitated a year-long crisis during which I struggled with the question of whether to leave my marriage. Contemplating divorce felt like walking off the edge of a cliff without knowing whether there would be anything to break my fall. At the same time, coming out as a lesbian allowed me to experience a powerful connection between sexuality, embodiment, and creativity. I was filled with new and exciting ideas, and when I finally took the terrifying step of ending my marriage, I discovered that, having walked through one closed door and survived, I could walk through others. Elisabeth Schüssler Fiorenza's *In Memory of Her* was published in this same period, and reading the book triggered an intellectual breakthrough that was another piece of claiming my power.[19] When I first read the book, I strongly resisted its premise that women are fully part of the Christian past. I kept scribbling in the margins: how do you know this? Isn't this a huge assumption? But gradually I realized that, in rejecting the notion that religious history is the history of women, I was clinging to being a victim who depended on others to bring about change, rather than confronting the task of integrating women's experiences into every aspect of Jewish life. The book provided me with the intellectual impetus to think about reconfiguring Judaism at a point when I was ready emotionally to move beyond critique.

One of many lessons I have learned from B'not Esh—and it was a lesson thoroughly reinforced by being in love—is that there is experience beyond language. Of course, the challenge of writing about such a realization is that it is impossible to put pen to paper without finding oneself back in the framework of ordinary words. For the first time, I understood the poets and mystics who spoke of the inadequacy of language to capture the fullness of certain feelings or experiences of the divine, and I found that they evoked the power of such experiences far more eloquently than I. Here, I will simply mention some moments at B'not Esh that brought me to a new respect for the more-than-rational dimensions of reality. At one of our early gatherings, one of our members received a phone call in the midst of an evening session informing her that her husband had had a major stroke. She went upstairs to pack and lie down briefly before catching a plane home, and the group crowded into her room to send her healing energy. The energy was so palpable and powerful that we could practically see and touch it. She said it sustained her for the next year and she felt as if she had levitated. We never discussed this moment afterward; whether it was because it was too frightening or we had no words for

---

19. Elisabeth Schüssler Fiorenza, *In Memory of Her: A Feminist Theological Reconstruction of Christian Origins* (New York: Crossroad, 1983).

it, I was never clear. But we had similar experiences other times too when we gathered to heal someone, when we sang together, or when we dug deeply into the wisdom of our lives to create new words of Torah. Another time, we had a very painful discussion about abuse in Jewish families and were stunned by how many of us had been physically abused as children. The next morning at Sabbath services, the leader instructed us to go out during the silent prayer and receive a revelation! The assignment seemed absurd. How does one have a revelation on command and in the space of half an hour? Thirty minutes later, Faith Rogow, who in the early years wrote much of our music, returned with the words and melody of a chant that not only became something like our anthem but that, in the time since, has found its way into non-Orthodox Jewish liturgies in remarkably far-flung places: "As we bless the source of life, so we are blessed."[20] Other times too, we were told to seek a revelation, laughed at the thought, and then returned with some extraordinary insight. Though we experimented with new images for God in the early years of B'not Esh, these experiences of the presence of God have been more important in shaping my theology than any particular language. They taught me that images are meaningful only insofar as they are rooted in genuine experiences and that it is possible for certain experiences to override and undermine language or to provide different messages from those that language may convey.

God Language and Religious Experience

Looking back over the many lectures about God that I delivered in the 1980s, I perceive a definite tension between my interest in and focus on language and the nonverbal level on which my understanding of God was actually growing and changing. Language was something I knew how to discuss, and I offered audiences a crazy quilt of images that I believed needed to supplement or replace the overwhelmingly

---

20. The words of the full chant can be found in the Reconstructionist Prayerbook, *Kol Haneshamah* (Wyncote, PA: The Reconstructionist Press, 1994), 246, although Faith had originally written "and makes our visions clear" rather than "vision."

male metaphors that dominate Jewish liturgy. One spring, for example, I spent a wonderful evening "consulting on God" with a group of Havurat Shalom members (the oldest of the independent Jewish fellowship groups) who were working on a new prayer book. I advocated for an inclusive monotheism that would be expressed through a wide range of images for God, including female images. I acknowledged the contradiction between praying to the Ground of Being, the source and sustaining energy of all that is, and the inescapable language of personal address, but urged them not to relinquish either dimension of God-language. In that conversation and other talks, I began to weave together the new words I had learned from various women's groups with those emerging in feminist literature and theologies: the -ing words bursting forth at Grailville (shaping, creating, changing, connecting, challenging, etc.) that spoke of a sense of empowerment rooted in cosmic power; Mary Daly's God-the-Verb; Alice Walker's vision of the sacredness of everything that is; and the Goddess pouring herself into the endless and varied forms of the world. All these images came out of and evoked experiences that I could point to through the power of metaphor but did not know how to describe directly.

When, in the mid to late 1980s, B'not Esh member Marcia Falk began to create new Jewish blessings in Hebrew and in English, I found that her language spoke to me more deeply than any of the other experiments with fresh imagery at the time. Falk replaced the traditional blessing formula, "Blessed are you, Lord our God, King of the universe" with a variety of new images appropriate to the object or experience being blessed, often invoking God as the "source" or "wellspring of life." Her blessings moved me both because she is a wonderful poet and because her largely nongendered language replaced the God above us in heaven with the source of life manifest in the totality of creation. While I continued to believe that female language was politically and religiously important in disrupting the hegemony of male images, it was Falk's language that most fully captured my own understanding of God. Female language was still personal, and, especially when it involved changing traditional blessings to female forms, often underscored problematic aspects of the traditional concept of God. Falk's images, on the other hand, evoked a God who could not be separated from the world in which God was present. Her blessings spoke of a God who was evident in the very ground beneath our feet and who could be found in every aspect of experience, sometimes without needing to be named explicitly. Her blessing for washing the hands, for example, replaced "Blessed are you, King of the Universe who has sanctified us with your commandments and commanded us concerning washing our hands" with "Washing the hands, we call to mind the holiness of body."[21]

In my chapter on God in *Standing Again at Sinai*, the issue of imagery continued to take precedence over my experiences of God and the elaboration of my own theology. The chapter criticized the inadequacies of traditional images for God and suggested new metaphors that might expand the Jewish religious imagination in ways that cohere with feminist understandings of Torah and Israel. It only hinted at the concept of God that lay behind these metaphors because, at the time, I was less interested in who God *is* than in how the ways Jews speak to and about God shape individual and communal self-understandings. Insofar as the images I discussed came out of genuine experiences, however, a deeply communal spirituality lay at the center of the chapter. I can hear reverberating behind all I say about the quest for a personal language that does not support male power or domination, the dynamism of the first decade of meetings of B'not Esh, as well as my experiences at Grailville and at other feminist retreats and meetings. At that point in my life, I felt the presence of God most fully in community with other women, an experience I described as analogous to the collective nature of the revelation at Mount Sinai, where the Israelites heard the voice of God and entered the covenant as a people. It is interesting to me in retrospect that, although I was

---

21. Marcia Falk began publishing articles about her blessings in the mid to late 1980s, but all of her liturgy can be found in *The Book of Blessings: New Jewish Prayers for Daily Life, the Sabbath, and the New Moon Festival* (San Francisco: HarperSanFrancisco, 1996). The blessing for hand washing is found on 16–17 and other places in the text.

attracted to Alice Walker's powerful evocation of God's immanence in the natural world and found Adrienne's Rich's "rockshelf further/ forming underneath everything that grows" a wonderful image of God, in *Standing Again at Sinai*, natural imagery is secondary to my attempts to evoke the presence of God in a "diverse, egalitarian, and empowered community of Israel." Indeed, I even argue that "insofar as women's experience of the holiness of nature has been named in a feminist context . . . it is the experience of *community* that has allowed the articulation and development of a nature spirituality."[22] In hindsight, it seems to me that my ideological commitment to transforming Jewish institutional and liturgical forms worked against the fuller development of my personal theology.

The part of my chapter on God that expresses most clearly my current perspective is my brief discussion of the nature of monotheism. In the chapter of *Standing Again at Sinai* on the community of Israel, I argued for using a part/whole rather than a hierarchical model to conceptualize Jewish difference. The many subgroups within the larger Jewish community—ethnic, religious, class or gender-based, and so on—have their own distinctive characteristics and identities and, at the same time, are parts of a greater whole, just as Jews are part of larger heterogeneous cultures. In the chapter on God, I used this part/whole model to talk about monotheism and also to reconceptualize transcendence. "Just as subgroups within a community are all parts of a larger unity, so any individual image of God is part of a divine totality that in its totality embraces the diversity of an infinite community." Monotheism is not the worship of a single image of God or of a supernatural being projected into the heavens but "the capacity to see the One in and through the changing forms of the many."[23] On this view, God's "moreness" or transcendence lies not in dominating but in pervading and unifying creation. Just as a community can be more than the sum of its parts without necessarily controlling or subjugating them, so God is the ultimate horizon of

22. Judith Plaskow, *Standing Again at Sinai: Judaism from a Feminist Perspective* (San Francisco: Harper & Row, 1990), 122, 156 (emphasis new).
23. Ibid, 151, 152.

creation, containing the vast complexity and multiplicity of creation. And this means that the negative, destructive, and terrifying aspects of creation are also part of God.

Where Is Evil?

This brings me to an aspect of my chapter on God that struck me as soon as I had finished writing: only in one paragraph do I refer to the frightening and overwhelming side of God, and I never deal explicitly with the problem of evil. This was especially startling to me because, as I have discussed, the problem of evil obsessed me from girlhood and throughout many years of my life. There was a time when I would have picked up any Jewish theology that did not deal with the Holocaust and flung it across the room in disgust. I did not *plan* to avoid the problem of evil, and I was nonplussed when I completed the manuscript and realized that I had not mentioned it. The omission is due partly to the specific focus of the book: I was trying to reconceptualize central Jewish concepts from a feminist perspective, and the feminist communities I was part of were much more interested in the empowerment of women than the theological question of evil. But on a deeper level, my failure to address evil pointed to the profound shift that had occurred in my understanding of God between the time I left Yale and when I wrote *Standing Again at Sinai*. In one sense, the entire book is about evil: the ways in which human beings destroy each other and ourselves when we create unjust social structures that subordinate some supposedly naturally inferior group to one imagined as superior. But *God's* responsibility for evil had simply ceased to be a problem for me in that I no longer thought of God as an omnipotent being with the power and responsibility to intervene in creation. God(dess), the ground and wellspring of life, could act only through the world, not upon it from outside. The enterprise of theodicy—the effort to justify God's goodness and power given the existence of evil—had become much less interesting than the ways in which our language about God supports social, political, and religious inequalities of power.

I thus could sympathize with my failure to deal with God's

relationship to evil; yet, almost immediately, I also saw the omission as a serious one. Just at the point that *Standing Again at Sinai* was going to press, the *Journal of Feminist Studies in Religion* published a roundtable entitled "If God Is God She Is Not Nice," initiated by Catherine Madsen. Madsen complained that when feminists think of God as Goddess or give her female characteristics, they tend to endow her with the so-called feminine virtues of nurturing, healing, and caretaking, cordoning her off from the unpredictability of the world.[24] Although none of the images I offer in *Standing Again at Sinai* can be described as traditionally "feminine," the roundtable nonetheless made me recognize the extent to which I had focused on a supporting and empowering God and neglected those aspects of reality that are disempowering and destructive. A year later, I published a short article entitled "Facing the Ambiguity of God" in which I took myself to task for neglecting evil and drew a distinction between the classical problem of theodicy and the profoundly ambiguous nature of all creativity and creation.[25] True, I no longer believed in a perfectly good and omnipotent God who acted in history and could therefore be blamed for remaining silent in the face of injustice. But I still knew the world, in Madsen's words, "with its droughts and floods, its extremes of climate, its strange combination of tender bounty and indifference, and the uneasiness of human society with its descents into savagery."[26] Where was the place for these aspects of reality in *Standing Again at Sinai*, and, for that matter, where was the place for my awareness that feminism afforded no protection against perpetrating injustice, or for my realization after Sabra and Shatila that, once in power, Jews would abuse that power?

This question was brought home to me again when the *Journal of Feminist Studies in Religion* published an article by Kathleen Sands on the feminist romanticization of eros. Sands pointed out that Audre

---

24. Catherine Madsen, "If God Is God She Is Not Nice," *Journal of Feminist Studies in Religion* 5, no. 1 (Spring 1989): 103–5.
25. Judith Plaskow, "Facing the Ambiguity of God," *Tikkun* 6 (September/October 1991): 70, 96. Reprinted in Plaskow, *The Coming of Lilith*, 134–37.
26. Madsen, "If God Is God She Is Not Nice," 104.

Lorde's essay "Uses of the Erotic: The Erotic as Power" had become virtually canonical for many feminists in religious studies, who had "tried to make unrepressed *eros* the central norm of a feminist ethic." When erotic satisfaction is viewed as providing a touchstone and vision through which to evaluate all aspects of existence, Sands argued, incest, violence, and other forms of sexual injustice come to be seen as "unreal *eros*" and consigned to a shadow world of misunderstood desire. Sexuality, she declared, should not be viewed as "the integrating center of life" but as an "elemental power" that "calls for moral discernment and choice."[27] Although I was not one of the theologians who Sands singled out for criticism in her essay, it was clear to me immediately that her critique applied to my treatment of sexuality in *Standing Again at Sinai*. Drawing on Lorde and my own experience of the power of the erotic when I fell in love and felt myself opening to the world on every level, I had written about the erotic as a fundamental life energy that flows through all activities and "that gives us access to a greater power that grounds and embraces us."[28] While I acknowledged the disruptive power of the erotic, its capacity to overturn rules and threaten the boundaries of community—as it had done in my own life—I saw this power as essentially positive: as a force that might lead women to rebel against a patriarchal social order in the name of a deeper intuition of how life could be. Sands made me see that I had ignored the power of eros to bind women to our subordination or to unleash destructive forces in ourselves and in others. My discussion of eros was much like my discussion of God: in both case, I had focused on empowerment to the exclusion of the contradictions and dangers of power. I still needed to find a way to integrate the understanding of God that emerged from my feminist experience with my life-long concern with evil and my shifting sense of my Jewish identity.

27. Kathleen Sands, "Uses of the Thea(o)logian: Sex and Theodicy in Religious Feminism," *Journal of Feminist Studies in Religion* 8, no. 1 (Spring 1992): 11, 14.
28. Plaskow, *Standing Again at Sinai*, 201.

6

———

Feminist Theology at the Center

Carol P. Christ and Judith Plaskow

Though some theologians might place feminism outside the theological mainstream, for us it is at the center. It was not just chronology that led us to include the first stirrings of feminist theology in our discussion of the theological trends of the second half of the twentieth century. Feminist theology arose in the wake of the demise of the Neo-orthodox consensus. It was part of the theological ferment that included Vatican II, Holocaust theology, and the death of God movement. It built on the revaluing of the body in the human potential movement. It intersected with the Civil Rights, antipoverty, and antiwar movements. Feminist theologians have addressed the compelling issues of our time. Moreover, if it is true that traditional theologies have ignored half of the human experience and denied the full humanity of women, then theologians who do not take feminist questions seriously will be likely to repeat the same mistakes. Because feminist theology has deeply influenced us, and because we, in turn, have contributed to its development, in this chapter we locate the questions we discuss in this book in the context of a larger feminist conversation.

Feminist Question Marks

Feminist theology began with a critical examination of patriarchal texts and traditions. The feminist insight that, for most of its history, theology has been practiced and interpreted by men who take male dominance for granted places a question mark over all inherited theologies. This does not mean that everything traditional theologians said was wrong, though much of it may be. Feminist criticism of texts and traditions focuses on religious ideas and symbols that perpetuate domination, violence, and oppression.

When feminists first began to look critically at their traditions, some argued that inherited sacred texts, if correctly understood, do not support male domination. Phyllis Trible retranslated and reinterpreted the Genesis story of Adam and Eve, asserting that Eve was not created subordinate to Adam but equal to him.[1] Looking again at the Qur'an, Riffat Hassan and Amina Wadud stated that texts used to support male domination had been misconstrued, and argued that the Qur'an consistently promotes women's equality.[2] Others acknowledged sexist elements within sacred texts, but claimed that there are normative principles within them that challenge all forms of dominance. Letty Russell and Rosemary Radford Ruether cited God's concern for the poor and oppressed in the prophetic tradition and Paul's words that "in Christ there is no longer Jew or Greek, there is no longer slave or free, there is no longer male or female" (Gal. 3:26, 28) as an emancipatory message against which other parts of the Bible can be judged.[3] Mary

1. Phyllis Trible, *God and the Rhetoric of Sexuality* (Philadelphia: Fortress, 1978), chap. 4.
2. Riffat Hassan, "An Islamic Perspective," in *Sexuality: A Reader*, ed. Karen Lebacz with David Sinacore-Guinn (Cleveland: Pilgrim, 1999), 337–72; Amina Wadud, *Qur'an and Woman: Rereading Sacred Text from a Woman's Perspective* (New York: Oxford University Press, 1992).
3. Letty M. Russell, *Human Liberation in a Feminist Perspective—A Theology* (Philadelphia: Westminster, 1974); Rosemary Radford Ruether, *Sexism and God-Talk: Toward a Feminist Theology* (Boston: Beacon, 1983), 22–27.

Daly, Naomi Goldenberg, Carol, and others countered that the idea of a liberating core makes no sense because nonsexist passages cannot be separated from the rest of the scriptures or traditions in which they are embedded.[4]

Deciding to Stay or Leave

Those on both sides of this divide argued vociferously that it was necessary to continue to work within or alternatively to leave biblical or other inherited traditions. Responding to this debate, Christian feminist biblical scholar and theologian Elisabeth Schüssler Fiorenza stated that there is no objective way to determine which parts of sacred texts or traditions are the product of divine revelation and which are human inventions. According to her, the community of women (later "wo/men") who read the texts from a feminist perspective can and must decide for itself which texts or traditions it will accept and which it will reject. Every community, she claimed, in fact makes such determinations—whether or not this is acknowledged.[5] This insight reframed the question of whether there "is" a liberating core in traditions. Recognizing that all traditions have both liberating and oppressive aspects, Schüssler Fiorenza focused on the responsibility of people in community to choose which elements of their traditions they will deem foundational and to decide what their traditions can become. Shifting the focus from the text to its interpretation caused us to rethink one of the questions we debated for many years: whether or not the Jewish and Christian traditions are essentially sexist. We came to the conclusion that this was the wrong question. Even if it could be determined that a tradition is more sexist than not, feminists could still decide to work within it to transform it.

---

4. Mary Daly, *Beyond God the Father: Toward a Philosophy of Women's Liberation* (Boston: Beacon, 1973); Naomi Goldenberg, *Changing of the Gods: Feminism and the End of Traditional Religions* (Boston: Beacon, 1979); Carol P. Christ, "Yahweh as Holy Warrior," reprinted in *Laughter of Aphrodite: Reflections on a Journey to the Goddess* (San Francisco: Harper & Row, 1987), 73–81.
5. Elisabeth Schüssler Fiorenza, *Bread Not Stone: The Challenge of Feminist Biblical Interpretation* (Boston: Beacon, 1984).

Conversely, even if a tradition could be shown to have a liberating core, feminists could still decide to reject it, for a variety of reasons.

When the critical role of the process of interpretation is understood, the authority of texts and traditions is transferred to the individuals and communities who interpret them. This insight means that Judith can agree with Mary Daly that it is impossible to separate a liberating core from the sexism that permeates every aspect of Jewish tradition, yet like Schüssler Fiorenza, she can work within her tradition to transform it. Buddhist feminists like Rita Gross face similar issues of authority in relation to the words attributed to the Buddha and the many ways they have been interpreted.[6] Those, like Carol, who leave inherited traditions behind, cannot avoid taking responsibility for becoming their own authorities in relation to the new traditions they create or rediscover. Early in the Goddess movement, Charlene Spretnak rescued "the lost Goddesses of early Greece" from a patriarchal overlay. But depth psychologist Christine Downing challenged Spretnak, arguing that the inherited patriarchal myths are more complex and therefore better mirrors of the psyche.[7] In *The Spiral Dance*, Starhawk appealed to ancient Goddess and Wiccan "traditions" to justify her interpretations of the history, symbols, and practices she described as the religion of the Great Goddess.[8] Over time, it has become clear that Wiccan and Goddess feminists are creating new and sometimes different interpretations of the ancient past, and that Wiccan tradition is itself a modern synthesis that can be criticized and transformed, not a direct inheritance from the ancient past.[9] Reflecting

6. Rita Gross, *Buddhism after Patriarchy: A Feminist History, Analysis, and Reconstruction of Buddhism* (Albany: State University of New York Press, 1993).

7. Charlene Spretnak, *Lost Goddesses of Early Greece: A Collection of Pre-Hellenic Myths* (Boston: Beacon Press, 1978, 1984); Christine Downing, *The Goddess: Mythological Images of the Feminine* (New York: Crossroad Press, 1981).

8. Starhawk, *The Spiral Dance: A Rebirth of the Ancient Religion of the Great Goddess* (San Francisco: Harper & Row, 1979; 2nd and 3rd editions, expanded, 1989, 1999).

9. Ronald Hutton, in *The Triumph of the Moon: A History of Modern Pagan Witchcraft* (Oxford and New York: Oxford University Press, 1999), argues that the Englishman Gerald Garner created "the Wiccan tradition" by piecing together elements of ancient religions, folk traditions, Masonic rituals, alchemical magic, the work of Margaret Murray, and his personal quirks such as his interest in nudism. Hutton, 356–59, is skeptical of Gimbutas's reading of the ancient past, while Starhawk was involved in the production of "Signs Out of Time: The Story of Archaeologist Marija Gimbutas," which is sympathetic to her views. Starhawk continues to view nudity as an integral

on all of this, we have concluded that, whether we situate ourselves within or outside of traditional religions, we as individuals and members of communities must still decide which aspects of our traditions we wish to bring forward into the future, which we wish to transform, and which we prefer to leave behind.

Women's Experience, Women's Experiences

Because feminist theologians recognized from the beginning that theologies written by men have neglected the experiences of one half of the human race, women's experience has been a central focus and concern. Though Valerie Saiving and others believed that women's experience could be defined relatively easily, the intervening years have proved this assumption wrong. The notion that all women share the experience of motherhood, for example, was soon criticized by those who pointed out that not all women are mothers, that the experience of motherhood varies enormously cross-culturally, and that it is influenced by women's status in a given society and the other work expected of or available to her. Women of color noted that Betty Friedan's "problem that has no name"—the sense of isolation and lack of self-worth suffered by mid-twentieth century middle-class white women—was not the problem of poor black women.[10] They were not trapped in their homes, but instead were working in white people's homes or in fields or factories while trying to raise children, sometimes on their own, and often without enough money to make ends meet. Along with other women of color, black feminists insisted on the importance of an "intersectional" analysis of women's experiences. Variables including class, race, culture, and sexuality cannot simply be "added on" to being a woman. Rather, these factors are so intertwined that the experience of being a woman is inseparable from the kind of woman that one is.

In light of these critiques, feminist theologians began to examine

aspect of Goddess rituals, while not all Goddess feminists concur. Also see Margaret Murray, *The Witch-Cult in Western Europe* (Oxford: The Clarendon Press, 1921) and Hutton's critique in his book, 194–201. Hutton's text is also an interpretation of history that can be questioned and criticized.
10. Betty Friedan, *The Feminine Mystique* (New York: Norton, 1963).

women's experiences in particular contexts, without making universal generalizations. Womanist ethicist Katie Canon argued that black women have regarded "survival" against overwhelming odds as the center of a "moral wisdom" that is not based on the "fixed rules" or "absolute principles" often assumed to be the only legitimate foundation of ethical thinking.[11] Lesbian theologian and Episcopal priest Carter Heyward focused on the struggle for justice for lesbians and gays in her work.[12] Korean-Canadian-American theologian Grace Ji-Sun Kim explored the concept of hybrid religious identity to describe what it means to live on the boundaries of Asian and Christian, Korean and American, cultures.[13] Some feminists, while recognizing difference, continued to believe that women within groups, or women as a group, share certain experiences and perspectives, even if these are not easy to specify. Carol Gilligan's discovery that the women and girls she studied were likely to put people before rules in ethical decision making felt right to many feminists, as did Nel Noddings's attempt to define a feminine ethic of care.[14] Carol has been drawn to this line of thought, while Judith finds it problematic.

Philosopher and gender theorist Judith Butler challenged the concept of women's experience from a different angle, arguing that gender is not a biological given but something we learn to perform.[15] Butler's critique of the gender binary inspired a new generation of scholars to reexamine the notion of gender-specific experiences. Where earlier feminist scholars sought to name and discuss women's experiences through variables including class, race, sexual orientation, and culture, scholars calling themselves "queer theorists" argued that

---

11. Katie Cannon, "Moral Wisdom in the Black Women's Literary Tradition," in *Weaving the Visions: New Patterns in Feminist Theology*, ed. Judith Plaskow and Carol P. Christ (San Francisco: Harper & Row, 1989), 284; reprinted in her *Katie's Canon: Womanism and the Soul of the Black Community* (New York: Continuum, 1995), chap. 4.

12. Carter Heyward, *Our Passion for Justice: Images of Power, Sexuality, and Liberation* (New York: Pilgrim, 1984).

13. Grace Ji-Sun Kim, *The Holy Spirit, Chi, and the Other: A Model of Global and Intercultural Pneumatology* (New York: Palgrave Macmillan, 2011), chap. 4.

14. Carol Gilligan, *In a Different Voice: Psychological Theory and Women's Development* (Cambridge, MA and London: Harvard University Press, 1982); Nel Noddings, *Caring: A Feminine Approach to Ethics and Moral Education* (Berkeley, Los Angeles, London: University of California Press, 1984).

15. Judith Butler, *Gender Trouble: Feminism and the Subversion of Identity* (New York and London: Routledge, 1990), chap. 1.

the very categories of "woman" and "man" are rooted in and productive of gender inequality. This perspective built on feminist work on the socially created and often-destructive nature of gender roles, but went beyond it to name the idea of fixed biological sex as part of the social construction of gender. In the space that was opened up, a new group of "others" appeared, calling themselves gender queers. This term was initially claimed by people whose experiences challenged normative gender categories—drag queens, butch lesbians, and those who were physically or psychologically intersex or transgender. More recently, some have extended the notion of queer to include all those who question traditional gender norms. Advocates of queer theory are not simply asking for the addition of new gender classifications such as intersex and transgender, because this would leave the gender binary (nearly) intact. Rather they are questioning the idea that humanity can be divided neatly into two gender categories. Queer theorists worry that feminist attempts to reclaim and revalue "women's" experiences both accept the gender binary and assume the self-evident nature of who belongs to the category of "women." Queer theory also challenges the binary of acceptable and unacceptable sexual activities. In *Indecent Theology*, Argentinian-born queer theologian Marcella Althaus-Reid tried to liberate God from the closet of heterosexual, parental imagery in which God has been straightjacketed by writing about God as Sodomite, Voyeur, and Whore.[16]

We recognize and value the ways in which queer theory refocuses the feminist critique of gender stereotypes and gender essentialism. Efforts to reclaim and revalue women's experiences can obscure and blunt the radical nature of early feminist criticisms of gender. At the same time, we think that, as long as the gender binary continues to operate in the world, it is important to write about women's multifaceted and intersectional experiences. A large part of the world's population continues to be thought of and to think of itself as female: as girls and as women. Also and more importantly, as long as

---

16. Marcella Althaus-Reid, *The Queer God* (New York: Routledge, 2003), 53, 86, 98.

patriarchal cultures and societies continue to put boys and men first and, in many and different ways, to oppress women and girls, it remains necessary to focus on women and girls and their experiences. In addition, there may be significant aspects of human experience, such as the ethical values of survival and care, that are more easily noticed and named when the experiences of women are highlighted. Judith is more sympathetic than Carol to queer theory's critique of the gender binary. Carol continues to wonder whether there are sex differences with fluid boundaries inherited from our human or even primate ancestors, such as a tendency to respond with empathy that is formed in the relationship of mothers with their infants.[17] Still, neither of us is a gender essentialist or biological determinist. We do not believe that all girls and women necessarily share a set of common traits. If there are differences between the sexes, they exist on a continuum; individuals and cultures make choices in relation to them; and gender is only one of the factors that make up the complexity of human life. Though we recognize that the notion of women's experience is problematic, we continue to insist that theologies need to take account of the experiences of those who are perceived as, and consider themselves, women. In this book, as in our earlier work, we write as women, situated in particular bodies, cultures, histories, and communities. Rather than viewing either of our experiences or both together as normative, we instead hope that what we share will resonate with the experiences of others in different situations, inspiring them to think and write from their own embodied and embedded perspectives.

Embodied Experience, Embodied Thinking

Because experience is always situated in bodies, thinking about and through the body is a foundational idea in feminist theology. In the

---

17. Primatologist Franz de Waal argues that the capacity for empathy is inherited from mammalian and primate ancestors and that males—including human males—seem to be able to override empathy in favor of aggression more easily than females. See "Franz de Waal Talks About the Nature of Empathy with Edwin Rutsch," http://cultureofempathy.com/references/Experts/Frans-de-Waal.htm.

past, few (male) theologians thought about their work as rooted in the body. When women began to protest that theology was male, and when people of color protested that it was white and European, the response of most white male theologians educated in European theological traditions was to assert that rational thinking is not affected by its location in a particular body, culture, or history. Yet as the critique of classical dualisms makes clear, this is one of the fallacies of traditional Western thinking. Feminist thinkers have criticized the traditional theory of knowledge that assumes that the disembodied minds of rational thinkers can commune with transcendent ideas. In contrast, feminists, including Carol and Beverly Harrison, proposed that thinking arises from the feelings of the body.[18] We are able to know and reflect on the world only because of our capacities to feel, touch, see, hear, taste, and smell. Our embodied thinking is always situated in relationships, communities, cultures, societies, and in the web of life.

Feminist theologians have put the theory of embodied thinking into practice in a variety of ways. Some have drawn on women's fiction, poetry, and memoirs to put flesh on the bones of their theologies. Others have reflected on their own experiences. Katie Canon analyzed the experiences of black women through detailed analysis of black women's fiction.[19] Rita Nakashima Brock and Rebecca Parker used autobiography to explore their claim that the doctrine of redemptive suffering encourages Christian women to accept violence in their relationships with men.[20] Christine Downing found the stories of her life mirrored in and deepened by the myths of the Greek Goddesses.[21] Carol explored women's spiritual quest in fiction and poetry in her first book and wrote about her own spiritual quest in another.[22] Thinking

18. Carol P. Christ, *Rebirth of the Goddess: Finding Meaning in Feminist Spirituality* (New York and London: Routledge, 1998 [1997]), chap. 2; Beverly Wildung Harrison, "The Power of Anger in the Work of Love," in her *Making the Connections: Essays in Feminist Social Ethics*, ed. Carol S. Robb (Boston: Beacon, 1985), 12–15.
19. Katie Geneva Cannon, *Black Womanist Ethics* (Atlanta, GA: Scholars Press, 1988).
20. Rita Nakashima Brock and Rebecca Parker, *Proverbs of Ashes: Violence, Redemptive Suffering, and the Search for What Saves Us* (Boston: Beacon Press, 2001); and its theological sequel, *Saving Paradise: How Christianity Traded Love of This World for Crucifixion and Empire* (Boston: Beacon Press, 2008).
21. Downing, *The Goddess*.
22. Christ, *Diving Deep and Surfacing: Women Writers on Spiritual Quest* (Boston: Beacon Press, 1980, 1985,

about theological issues from the perspectives of different bodies, different situations, different communities, different cultures, and different histories, feminists have begun to add the pieces that were missing in the theologies of the white men who went before us.

Turning to the World

In addition to situating experience in the body, feminist theologies find divinity in the world. In contrast to traditional theologies that define God as transcendent of the world and a transcendent realm as the true home of the soul, most feminist theologians affirm the immanence of divinity and assert that the meaning of life is to be found in this world. Feminist liberation theologians speak of God's preferential option for the poor and find God's presence in the struggles of poor women, especially third world and indigenous women.[23] When they speak of "the liberating Word of God" and "the experience of God's presence among one another and through one another," they are not necessarily referring to the God of Exodus who intervenes in history with a mighty arm, but rather to divinity as immanent in poor women's experiences and struggles.[24] In a different vein, Christian theologian Sallie McFague described the earth as the body of God,[25] while poet Alice Walker named all the colors of earth, sea, and sky as the body of Goddess.[26] Although some have said that concern for the poor is a critical issue of justice, while concern for the earth is a less important or less pressing issue, we consider this to be a false dichotomy. For us, the common thread uniting liberation and ecofeminist theologies is a shared conviction that divinity is to be found in the world, not outside of it. We view the issues of ecology and social justice as inseparable. Not only are toxic waste dumps and uranium tailings often located in poor

1990) and Christ, *Odyssey with the Goddess: A Spiritual Quest in Crete* (New York: Crossroad: 1995), revised as *A Serpentine Path: Mysteries of the Goddess* (Cleveland, OH: Far Press, 2016).

23. Kwok Pui-lan, ed., *Hope Abundant: Third World and Indigenous Spirituality* (New York: Orbis Books, 2010).

24. See Rosemary Radford Ruether, *Sexism and God-Talk*, 137; Elisabeth Schüssler Fiorenza, *In Memory of Her: A Feminist Theological Reconstruction of Early Christian Origins* (New York: Crossroad, 1983), 345.

25. Sallie McFague, *The Body of God* (Minneapolis: Fortress Press, 1993).

26. Alice Walker, "We Have a Beautiful Mother," *Her Blue Body Everything We Know: Earthling Poems 1965–1990* (New York City and Orlando, FL: Harcourt Books, 1991), 459–60.

communities, but also, the health of the environment that sustains human and other forms of life is crucial to the survival of human beings.

Some feminist theologians have linked the turn to the world in feminist theology to the need for criticism, reconstruction, or rejection of monotheism. Jewish poet and theologian Marcia Falk criticized the exclusive male monotheism of biblical traditions not only because it privileges male language for God, but also because it depicts God as separate from the world. Falk stated that an "authentic monotheism" must affirm the multiplicity of the world through a plurality of images for divinity, "as many as are needed to express the diversity of our individual lives."[27] Laurel Schneider and Catherine Keller rejected what they called a "totalizing monotheism" in the name of a theology of multiplicity. They view the opposition between the one and the many as a product of "the logic of the One" that has dominated Western theological discourse, engendering and authorizing the related notions of one Truth, one Empire, one Law, one Father, one Ruler, and one Way to live. For them, it is no accident that monotheistic cultures tend to be religiously intolerant, viewing beliefs other than their own as lesser, lower, inferior, wrong, and uncivilized. Schneider and Keller proposed that the Christian concept of Trinity provides a model for understanding God and the world in terms of "multiplicity, open-endedness, and relationality."[28] Speaking from a different standpoint, Karen McCarthy Brown argued that the many spirits of Haitian Vodou reflect the diversity of the world and the multiplicity of wills that it encompasses, creating a fluid moral universe in contrast to the more rigid rule of law characteristic of monotheistic systems.[29] While we share the critique of exclusive and male totalizing monotheism, we also agree with Schneider that, in the final analysis, "a logic of

---

27. Marcia Falk, "Notes on Composing New Blessings: Toward a Feminist-Jewish Reconstruction of Prayer," *Journal of Feminist Studies in Religion* 3, no. 1 (Spring 1987): 41; reprinted in Plaskow and Christ, *Weaving the Visions*, 128–38.
28. Catherine Keller and Laurel C. Schneider, eds., *Polydoxy: Theology of Multiplicity and Relation* (New York: Routledge, 2010), 1.
29. Karen McCarthy Brown, *Mama Lola: A Vodou Priestess in Brooklyn* (Berkeley, Los Angeles, London: University of California Press, 1991), 241–42.

multiplicity is not opposed to unity."[30] What is most important for us is to find ways to affirm both the diversity and unity of the world.

Female Language for Divinity

For many feminist theologians, the turn to the world is associated with the search for a new female language for divinity. Imagining God as a woman affirms the minds and bodies of over half of humanity. Because femaleness has been disparaged in dualistic thinking by linking it to the body and nature, it makes sense that a new female language for divinity not only revalues and reclaims the female body, but also affirms divinity in nature. At the same time, the feminist celebration of divinity as female calls for the repudiation of dualisms and the integration of body, mind, and spirit. Archaeologist Marija Gimbutas questioned the widely held view that the Goddess is to be associated with a lower and nonrational stage of culture. She argued that the Neolithic Goddess cultures of Old Europe were peaceful, egalitarian, and highly artistic—and in many ways superior to the patriarchal, warlike cultures that destroyed them.[31] Moreover, the women who invented agriculture, weaving, and pottery in the Neolithic era were not acting out of unconscious instinct, but were clearly intelligent—and rational. We underscore this point for two reasons. We are critical of those who identify the "Divine Feminine" or "the Goddess" primarily with feeling, relationships, intuition, and the unconscious, while asserting that "the Divine Masculine" represents rationality, independence, assertiveness, and even warlike aggression. This leaves the dualisms intact and does not criticize the violence inherent in patriarchy. But we are equally critical of those who fail to see that the vast majority of Goddess feminists, as well as feminists who are experimenting with female imagery for divinity within traditions, do not hold such simple views. Feminists are striving to reunite the separated poles of thinking and feeling, to affirm that all human beings

---

30. Laurel C. Schneider, *Beyond Monotheism: A Theology of Multiplicity* (New York: Routledge, 2008), 198.
31. Marija Gimbutas, *The Language of the Goddess* (Los Angeles: University of California Press, 1981); also see Carol P. Christ, *Rebirth of the Goddess*, chap. 3.

are embodied and embedded in nature, and most of all to insist that "being female means you still can be strong," independent, and intelligent, as well as loving, giving, and caring.[32]

Goddess feminists have been inspired by images from the ancient past, from the Paleolithic Goddess of Willendorf to the Snake Goddesses of ancient Crete, as well as by living traditions, from the intelligent Thought Woman of the Keres Pueblos, to the compassionate Kuan Yin of China, to the fierce Kali of India. In organized groups like Starhawk's Reclaiming community, in unaffiliated circles of friends, and when alone, growing numbers of women invoke the Goddess in rituals on full moons and at the turn of the seasons. While most churches and synagogues have been slow to embrace female images for divinity, many Christian and Jewish women have invoked God-She and Goddess in small groups or in private prayers. Jewish Renewal rabbi Lynn Gottlieb reimagined Shekhinah—the female divine presence in the Jewish mystical tradition—as She Who Dwells Within.[33] The Kohenet Hebrew Priestess Institute seeks to "revive and re-embody Judaism through the gifts of women spiritual leaders and through experience of the sacred feminine, whom we call Shekhinah, Goddess, and many other names."[34] In San Francisco, Ebenezer Lutheran herchurch is committed to giving voice to the Divine Feminine in the words of prayer and liturgy and to adorning its sanctuary with works of art that celebrate God as a woman.[35]

While a call for new images of Goddess and God is to be found in most feminist theologies, feminist work on the sacred is often qualified by what theologian Laurel Schneider calls the "metaphoric exemption." This is the idea that language about Goddess or God must always be symbolic or metaphoric because the true nature of divinity is unknowable.[36] Drawing on this idea, Jewish and Christian theologians,

---

32. The words "being female means you still can be strong" are from Meg Christian's "Ode to a Gym Teacher," http://www.lyrics.com/ode-to-a-gym-teacher-lyrics-meg-christian.html.

33. Lynn Gottlieb, *She Who Dwells Within: A Feminist Vision of a Renewed Judaism* (San Francisco: HarperSanFrancisco, 1995).

34. "Kohenet Hebrew Priestess Institute: Mission," http://www.kohenet.com/mission/. Also see Rabbi Jill Hammer and Holly Taya Shere, *Siddur Kohenet: A Hebrew Priestess Prayerbook* (N.p., n.d.).

35. See Elizabeth Ursic, *Women, Ritual, and Power: Placing Female Imagery for God in Christian Worship* (Albany, NY: State University of New York Press, 2014), chap. 4.

including Rita Gross, Elizabeth Johnson, Sallie McFague, and Judith have justified the quest for new images of God as female by arguing that, if all language about God is symbolic, then new female images are no more or less accurate than traditional male images.[37] Invoking the idea that divinity is not knowable frees feminists to explore new symbols in ritual and worship without being required to justify them with new theological conceptions.

However, not all feminist theologians agree that divinity is unknowable. Mary Daly described her work as a philosophy of women's liberation and redefined God as a Verb, as active Be-ing ever creating itself anew. She believed that a new understanding of divinity would provide support for the idea that new revelations leading to new be-ing are occurring in the movement toward the liberation of women. Daly minced no words in describing traditional Western philosophical and theological views of God as static Being as wrong.[38] Building on the process relational philosophies of Alfred North Whitehead and Charles Hartshorne, Valerie Saiving, Marjorie Suchocki, Catherine Keller, Monica Coleman, and Carol asserted that process relational philosophy can hold the insights of feminist theology together in a consistent worldview.[39] Arguing from revelation, Roman Catholic theologian Catherine Mowry LaCugna constructed a relational ontology of divine and human personhood to replace the traditional ontology of divine substance existing apart from the world.[40]

36. Laurel C. Schneider, *Re-imagining the Divine: Confronting the Backlash against Feminist Theology* (Cleveland: Pilgrim Press, 1998), 23.
37. Rita Gross, "Female God Language in a Jewish Context," in *Womanspirit Rising: A Feminist Reader in Religion*, ed. Carol P. Christ and Judith Plaskow (San Francisco: Harper & Row, 1979), 167–73; Elizabeth Johnson, *She Who Is: The Mystery of God in Christian Tradition* (New York: Crossroad, 1992), 6–8; Sallie McFague, *Models of God: Theology for an Ecological, Nuclear Age* (Philadelphia: Fortress Press, 1987), 35 and passim; Judith Plaskow, *Standing Again at Sinai: Judaism from a Feminist Perspective* (San Francisco: Harper & Row, 1990), 134–36.
38. Daly, *Beyond God the Father*, chap. 1.
39. Valerie Saiving, "Androgynous Life: A Feminist Appropriation of Process Thought" and Marjorie Suchocki, "Openness and Mutuality in Process Thought," both in *Feminism and Process Thought*, ed. Sheila Greeve Davaney (New York: Edwin Mellen Press, 1982), 11–31 and 62–82; Catherine Keller, *From a Broken Web* (Boston: Beacon Press, 1988); Monica Coleman, *Making a Way out of No Way: A Womanist Theology* (Minneapolis: Fortress Press, 2008); Carol P. Christ, *She Who Changes: Re-imagining the Divine in the World* (New York: Palgrave Macmillan, 2003).
40. Catherine Mowry LaCugna, *God for Us: The Trinity and Christian Life* (San Francisco: HarperSanFrancisco, 1991); and "God in Communion with Us: The Trinity," in *Freeing Theology:*

We have changed over time in our attitudes toward the metaphoric exemption. In "Why Women Need the Goddess," Carol stated that symbols have a richer significance than any possible explication of their meaning. Since then, she has become committed to developing a philosophically coherent account of the worldview of Goddess feminism. She considers the idea that divinity is essentially unknowable to be a legacy of classical dualism's insistence on absolute divine transcendence, an idea that, in other contexts, feminists reject.[41] Judith's early work on God focused on the issue of imagery, especially on the harm caused by the image of God as a dominant male other. She did not offer a full-scale theology in *Standing Again at Sinai* because the issue of images seemed more immediate and pressing, as well as less difficult to address. However, as she came to recognize the many theological questions she left unanswered, she realized that, even though she believes we can never be certain of whether our theologies capture the divine "as it really is," it is nonetheless important to reflect on the nature of God more fully.

While we recognize that many readers of this book might prefer to leave questions about "the real nature" of Goddess or God shrouded in mystery or paradox, we find this traditional answer to human questions unsatisfying. Feminist theology did not begin with the statement that the nature of divinity is unknowable. Rather it began with the assertion that the image and idea of God as an old white man who rules the world from outside it justified male domination. The interrelated set of ideas associated with the traditional image of God not only fails to make sense of the world as we know it, but also has been harmful and destructive to individuals, communities, and the whole web of life. Unless and until we develop viable alternatives to these ideas, they will continue to influence us. This is why we have dared to engage in systematic thinking about the nature of divinity and to encourage others to do so. While we acknowledge that all thinking about God and Goddess is situated in embodied human experience and

---

The Essentials of Theology in Feminist Perspective, ed. Catherine Mowry LaCugna (San Francisco: HarperSanFrancisco, 1993), 83–114.

41. Christ, *She Who Changes*, introduction.

therefore will always be fragmentary and limited, we also believe that we can and must speak about our understandings of divine power and the relation of divinity to the world.

7

Answering My Question

Carol P. Christ

As will become clear in this chapter, it took me many years to answer for myself the question I posed at the end of my Harvard lecture. When I moved to Greece, I planned to begin working on the Goddess theology I had contracted to write. At the same time, I felt that the idea of writing a systematic Goddess theology was not mine, but had been thrust upon me by friends, colleagues, and editors, because of my unique position as a theologically trained participant in the newly emerging Goddess movement. I was not convinced that theology was the appropriate genre in which to discuss the meaning of the Goddess. Left to my own devices, I might have focused on ritual or tried my hand at poetry or fiction. As I was to discover, I would need to resolve the question of the nature of the Goddess before I would be able to write a coherent theology.

One of the reasons I moved to Greece was to change my life. I did at first live without a car, washing machine, central heating, or even an oven. There were few shops in my village, and they carried primarily local products and seasonal produce—no tomatoes in the winter and no lettuce in the summer. "Remember peanut butter?" we used to lament. Living with fewer things put me in closer connection to bodily life; I felt in touch with the seasons and the landscape eating local foods in their time; and I learned that I could do without many things that seemed to be necessary in the United States. I found myself living in an extroverted or expressive culture in which strong emotions, both positive and negative, are rarely repressed. This cultural style has its own negatives, but in the beginning, I focused on the positives. Being among people who were able to express their feelings of the moment encouraged me to continue the personal work of coming more in touch with the feelings of my body. Many of the people in my village still lived by the rhythms of the agricultural life that had sustained their ancestors for millennia. They knew how to read the signs of the weather, and their daily lives were rooted in the rhythms of the earth. While I had come to Greece with the intention of rediscovering traces of long-forgotten Goddesses, I began to understand that Goddesses were alive in sacred places in the landscape, in folk rituals that had a very thin Christian overlay, and in simple devotion to the Panagia (the Virgin Mary), whose name translates as She Who Is All Holy. Without being fully conscious of it, I had entered into a process of reconstructing my life from the inside out; I was moving from my head into my body; and I was beginning to experience the world from the perspective of greater connection to the web of life. Everything I thought I knew was being challenged.

I did finish a draft of my Goddess theology a few years after I moved to Greece. My editors responded that, though the book had many beautiful and provocative parts, "there was something missing." Unfortunately they could not say just what the missing piece was. I had no idea either, and so I felt stymied. In retrospect, I can see that the missing piece was my lack of clarity about the nature of divinity. But even had we realized that, neither I nor my editors could have snapped our fingers and made the answer appear. I would say as well that the first draft of my book was written primarily from the head, but that the book needed to be written from a deeper place of embodied knowing and connection to the web of life. When I received my editors' response, I was slipping into a depression sparked by yet another disappointment in love, so I set the book aside. From time to time the editors inquired about when they could expect the manuscript, and all I could say was "I don't know." Meanwhile *Laughter of Aphrodite* was doing well, and so was the second anthology Judith and I coedited, *Weaving the Visions.* I was still being asked to speak in the United States and Canada.

The depression I fell into after moving to Greece lasted for several years. It stemmed from feelings of betrayal by a Greek man I loved but who, because he was a drug addict (though I did not know this at the time), was incapable of returning love. I lost faith in the Goddess who I thought had led me to this man. I felt I could not trust my intuition or the feelings of my body. Numb and empty, I had no desire to write anything at all and certainly not a Goddess theology. During this time, I never doubted my decision to move to Greece. On some level, I must have known that my depression was part of a process that I needed to go through—even though it did not feel like that at the time. I was saved by three very good friends, Susie Irving, Dana Zangas, and Pat Felch, and by the project of using my hands (rather than my head) painting, refinishing furniture, hammering nails, learning to connect electrical wires, and sewing curtains to create a home in the apartment I bought in Athens.

Love in the Face of Death

During that time, my mother was diagnosed with cancer. While my mother was dying, I came to the realization that I had never loved anyone as much as I loved her. Susie encouraged me to write a letter to my mother expressing my feelings. My mother replied that my letter "was the nicest letter she had ever received in her life," and she invited me to come home to be with her. My mother was told that her cancer

149

was not in remission shortly after I arrived. She died only a few weeks later, in her own bed as she wished. She was on an oxygen machine, and I heard her call out. When my dad got to the room, he turned up the oxygen, but it didn't help. Then he called the doctor who reminded him that my mother had a living will stating that she did not want to go to the hospital under any circumstances. My father sat by her bed and held my mother's hand. As my mother died, I felt that the room was "filled with love," and I sensed that she was "going to love." Prior to that moment, I had often felt that I was not loved enough, especially in the wake of failed love affairs. I would feel helpless and abandoned and could think only that "no one loves me, no one will ever love me, I might as well die." Although my life continues to have its ups and downs, from the moment when the room filled with love as my mother died, I have never doubted I am loved, nor have I contemplated suicide again.

The experience I had when my mother died did not come with any words except "filled with love," and "going to love." I did not feel Goddess loves me or God loves me or that my mother was loved by Goddess or God. I also did not feel that my mother was entering into eternal life. I simply felt the palpable presence of great love in the room. Reflecting on this experience, I came to the conclusion that Goddess is love. This is not primarily an intellectual interpretation of my experience of my mother's death, though it is that as well. Most importantly, it is a feeling that permeates my daily life that was made possible by the experience I had when my mother died.

As I thought about what I had learned, I realized that, in my desperate search to find the "true love" I did not have, I had been ignoring many forms of the love I did have, from friends, family, animals, and the whole of the natural world. It felt as if a veil had been lifted that had clouded my vision. Like Alice Walker's Shug, I began to sense in my body that love is everywhere and that "everything wants to be loved."[1] Though I recognize that the power I call Goddess may also be called God, for me the word God is too bound up with images

1. Alice Walker, *The Color Purple* (New York: Harcourt Brace Jovanovich, 1982), 179.

of war, violence, and domination for me to feel comfortable using it in my prayers and meditations. I have had troubled relationships with my father and academic father figures, while my relationships with my mother and grandmothers were full of love. This makes it easy for me to think of the loving arms of Goddess embracing the world.

Anger at Goddess

I wish I could say that after my mother died and I returned to Greece, I sat down and rewrote my book and lived happily ever after. But it was not that simple. Insight may come in a flash, but living into its meaning happens more slowly. In the next years, I began leading Goddess Pilgrimages to Crete, and the experiences I had in Crete helped to restore my relationship with the Goddess. When I was first asked to lead a Goddess Pilgrimage in Greece, I responded that I did not feel capable of introducing others to a Goddess I was no longer sure I trusted. As often happens in my life, chance intervened. Friends insisted I join them in Crete at a conference on the partnership principle, organized by Riane Eisler and Margaret Papandreou. After the conference, my friends and I stumbled on the convent of Paliani with its Sacred Myrtle Tree in which the Panagia is said to dwell. The Sacred Myrtle Tree grows at the back of a courtyard filled with flowers and surrounded by the small homes of the nuns who care for Her. In the church near the tree, the eyes of the icon of the Panagia seemed to be looking directly at me. The acts of lighting a candle and taking a dry twig from the tree for protection were my first steps toward repairing my relationship with the Goddess. The woman who asked me to lead Goddess Pilgrimages had also come to Greece for the conference. When I met her a few days later in Athens, I agreed to lead a Goddess Pilgrimage, but only if it would be in Crete.[2]

Thinking about Paliani during the subsequent months, I started to wonder if a myrtle tree could be as old as the nuns said theirs was. In a book about the trees and shrubs of Greece, I learned that myrtle is a

---

2. I have been leading the Goddess Pilgrimages to Crete in spring and fall for more than twenty years; see www.goddessariadne.org.

shrub that only rarely becomes a tree. To my great shock and surprise, I also discovered that the myrtle had been sacred to Aphrodite. This definitely was not what I wanted to hear. I thought I had left behind Aphrodite and all the heartache she brought me. Alone in my apartment on a hot summer night, my pent-up anger exploded. I poured my heart out to Aphrodite, saying, "I hate you. . . . You abandoned me. You left me to die. Not once, but many times." In the silence that followed, I heard Her reply in unexpected words that came into my mind: "I did not abandon you," She said. "Who do you think led you to the Paliani convent? You were so angry with me that I had to disguise myself in order for you to find me. But you did find me there. Do you remember your prayer? You asked for what you believed I had taken from you. You knew I was there. I did not abandon you. The path you are on now is not easy, but I will be with you all the way."[3]

Expressing anger at Goddess was as powerful as expressing anger at God had been years earlier. In both cases, I needed to be fully present with all of my feelings in order to receive what I hesitantly call revelation. This time I learned that Goddess is omnipresent, always there, but not omnipotent, all-powerful. Just as She could not intervene in history to stop the suffering of women, so She could not intervene in my life to fulfill the desires of my heart. She is with me and always has been with me, loving and understanding me, sympathizing with my struggles, and helping me to see that I can find my way. I have yet to find my true love—or perhaps my true love came in the form of my mother, certain friends, and a little white dog—but that does not seem to be important any more. I have learned that life is not about getting what "I" want. I often say that I have become a kind of Buddhist, as I have given up many of the desires of my ego that had clouded my vision. In giving up having to have what I thought I could not live without, I began to see the beauty of the world and all the people and creatures in it a different light.

Not long after my mother died, Christine Downing asked me to write

---

3. Carol P. Christ, "Words with You Aphrodite," *Odyssey with the Goddess: A Spiritual Quest in Crete*, 60; revised and republished as Carol P. Christ, *A Serpentine Path: Mysteries of the Goddess* (Cleveland, OH: Far Prees, 2016), forthcoming.

about my experience of my mother's death for a book she was editing on Demeter and Persephone.[4] I agreed, and in the process broke through the writing block that had lasted for years. I felt compelled to write about the experiences of the Goddess I was having in the sacred places of Crete. The words poured out of me, and as I wrote, I came to a deeper understanding of the power that was healing me. Soon I had a book I called *A Serpentine Path*, in recognition that the journey of life, like the path of a snake, is never straightforward.[5] This book was pivotal in my life and work. Through the experiences I described in it, I gained the deeper knowing that would enable me to create a Goddess theology at last. In the process of reflecting upon my experiences, I found the embodied voice I had been seeking.

Thealogy

When I began to rewrite *Rebirth of the Goddess*,[6] I decided that I would write about the major topics of theology: "God, man, the world, history, and ethics." These topics became chapters: "The Meaning of the Goddess," "Goddess History," "The Web of Life," "Humanity in the Web of Life," and "Ethos and Ethics." I remembered that a systematic theology must be clear, coherent, and comprehensive.[7] Not forgetting my earlier interests in story and theology, I began the book with stories of the rebirth of the Goddess in women's lives, and I incorporated pieces of my story throughout. As the Goddess is embodied in images as well as in ideas, I included some of my favorite images of the Goddess in the introduction. In the process of writing, I found that I could integrate my thinking and my experience in a confident new voice that

4. Carol P. Christ, "Learning from My Mother Dying," in *The Long Journey Home: Revisioning the Myth of Demeter and Persephone for Our Time*, ed. Christine Downing (Boston: Shambala Press, 1994), 125–35. In slightly different form, this essay was incorporated as "Death," in Christ, *Odyssey with the Goddess*, 18–23, and Christ, *A Serpentine Path*, forthcoming.

5. This book was originally published as *Odyssey with the Goddess: A Spiritual Quest in Crete*, a title chosen by the publisher. A revision of the book with new preface and epilogue will be published with my preferred title as *A Serpentine Path: Mysteries of the Goddess* (Cleveland: OH, 2016).

6. Carol P. Christ, *Rebirth of the Goddess: Finding Meaning in Feminist Spirituality* (New York: Addison Wesley, 1997; paperback, New York, Routledge, 1998).

7. As I said in an earlier note, I have remembered the three *C*'s of systematic theology differently over the years.

was no longer divided in two. Being able finally to write the book was exhilarating, but the process was not easy, for there were no models for what I was doing, no sacred texts to interpret, and no authorities to tell me what I must say or could not say.

I called my book a Goddess thea-logy, from *thea* (or Goddess) and *logos* (or meaning), in order to call attention to the radical way in which I was rethinking a theological tradition that had always focused on *theos*—the male God. Before I could begin my thealogy, I had to discuss epistemology, or how we know. Because my thinking about the Goddess was not rooted in revelation recorded in sacred texts or in a living tradition, this question was critical. Even before I became a feminist, I had been dissatisfied with the way we were studying theology at Yale because I viewed theology as a way of making sense of experience—both personal and social. As a feminist, I argued that theologies had been rooted in men's experiences and that they needed to begin from women's experiences as well. When I mentioned the word "experience" at Yale, I was told that the meaning of the term was by no means self-evident. This term would need to be defined. By the time I wrote *Rebirth*, "women's experience" had been contested among feminists. I had never believed in the eternal feminine, and though I did and do believe that there are commonalities or family resemblances in women's experiences, I have never been what is called an "essentialist."

Once again I found confirmation of my method in the insight of Martha Quest: I trusted that if I wrote from "the growing place in myself," I would be speaking for others as well.[8] I decided that, rather attempting to define certain experiences as common to "all women" or even to a more limited group such as "feminists," "white women," "children of the 1960s," or "Goddess feminists," I would write from my own deepest experiences in dialogue with other feminists in religion, and trust that if I did so, I would also be speaking for and to many other women, and to men as well.

I defined "experience" as embodied and embedded in relationships

8. Doris Lessing, *The Four-Gated City* (New York: Bantam Books, 1970), 67.

and in time and place. I assumed that experiences that I may think are mine alone are shared by others who inhabit the same or similar social and natural worlds. I had begun to learn this in the early exciting days of feminism when so many of our experiences seemed to be shared; it was confirmed in my therapy group; and it had proved true in my writing and speaking. At the same time, I was aware of the limitations of every standpoint. Though certain aspects of my situation are shared by others, my experience does not encompass every standpoint or the experience of the whole world. Thus we must always situate our experience in communities in which our ideas can be challenged and tested. In addition, we must seek to expand the range of our empathy so that we can understand the experiences of others and, to the best of our abilities, incorporate perspectives that are not our own.

I wrote *Rebirth* from my standpoint as a white, middle-class, heterosexual, bicultural Greek and American Goddess feminist, while consciously situating my words in conversation with those of other Goddess feminists, with feminists in religion, with women writers, with male theologians, and with the field of religious studies as a whole. While I was very much aware that I was writing the first contemporary Goddess thealogy, I also knew that I could draw on the wisdom of many others. This is why I continually referred to other voices while constructing my thealogical worldview. My experiences are articulated in the book, not in the form of autobiography or memoir, but as the embodied standpoint from which I engage in theological reflection. As I discovered how to write theology in an embodied and embedded way, I realized that I am a theologian after all. I like to think about divinity and the world and the meaning of life. All of my training and previous work had prepared me to write an embodied, situated, systematic thealogy of the Goddess.

The System in Systematic Thealogy

The "system" in systematic theology means that the same themes are expressed in different ways in relation to different topics. For example, if, citing the work of Martin Buber and the work of feminists, I argue that relationships are fundamental in human life, it makes sense also to think about God, nature, and ethics in terms of relationships. Drawing on Buber's I-Thou relationship with human beings, God, and a tree, I began to develop a more complete philosophy of relationship. I rejected the common view that humanity stands apart from nature. Instead, I advanced the ecological and ecofeminist view that all beings, including human beings, are related, connected, and interdependent in the web of life. I rejected the idea that ethics stems from a transcendent principle of justice delivered on high by God or intuited as a universal principle by rational minds. Instead, I argued that ethics stems from *eros*, feelings of connection with other human beings and with nature. I would also use the concept of relationship to understand the nature of divinity: Goddess is omnipresent, always related to all, and Her love, understanding, and inspiration define Her relationship to the world.

I was careful to be consistent in regard to other assertions as well. If I argued that women must reclaim our connection to our bodies, our body wisdom, and our powers to heal with our hands, I would not leave this assertion hanging. I would go on to assert that the world is the body of Goddess and that She knows the world because She listens to her body. I would say that embodiment connects humanity to nature. Or, if I said that in human beings, mind and body are connected, did it not make sense to say that the same is true of Goddess? The Goddess must have a mind as well as a body, a consciousness akin to our own, if She is to feel the feelings of the world that is Her body. And then how could it make sense to say, as is commonly asserted, that nature is body without mind? Intelligence and forms of consciousness and choice must be found in nature too. In this way, I worked through all of the topics I considered with a concern for explaining the world as I experienced it and with an eye for consistency in my thinking. What may have seemed to be a series of positions arrived at independently in my previous work now were connected in a comprehensive worldview, in principle applicable to everything. Of course, I was not just filling in the pieces of the puzzle. Everything I wrote arose from my experience and was tested in relation to the thoughts of others.

Rebirth of the Goddess builds upon the insights I had gradually developed in my earlier work: the symbol of Goddess affirms women's power, bodies, will, and relationships with each other; images of Goddess have the metaphoric power to transform male images of God; the Goddess symbol has the power to transform classical dualism's separation of mind and body, thought and feeling, spirit and nature, male and female, and the absolute categorical distinctions between God, humanity, and nature; the earth is sacred and our true home; we must embrace a finite life that includes death; all beings are connected in the web of life.

To this it adds the insight that Goddess is "the intelligent embodied love that is the ground of all being."[9] When I considered defining the Goddess as love, it felt important to add "embodied" because love is not a disembodied feeling but always occurs in and between bodies. I added "intelligent" before love in order to affirm that love is by no means only emotional or irrational feeling. Goddess not only loves the world but understands it as well. Her understanding is like that of a good therapist who sees who we are and encourages what we can become. I took the phrase the "ground of being," to which I added "all," from theologian Paul Tillich. While Tillich referred to God or Being as the metaphysical whole out of which individual beings arise, I have always heard the English translation of his German words in a physical sense as well—as referring to the ground beneath our feet and the earth which supports us. I agree with Mary Daly that both Be-ing and be-ings are not static as Tillich may have thought, but changing. Some years after *Rebirth* was published, I was delighted to recall that my concept of Goddess as intelligent embodied love owed a debt to my undergraduate teacher, Michael Novak, who, in his book *Belief and Unbelief*, defined God as love and understanding.

---

9. Christ, *Rebirth*, 107. I reword this definition in chapter 11. Questions posed by John Cobb and Judith caused me to rethink this definition in relation to a technical point made by John Cobb in "Being Itself and the Existence of God," in *The Existence of God*, ed. John R. Jacobson and Robert Lloyd Mitchell, (Lewistown, NY: Edwin Mellen, 1988), 5–19.

Panentheism and the Divine Relativity

When I got to the chapter where I needed to discuss the nature of divine power, I reached back to a book I had not read since graduate school, *The Divine Relativity* by Charles Hartshorne.[10] I worked from memory, while asking a friend to send me a photocopy of it. I had not known I was going to explain divine power using the concept of panentheism. However, when I came to the appropriate place in the book, I realized that this was the concept I needed. Panentheism is formed by adding *en*, which means "in," to pantheism, which means all is God or God is all. Panentheism means that the God is in the world and the world is in God—while avoiding the conclusion that the world *is* God. Like other feminists, I wanted to criticize the traditional view that God is distant from or wholly transcendent of the world. I was sympathetic with Starhawk's view that Goddess is immanent in the world, but I did not want to affirm that there is no distinction between God and the world. I did not want to be forced to conclude that Goddess is as much the rapist as the rape victim or that making war is as much a part of the divine nature as making love. Nor have I ever been comfortable when others spoke the words, "You are Goddess" or "I am Goddess." The divinity is infinite, while I am not. Panentheism allowed me to assert that Goddess is in the world but more than the sum total of the world and that Goddess is in me but more than I am or ever will be. That "more" is expressed in the statements that, while the world is a mixture of good and evil, Goddess is good, that while we sometimes love, Goddess always does, and that while our understanding is limited, Hers is not.

I also adopted the notion of divine power as persuasive rather than coercive from Hartshorne. For me, the notion of divine omnipotence is proved implausible by the Holocaust—as well as by rape, genocide, and war. This insight was also confirmed in my experience that Goddess could not give me what I wanted and prayed for—not as a child and not

10. Charles Hartshorne, *The Divine Relativity: A Social Conception of God* (New Haven: Yale University Press, 1948).

as an adult. Divine power is not the power to control and determine everything that happens in the world. Hartshone calls the notion of divine omnipotence the "zero fallacy."[11] If God has all of the power, then God has the power to determine the course of history. But if God has all of the power, then we have zero or none, and in fact there is no history, but only a divine dance with not even an audience to watch it. If God does not have all of the power, and the world has some power, then the power that God does not have must be sufficient to affect the course of events. If this is so, then God is not able to control the course of events, but only to influence them. The divine power is always a power of love and understanding, but this power is the power to persuade or inspire, not the power to cause or coerce the outcomes God might prefer.

Judith read the chapters of *Rebirth of the Goddess* as I wrote them, as did my longtime editor Marie Cantlon. Although I treasured Judith's and Marie's insights and support, I still had my doubts as to whether I had succeeded in writing a systematic theology of the Goddess. It was nearly ten years since I had participated in a seminar at Harvard led by Gordon Kaufman and John Cobb. I had had no contact with either of them after I left Harvard. Still, they were the only well-known male theologians I could think of asking to read my book. Tentatively, I had my pages copied and mailed them out. What would these Christian men think of my heretical work? Would they declare it theology or rubbish? I waited with bated breath. Eventually both men responded that they liked my book a great deal. They concurred that it was a systematic theology. And they both thought it was an important statement addressing the problems of our world. I breathed an enormous sigh of relief. Both of them offered to write comments for the book jacket. Gordon agreed to join a panel on my book at the American Academy of Religion.[12] John invited me to visit him when next I was next in southern California.

11. Charles Hartshorne, *The Zero Fallacy and Other Essays in Neoclassical Philosophy*, ed. Mohammad Valady (Chicago: Opencourt Press, 1997), 161–72.
12. "Reflections on Carol Christ's Theology" by Gordon D. Kaufman, will be available in the future in Carol P. Christ's archives at Smith College.

John Cobb lives in Claremont, California, only a few miles from where I grew up and from where my father still lives. When I visited him, John told me that he not only liked *Rebirth of the Goddess*, but also that he considered it a work of process theology. When I responded that I had drawn on process ideas in only a few pages of the book, John replied that the whole book expressed process ideas. He said that if I had worked my own way into the process worldview rather than learning it from books, that made my achievement all the more important. It proved, he said, that process ideas really do make sense of the world. When I left John's house, I stopped at the university bookstore where I bought all of the books in stock by process philosophers Charles Hartshorne and Alfred North Whitehead.

A Process Relational Worldview

Back in Greece, I began to read them. I began with Hartshorne's essay "Do Birds Love Singing?"[13] I intuitively agreed with him that they do. From there, I plunged into his works with a sense of delight. The feelings I had in graduate school that I was reading a book written by a kindred soul came flooding back. I was amazed to discover that, indeed, I had come to many of the most important conclusions of process philosophy on my own. I was elated to learn that male philosophers of religion who were not thinking primarily of women, feminism, or Goddesses held views similar to those I had developed through long, hard, and often solitary struggle. Process philosophy provides a metaphysical framework in which the ideas I have been struggling to express all my life—and ideas I have discovered in the struggle—cohere and make sense in a comprehensive worldview.

"Metaphysics" is one of those terms that make some people cringe. As used by process philosophers, it simply means that the whole world is governed by and expresses certain fundamental principles. For process philosophy, the most essential of these principles are relationship, freedom or creativity, and change. We are born into

13. Hartshorne, *The Zero Fallacy*, 43–50.

relationships with our mothers and the world.[14] Our presence changes the lives of those who care for us, and we are shaped by the way they choose to relate to us. We change and are changed by every other individual we meet in the course of our lives. Our freedom exists within the context of relationships, and because our choices affect others as well as ourselves, our choices are important. Relationship, freedom, and change are fundamental principles that are expressed not only in human life but also in the world as a whole. We are all interconnected in the web of life. Everything changes and is changed. All individuals in the web of life, human and other than human, affect and are affected by the others. If this is what a process metaphysic means, I find more reason to rejoice than to cringe, because the process metaphysic makes sense of the world as I experience it.[15]

I agree with process theologian Marjorie Suchocki that feminist theology needs a metaphysic, a coherent worldview that can hold together what we might otherwise see as a series of unrelated assertions made by feminists.[16] This does not mean that ideas are more important than reality. For process philosophy, metaphysics does not precede physics. Metaphysical principles are not revealed in rational contemplation divorced from the world, as philosophers have often assumed. Quite the opposite: metaphysical principles are conclusions reached through paying close attention to the world. Metaphysical principles are one of the ways we explain the way the world works to ourselves. Because our explanations are always limited by our perspectives or standpoints, metaphysical principles as we know them are not certain and unchanging. This means that we should think of metaphysical principles not as the complete and final truth about the

14. Martin Heidegger's famous phase that "being " is "thrown" into the world expresses the fact that we that we are born into a world we did not create and into relationships we did not choose. However, if we were actually thrown rather than welcomed into the world, few of us would have survived. In other words, Heidegger's phrase fails to appreciate the importance of the care and concern of mothers in the life of "man." Martin Buber, on the other hand, recognizes that "I" only become "I" in relationship to "Thou."
15. Also see the discussion of *She Who Changes* in this chapter and my description of the creative process in chapter 9.
16. Suchocki made this statement as part of her opening remarks at the Conference on Process and Feminism in Claremont, California in April 2004, which she and I organized together.

world but rather as the best understanding of the world I have at this point in time from my standpoint and in conversation with others.

Feminism and the Process Relational Worldview

Discovering process philosophy led to my next book, *She Who Changes*, in which I show how the process relational worldview provides philosophical support for feminist assertions, including those about the importance of relationships, the embodied nature of life, and the centrality of care in ethics.[17] It offers a coherent alternative to the classical dualistic thinking inherited from Plato and criticized by Rosemary Ruether that separates mind from body and spirit from nature, and identifies women with the despised body and nature. Moreover, process philosophy says that thinking begins in the feelings of the body in a relational world, which is exactly what feminists mean when we say that theology begins in experience and must connect feeling and thinking.

For process philosophy, divinity is not the exception to metaphysical principles, but rather the most comprehensive example of them. As the most relational of all relational beings, and the most sympathetic of all sympathetic subjects, Goddess or God feels all of the feelings of the world and responds to them. This also means that divinity changes with the changing world. When the world rejoices, divinity rejoices; when individuals in the world are violating each other, divinity feels the sadness and anger of the world and seeks to inspire a better way. What is unchanging is that Goddess or God always responds to the world with love and understanding, and always desires the flourishing of the individuals within it. Hartshorne's discussion of God's relationship to the world, using the image of the world as the body of God, provides grounding for Goddess spirituality's image of the Goddess as Mother Earth, the matrix in which other individuals exist. In Hartshorne's model, the cells of a body are independent

17. Carol P. Christ, *She Who Changes: Re-imagining the Divine in the World* (New York: Palgrave Macmillan, 2003). The title of the book was inspired by the Goddess chant, "She Changes Everything She Touches." It was not conceived as a response to Elizabeth Johnson's *She Who Is*, but the contrast between the two titles reflects the contrast between a process and a classical metaphysic.

162

individuals—not under the full control of the mind of the body, yet connected as parts of single body, influenced by the mind. So too, individuals in the world—human and other than human—are independent, yet interconnected in the body of God, influenced by and capable of being inspired by the divine wisdom. The divine body is the earth-body, but also the body of our universe and all other universes.

With process philosophy as a firm foundation, I feel more confident that it is right to think not only about God, but also about everything else in the world through the lens of change, relationship, freedom, and interdependence in the web of life. The notion of God's power as persuading or inspiring, but not coercing, makes sense to me. The idea that God is not in control of everything answers the questions I had about evil. We may perceive death, disease, and natural phenomena such as earthquakes, volcanoes, and floods as evil, but in fact, they are among the conditions of life as it developed on our planet. We may ask why God lets them happen, but in fact divinity alone did not create the evolutionary process or the world. Other individuals contributed to the process of creation, beginning with the atoms and parts of atoms that came together as they were swirling in space. The real evil in our world is not created by divinity but by human beings. The process worldview places the responsibility to change the world firmly in our hands.

Learning to Know the Body of Goddess

In the decade following the completion of *She Who Changes*, I have learned to pay closer attention to the world that is the body of Goddess. I have felt connected to nature all of my life. Yet often, though not always, I have related to nature in general rather than in specific ways. After reading Hartshorne's essay on birdsong, I stopped for the first time in the wetlands of Kalloni, Lesbos, to look for the flamingoes that live in the saltpans. One thing led to another, and I met someone with whom I spent the next six weeks visiting every pool and puddle where birds were stopping in Lesbos that spring. I would have said that I had always loved birds, but I had not studied them or even paid attention to their differences. Over the next several years, I spent countless hours in bird habitats and pouring over books, during which time I learned to identify over three hundred species of birds that live or migrate through Lesbos. I also learned that Lesbos has a wetland ecosystem that is one of the most important stopping-off points for birds migrating from Africa to Europe in the spring.

Bird watching can be and is for me a practice of meditation on the beauty of the world. To find birds, you must learn something about their habits and habitat. But you must also look closely and wait patiently for them to appear. To be able to watch an elegant and shy black stork fish in a seasonal river, you must also be lucky, for black storks generally fly off as soon as they see people. Part of the magic of bird watching is that, just when you feel disappointed in not finding a bird you have been looking for, a bird you were not looking for flies right in front of you. It may be a common and familiar bird, but watching it bathe in a mud puddle can be magical. This for me is the grace of life.

Through bird watching, I learned that if I love the earth, I would do well not just to admire sunsets, but to study the varieties of life that make up the earth body. Sadly, as I became intimate with specific birds and the places they loved, I also became intimate with the degradation of wildlife habitats in Lesbos where I watched them. I found that the more I love the world, the more I suffer when parts of it are destroyed. When I see degraded wetlands, I feel that parts of my own body are violated. I understand that when Alice Walker's Shug said, "If I cut a tree, my arm will bleed,"[18] this is not hyperbole but an accurate description of feelings in the body.

For a decade and a half, I have been engaged with others in the struggle to save the wetlands of Lesbos for birds and other wildlife as required by the European Community law known as Natura 2000. Along with others, I drafted scores of complaints about the degradation of individual wetlands on the island. When the local authorities failed to intervene to protect them, I spent a good part of several years writing, and then working with World Wildlife Fund and the Hellenic

18. Walker, *The Color Purple*, 167.

Ornithological Society to perfect, a detailed Complaint to the European Commission concerning the failure of Greek governmental authorities to protect the bird and wildlife habitats of the wetlands of Lesbos. Three years after the submission of the Complaint, the European Commission found infringement of the law, deciding the case in our favor, and initiating discussions to bring the Greek government into compliance. In the ensuing year, following the election of a new government, the Ministry of the Environment of Greece announced its intention to secure funding to carry out the research necessary to institute measures to preserve all of the four hundred and forty-nine Natura sites in Greece.[19] This is the first time the Greek government has expressed a serious commitment to Natura. If the money is found (and it is almost certain that it will be), the final result will be far more than we had even dared to imagine we could achieve. Because of my environmental work, I was asked to join the Green Party Greece and to run for office in Lesbos in regional and national elections. My efforts combined with those of many others led to the appointment of a Minister of the Environment in Greece who is a Green Party member. He is the one who is now working to initiate measures for the protection of the Natura sites at the national level. For me, loving the world and working to save it are two sides of the same coin. I get as much joy from giving back to the earth as I do appreciating its beauty.

At the time I began to learn about birds, a geologist came on the Goddess Pilgrimage to Crete. She spoke to our group about the great

19. The original complaint with documentation filling two large binders, submitted in September 2011, was given the number 2770/11/ENVI by the Eurooean Commission; after the infringement decision, it was re-classified as Infrigement Case 2013/4208 in 2014. The Greek Ministry of the Environment stated on numerous occasions in 2015 and 2016 that funding will be found to proceed with the research leading to the protection of all of the Natura sites in Greece. As this book goes to press, all indications are that a formal announcement is imminent. The Mayor of Kalloni, Lesbos was one of the first to act to protect the Natura wetlands of Greece; after his efforts were opposed by local landowners, government officials at both local and national levels apparently concluded that doing nothing was the best policy. In 2000, I wrote a petition that was signed by birdwatchers and locals that led to the founding of Friends of Green Lesbos, and it was in my capacity as Vice President of that group that I drafted individual complaints and the formal Complaint to the European Union. Friends of Green Lesbos worked together with Nautilos en drasi, an environmental group based in Lesbos, and WWF Greece for many years. The Hellenic Ornithological Society joined with us to sign the Complaint. I am a dual citizen of Greece and the United States and have run for office in Greece as a Greek citizen.

upheavals affecting the plates of the earth that pushed the mountains of Crete, along with the Alps, up from the sea floor about 200 million years ago, beginning to shape the continent of Europe as we know it today. Until then, I had imagined that as Greek islands, Crete and Lesbos must have had similar geological histories. Visiting the Museum of Natural History in Lesbos for the first time, I was astonished to discover that Crete and Lesbos were formed in different ways. While one of Lesbos's mountains arose from the sea at the time of Crete's mountain formation two hundred million years ago, the others were shaped by massive volcanic explosions twenty-two to sixteen million years ago, in the process of which the Aegean Sea was formed. My eyes were opened to the differences between the porous volcanic rocks from which my village is built and the smoother marl or marble-like limestone rocks of Crete that were formed from deposits of plankton in the sea beds. For the first time, I noticed that the stones from which the houses and streets and walls of my village are built are not uniformly grey, as I had always seen them, but that some are greyish-lavender, some are greyish-pink, and some are greyish-green. The word "geology" comes from *ge*, the ancient Greek work for earth. Learning about the evolution of the earth and about the geology of the islands I love is another way of learning to know and love the earth more deeply and more intimately. Now I know Her history in the crevices of Her body.

Ancestor Connection

Once, when I was speaking about the earth as the body of Goddess, womanist theologian Karen Baker-Fletcher asked if I thought the ancestors are a missing link between our bodies and the earth. It took me years to grasp the full meaning of her question. As Baker-Fletcher writes in one of her books, our bodies are "dust" insofar as they are made up of elements of the stardust that formed the planet earth.[20] However, this dust comes to us through the egg and the sperm that

20. Karen Baker-Fletcher, *Sisters of Dust, Sisters of Spirit: Womanist Wordings on God and Creation* (Minneapolis: Fortress Press, 1998).

unite in our mothers' wombs. The fertilized egg carries DNA inherited from near and distant ancestors, going back to the earliest human beings, to their primate ancestors, to the first mammals, all the way back to the beginning of evolution on our planet. If we are inspired to give thanks to Mother Earth, should we not also acknowledge our own mothers, and through them the long line of mothers and fathers, and the history of evolution that have made our lives possible?

From my earliest feminist days, I have known the ritual of naming female ancestors. "I am Carol, daughter of Janet, daughter of Lena, daughter of Dora." I have always felt this ritual to be spiritual, though I was not sure why I felt that way. Even when I knew only three names in my maternal line, the ritual of naming ancestors was an incredibly powerful way of affirming that, as I later put it in a blessing we use in Crete, "I come from a long line of women." In our ritual on the Goddess Pilgrimage, a few women added their membership in one of the clans of the "seven daughters of Eve," the seven ancestral mothers to whom almost all Europeans are related. This sparked me to read Bryan Sykes's book of the same name, and to begin thinking about human migration out of Africa.[21] Testing my DNA told me that I am descended from the Tara, the name Sykes gave to ancestress of the "T" line of mitochondrial DNA shared by about 10 percent of Europeans but passed down only through the female line. Tara may have lived near the Alps in northern Italy about eighteen thousand years ago. Tara herself was a descendant of Africans who migrated to the Middle East about sixty to fifty thousand years ago. Her lineage diverged from that of the African Eve who lived about two hundred thousand years ago, and who is the single ancestral mother or ancestress of all living human beings. I can begin to imagine my ancestors living in Africa, walking to the Middle East and settling there, moving on to paint their handprints in the caves of Europe during Ice Age, and a whole line of women connecting them to me. In our mother line ritual, we

21. Bryan Sykes, *The Seven Daughters of Eve: The Science That Reveals Our Genetic Ancestry* (New York: W. W. Norton & Co., 2001).

now repeat, "I come from a long line of women, known and unknown, stretching back to Africa."

Through the Internet and family members, I have discovered that some of my ancestors were Huguenots who fled France to England to the New World and then moved on to found the Hempstead Colony on Long Island. I have found others in the tenements of New York City and Brooklyn. I have ancestors who took land from the Indians and others who held slaves in New York, and some who, as Quakers, opposed slavery. I have relatives who died of diphtheria and tuberculosis in the tenements, and others who managed to survive poverty, hardship, and discrimination. Knowing this history changes the way I feel about myself. It is not that all of my ancestors were noble and good. Some of them did things I am not at all proud of. At the same time, it is their lives that made my life possible. Knowing who my ancestors are, I feel related to specific places in the body of our mother earth and to numerous times in her history. "I am Carol Patrice Christ born in Pasadena, California, daughter of Janet Claire Bergman born in El Paso, Texas, daughter of Lena Marie Searing born in Lyons, Michigan, daughter of Dora Sofia Bahlke born in Alma, Michigan, daughter of Maria Hundt, born in Parum, daughter of Catherina Schopenhauer, born in Pogress, daughter of Anna Seehasse, born in Zülow, Mecklenburg, in the clan of Tara. I come from a long line of women, known and unknown, stretching back to Africa."[22]

Gratitude and Sharing

The more I practice the spirituality of the Goddess, the more I understand that earth-based spiritualties are rooted in two fundamental principles: gratitude and sharing. We give thanks to the Goddess, and to the earth, and to our ancestors for the gift of life. As we recognize our interdependence and interconnection in the web of life, we are moved to share what has been given to us with others.

---

22. See Carol P. Christ, "Finding Ancestor Connection via the Internet," in *Feminism and Religion in the 21st Century: Technology, Dialogue, and Expanding Borders*, ed. Gina Messina-Dysert and Rosemary Radford Ruether (New York: Routledge, 2014), 88–98.

When I first began to lead Goddess Pilgrimages, I was inspired by a line in Homer to begin a pilgrimage tradition of pouring libations of milk, honey, water, and wine on ancient stones. At first, like the rabbi Wiesel wrote about, I did not know the meaning of the ritual, but could only tell the story. But as I began to pour libations myself and thought about the large number of pouring vessels in the museums and the altar stones onto which liquid was poured, it dawned on me that pouring libations while offering the first fruits of every harvest was not only "a" ritual of ancient Crete, but most likely the central one. Its purpose is to thank the Goddess as Mother Earth for the bounty She has bestowed on us. The pouring of libations is not, as is sometimes thought, "simple fertility magic," performed to induce the earth to produce the next harvest, but rather is an expression of gratitude for the gift of life and the gifts of life. The act of moving to and from the altar in conjunction with others while pouring liquids onto stones embodies the flow and grace of life. When each person in a community approaches the altar and pours a libation, the community is integrated without hierarchy. The essence of these rituals is expressed in a song by Faith Rogow taught to me by Judith that includes the lines, "As we bless the Source of Life, so we are blessed."[23] Chanting those words again and again, I have come to understand that expressing gratitude for what we have been given and celebrating our place in the flow of life is one of the primary purposes of prayer and ritual.

The other basic principle of earth-based spirituality, sharing, is an outgrowth of gratitude. We did not "make ourselves," but were given the gift of life through the inspiration of Goddess in the long history of our universe, from our Mother Earth, from the places where we live, our ancestors, and from our mothers' bodies. When we realize this on a deep level, we feel gratitude for what we have been given, and this motivates us to share what we have with others in our communities and in the web of life. Some have asserted that the source of ethics is a transcendent principle of justice. Others would say that we require the

23. See Carol P. Christ, "As We Bless the Source of Life, So We Are Blessed," *Feminism and Religion* (blog), May 7, 2012, http://feminismandreligion.com/2012/05/07/as-we-bless-the-source-of-life-so-we-are-blessed-by-carol-p-christ/.

words of the prophets or the model of Jesus. Some might even speak of the fear of God. But I would say that the impulse to share what we have and to work to create a more just and harmonious world stems from recognizing how deeply we are connected to each other and to all others in the web of life. The rituals of earth-based spirituality end in feasting: the sharing of food and drink, the original communion.

The answer I can now give to the question I posed at the end of my Harvard lecture is that the Goddess is a personal presence who loves, understands, enjoys, and inspires every individual, human and other than human, on this earth and throughout the universe. She is not the earth nor did She alone create the universe, but it is appropriate to think of the universe as a whole and our earth in particular as the body of Goddess because She is as intimately connected to all of the individuals who live or have lived on this planet or any other as we are to the cells of our own bodies.

8

Wrestling with God and Evil

Judith Plaskow

In the first years after I finished *Standing Again at Sinai*, I explored the problem of evil in several lectures on "Reconsidering Evil," in which I sought to understand the lack of attention to theodicy in feminist theology, including my own. I attributed the failure to address this question to a widely shared feminist understanding of divinity as empowering, nonpersonal, and immanent in creation—a divinity who it made no sense to blame for the evils in the world. As women claim our power as agents in community and history, I argued, we come to know ourselves as grounded in a greater power that nourishes and sustains us, even as it sustains the universe of which we are a tiny part. But, I asked, do we not also need to acknowledge that, as we become effective in the world in new ways, we gain new power to hurt and destroy others? Haven't we learned that our own oppression brings no guarantees that we won't in turn oppress others? Isn't the same cosmic ambiguity to which Catherine Madsen directs our attention—the droughts and floods, bounty and indifference of the world[1]—manifest in human nature, in our capacity to use our creativity for great good, for great evil, and for everything in between? As I learned from Sioux medicine man John Fire Lame Deer, whose book I was teaching at the time, "The thunder power protects and destroys. It is good and bad, as God is good and bad, as nature is good and bad, as you and I are good and bad."[2]

As students and colleagues raised questions or debated with me after my talks, I realized that there was often a fundamental divide in the way we understood the purpose of religious beliefs and symbols. For many of those with whom I spoke, the purpose of religion was to give expression to their highest aspirations, so that the notion of a God who was other than perfectly good simply made no sense. I, on the other hand, looked to religion to provide a map of the universe in all its messiness and complexity, and to furnish ways both to live with that messiness and, where appropriate, challenge it. A concept of God that did not leave out the world's terrors was far more satisfying to me than one that crystallized ideals. The anger at God I had nursed for many years now transformed itself into the insistence that an inclusive monotheism must embrace the complexities and ambiguities of existence as part of the nature of God. My life-long wrestling with human and divine evil had changed along with my concept of God, but I wasn't ready to let it go.

The Ambiguous God

Two experiences I had just after completing *Standing Again at Sinai* further contributed to my interest in rethinking God's relationship to the ambiguous forces at work in the universe and ourselves, even as they shifted my theological focus in yet another way. In conjunction with attending a feminist conference in Buenos Aires, Argentina, my

1. Catherine Madsen, "If God Is God She Is Not Nice," *Journal of Feminist Studies in Religion* 5, no. 1 (Spring 1989): 104.
2. John (Fire) Lame Deer and John Erdoes, *Lame Deer: Seeker of Visions* (New York: Washington Square Press, 1972), 253.

partner Martha and I visited Iguassu Falls and spent three days in the Amazon. Iguassu is one of the largest series of waterfalls in the world and lies on the border of Brazil and Argentina. I expected to find the falls beautiful; we had been told that they were not to be missed, but I did not expect to be utterly mesmerized by them, to feel as if I could stand and look at them forever, and to weep when we had to leave after three days. Particularly when we visited the "Devil's Throat," a spot where it is possible to stand on a platform over the roiling waters at the bottom of the largest waterfall, I felt that I was gazing at the wellspring of life in all its terror and sublimity. On the one hand, the energy, potency, and beauty of the water were incredibly energizing and empowering. It seemed to me that if human beings could only tap into the electricity of the current and allow it to flow through us, we could indeed "let justice roll down like waters, and righteousness like an ever-flowing stream" (Amos 5:24). On the other hand, the waters knew no moral purpose; they could as easily overwhelm and destroy as nourish and vivify. They seemed to transcend the distinction between "power with" and "power over" that had been so central to feminist theology; they could lift up and sustain or engulf and annihilate. I had seen the face of God, and it brought home to me the complex and multifaceted nature of all creativity, human and divine.

A week later, we spent three days at a hotel in the Amazon at the juncture of the Rio Negro and the Ariau River. We arrived in pitch blackness after a long boat ride up the Rio Negro to be directed to a room with only screens for the outer wall, filled with sounds of frogs and crickets. I awoke in great excitement at 3:30 in the morning, feeling like a child who has gotten up too early on Christmas morning and can't wait for the day to dawn. Two hours later, we were startled by what sounded like the whole river being drained by a huge vacuum, a terrifying noise that we afterward discovered came from howler monkeys calling to each other. We dressed hurriedly, went outside, and accompanied by black spider monkeys, climbed a tall wooden tower to see the sunrise. I have a phobia of heights and normally would not think of ascending an open and rickety-looking wooden structure, but in this case my excitement overpowered my fear. The sun rose as it had set the previous evening, a giant red ball, ascending into the sky with amazing rapidity. As it rose, the whole world came to life. The egrets we had seen flying to their trees at sunset took off again, as did flocks of flycatchers. The macaws that lived at the hotel began to squawk, and squirrel monkeys swung from tree to tree. It was a vast panoply of sights and sounds that made us feel as if we were present at the moment of creation. Our time in the Amazon was both magical and unnerving, rich and overwhelming: the density and tangledness of the vegetation; the strange sounds; the snakes, monkeys and other animals that might appear at any moment and that were still wild even when they lived at the hotel; the vultures feasting on the carcass of a crocodile; the hordes of ants; the piranhas lurking in the river. I experienced a deep sense of reverence for the astoundingly intricate and complex universe of which I was part. "This is not the Lord of history at work here," I wrote in my journal of the trip, "but the infinitely fertile and inventive source of life."

A Changing Relationship with God

In the years that followed this trip, I did not write about God or about my experiences in Argentina and Brazil. Having arrived at an understanding that worked for me on a personal level, I turned my attention to other subjects. I had not been ready to come out as a lesbian when I wrote *Standing Again at Sinai*, but in the decade and more following its publication, I wrote several articles on gay and lesbian issues and lectured widely on the topic of sexuality. I made it my mission to get people to address the difficult and painful passages in canonical texts (such as Lot's offering his virgin daughters to the men of Sodom in Gen. 19:8), passages that are too often passed over in silence and thereby left to work their mischief in the world.[3] When I was elected president of the American Academy of Religion, I decided

---

3. See, e.g., "Jewish Anti-Paganism," "Dealing with the Hard Stuff," and "Preaching Against the Text," in my *The Coming of Lilith: Essays on Feminism, Judaism, and Sexual Ethics, 1972-2003* (Boston: Beacon, 2005), 110–17, 152–56.

to give my presidential address on the changing shape of academia and issues of class more broadly—another area I felt I had neglected in *Standing Again at Sinai*. I tried to think and speak about how Jewish feminists could move from a focus on the transformation of Judaism to bringing Jewish feminist perspectives to other social justice issues. Remembering the absence of women's bathrooms in the Divinity School library at Yale, I began to write about access to toilets as a social justice issue. I felt compelled by the rise of transgender activism to rethink the gender models that underlay my own and other feminists' work. Throughout this time, I continued to engage with other feminist and womanist scholars on issues that divided us as well as questions of shared concern. In more recent years, I have found interesting commonalities with Muslim feminists who—like Jews—need to deal with the complexities of being seen as Muslims in a Christian society and as feminists by their own coreligionists.

But the fact that I was not writing or speaking much about God did not mean that my *relationship* with God was not growing and shifting. In the aftermath of completing *Standing Again at Sinai* and going to Brazil, I asked myself what it meant that the theology I had laid out in the book was so profoundly communal. Was I entirely dependent on meetings of B'not Esh and my havurot for regular spiritual infusions? Did I have no personal spiritual practice? Martin Buber says that the radio waves of the Eternal Thou are all around us, but most of the time we have our antennae turned off. After visiting Iguassu, I tried to be more attentive to turning up my antenna. I imagined the waters of the falls flowing through the whole of my life, signaling the presence of God in each moment of experience. At some point, I decided to begin each day by naming five things for which I was grateful. For a few years, I read a few verses every morning of *Perek Shirah* (*Song of the Universe*), a traditional text that imagines various aspects of creation—the heavens, the seas, grasshoppers, elephants—singing God's praises with verses from the Bible. I tried to be aware of the holy moments in the classroom when students suddenly connect with an idea and begin to spark off each other and me. When Campus Ministry put up signs around the hallways of Manhattan College saying, "Remember that we are standing in the holy presence of God," I did not share the annoyance of some of my colleagues, but felt, yes, it is good to be reminded that teaching is holy work and that even students who never do the reading are created in the image of God.

When my son started college, I moved from Queens to Riverdale in order to be nearer to work. Instead of beginning each day cursing on the Triboro Bridge, I walked to school through a beautiful neighborhood filled with old trees and frequently found myself humming a chant on the way: "*Ze hayom asa yah nagilah venismeha vo.*" "This is the day that God has made; let us rejoice and be glad on it" (Ps. 118:24). When I first learned this song, I associated "this day" with the holidays on which the psalm is always chanted—until I realized that every day is a day to rejoice in the glory of creation. Some years later, I moved to Manhattan, and I now live just a block from the Hudson River. I frequently walk along its shore in Fort Washington Park, watching its waters flow down under the George Washington Bridge and disappear into the distance. Simone de Beauvoir in *The Second Sex* talks about how young girls often find a freedom in relation to nature that is denied them by the press of social expectations. That had been true of me as a girl, but when I first became involved in various feminist communities, the power of God's presence in nature had taken second place. Now it has once again regained its prominence. I sometimes feel that the veil between me and the existence and unity of God's world is very thin and that I only need to remember to truly look at the world around me to shift into a deeper level of seeing. To use Gerard Manley Hopkins's words, "The world is charged with the grandeur of God."[4]

It is not just in relation to nature that I have these feelings. New York City is also a mediator of the sacred for me. Several years ago, a colleague who had moved to New York from Iowa asked me whether I found New York a "sacramental reality." It was a wonderful question

---

4. Gerard Manley Hopkins, "God's Grandeur," in *Gerard Manley Hopkins: A Selection of His Poems and Prose*, ed. W. H. Gardner (Baltimore, MD: Penguin, 1953), 27.

because it led me to turn up my antenna, push aside the veil, and become aware of God's presence in the contours of the City. So often, I am deeply moved by the *landscape* of Manhattan, its density, the shape of its buildings against the sky, its syncopated rhythms. When I am in Times Square, I find myself caught up in the beat of the city and feel as if I am standing at the center of the universe. The pleasure is quite analogous to taking in and becoming part of a beautiful natural environment. I especially love the city from the water or from a great height like the Empire State Building, from which I can see canyons every bit as majestic as the Grand Canyon. I was in Boston for the year when the World Trade Center was destroyed, and I went back to New York the very first weekend after the attack. My sense was that my beloved had been injured, and I needed to be with her. It strikes me that my reluctance to live anywhere but New York is analogous to the feeling I had leaving Iguassu: Why would I tear myself away from a spot where the presence of God is so palpable?

As I think about my feelings about New York in relation to my experience at Iguassu Falls, I realize that, in the one case, I felt the divine presence in nature, and, in the other, in the power of human creativity. One of the joys of living in the city is that—apart from its beauty as a whole—it provides many particular occasions to experience the presence of God in the works of human hands. In standing before a painting by Fra Angelico or Rembrandt at the Metropolitan Museum, in admiring the gargoyles or surprisingly intricate brickwork on various apartment buildings, or in singing Vivaldi's "Gloria" with the Riverdale Choral Society, I feel, as I do about New York itself, that I am in touch with the source of life. As someone who especially loves the theater, I often ask myself after a disappointing play why I continue to throw out my money when I have to sit through numerous ordinary productions for every remarkable one. But then I see a performance that makes me want to shout and cheer, and I realize that, for me, theater is like prayer: I cannot engage in it expecting a transcendent experience every time, but when those extraordinary moments come and the heavens open, there is no question that they render the quest worthwhile.

In describing these experiences, I do not mean to imply that community has ceased to be a "sacramental reality" to me, just that it is no longer *more* important than nature, cityscape, or art as a mediator of the sacred. Until 2014, when Martha retired from teaching at Smith College and we settled permanently in New York, we were both members of Havurat Ha-Emek (Fellowship group of the [Pioneer] Valley) for thirty years, and for seventeen years, we also belonged to Su Kasha ("su kasha" is a play on *su casa*, your house), a gay and lesbian havurah in New York. Both of these were groups of fifteen to eighteen members that met in people's homes and rotated leadership of services.[5] Much that Martha and I value in B'not Esh—its intimacy, open-endedness, and willingness to experiment—also characterized these groups, so that we had ongoing prayer communities that were religiously nourishing. Because the independent Jewish communities called havurot are member led and able to respond to member needs, different groups vary considerably in both size and in their practices. Emerging in the late 1960s as a countercultural response to the perceived anonymity and soullessness of large synagogues, havurot take advantage of the fact that Jewish communal worship requires only ten Jews (traditionally ten male Jews), not the leadership of a rabbi. While equality between men and women in religious leadership is a baseline value of havurot, some use the traditional prayer book, while others are more experimental. Our two havurot were on the latter end of the spectrum. We followed the deep structure of the Sabbath service from morning blessings to Torah study, but without the traditional prayer book's barrage of words that for many of us only served to obscure God's presence. We chanted; we sang; we used poetry and meditation. We left time to talk about the meaning of a poem or prayer that suddenly struck someone in the group as significant. Because we used little of the traditional liturgy, the issue of male language

---

5. Havurat Ha-Emek continues to meet, but, sadly, since we moved permanently to New York, we are no longer able to be part of it.

was less pressing than it might otherwise be. Sometimes we left the traditional language intact; sometimes we used the Reconstructionist prayer book's *Hay ha'olamim* (Life of all worlds) instead of *Melekh ha'olam* (King of the universe); occasionally we used Marcia Falk's blessings. I made it a practice to consistently use *Ruakh ha'olam* (Spirit or breath of the world) instead of *King* for the traditional blessing formula, even when others used traditional language.

Torah and Prayer as Mediators of the Sacred

Discussion of the Torah portion was central to our gatherings, and over the years, I have come to a deep appreciation of Torah as another mediator of the sacred. Certainly, I do not always like what I find there; there is much that I consider disturbing and even horrible. But for me, the Torah's ability to hold up a mirror to the world in all its contradictions and complexity is a source of continuing insight and self-discovery. For example, one time when we read the Torah portion containing the passage in Leviticus that disqualifies men with physical defects from serving at the altar (Lev. 21:16–23), Havurat Ha-Emek had a wonderful discussion of the concepts of perfection and disability, of attitudes toward disability in Jewish tradition and society, and of experiences of illness and disability in our own lives. On other occasions, when the Torah portion contained images of God as violent and punishing, we debated whether we could continue to read such passages as sacred text and what it means to transmit them to the next generation. Can we understand such images of God metaphorically, and if so, as metaphors for what? How do we pass on to our children a fuller range of images for God so that, rather than taking certain metaphors for granted, they are aware of the open-endedness of image-making? While we certainly did not reach closure on this topic, we found that ongoing wrestling with "texts of terror" (to use Phyllis Trible's phrase)[6] is part of the process of forging a meaningful Jewish identity. Just as I find a concept of God as present in all the ambiguities

---

6. Phyllis Trible, *Texts of Terror: Literary-Feminist Readings of Biblical Narratives* (Philadelphia: Fortress Press, 1984).

of existence more satisfying than a notion of God as purely good, so I find meaning in the hard places of Torah that point to aspects of our world that need to be confronted and transformed.

I want to be clear that in embracing ambiguity, I am not saying that the passages on disabled priests, or those on exterminating Amelek, or marrying a young woman to her rapist, or any of the other dreadful things we find in the Torah, are simply to be accepted as parts of a complex whole. On the contrary, they should be read as reflecting aspects of the world and ourselves that we need to address and change. I realize that, in affirming the power of the sometimes-awful Torah or insisting on the ambiguity of God, I come perilously close to an aesthetic theodicy that sees the loose threads on the back of a tapestry or the blot in the corner of a painting as contributing to the beauty of the larger picture. I have always hated this theodicy because it ignores the reality that the broken threads and blots are people's lives negated, cut off, or made abject. The violence in the world and in the Torah, like the poverty, misery, and dysfunction that are part of the reality of New York City, are indeed aspects of the whole. But I believe it is our task as beings who have the power to discern the distinction between right and wrong, life and death, to choose life (Deut. 30:19), to ally ourselves with the voices of justice, compassion, and loving kindness in the Torah and the world in order to help create a society in which everyone shares in the earth's resources without depleting or destroying them.

I recognize that my willingness to ask what I can learn from the difficult parts of Torah may indicate that I have grown more conservative over time. Although I refuse to excuse or apologize for the awful parts of the text, I do sometimes wonder whether finding meaning in them—even when I name them as awful—is only a more subtle form of apologetics than explaining them away. Similarly, after many years of using the traditional prayer book at least occasionally, I have grown more reconciled to it. While there are still many occasions when it makes me angry, I can read myself into its metaphors in ways that would have been unacceptable to me in an earlier incarnation.

I definitely experience a tension between my understanding of God as a nonpersonal, sustaining presence and the personal images of the liturgy. But I negotiate this tension by approaching prayer as an attempt to evoke and inculcate various feeling states that I, and probably most human beings, experience at different times in relation to the universe. These states include awe, gratitude, powerlessness, surrender, agency, love, healing, anger, sorrow, and many others. Prayer is a total experience, including community, music—a crucial aspect of worship for me—gestures, and silence. The language of prayer is important, but it is only one layer, and other elements of the prayer experience can override or relativize the messages language conveys. Joining in prayer with others reminds me to pay attention to the God in which I believe rather than to let my busyness and everyday concerns eclipse my awareness of the presence of God in the world.

My changing attitude toward Yom Kippur—the Day of Atonement—is in some ways emblematic of this reconciliation. For many years, Yom Kippur was my least favorite holiday. I approached its required fast as a hunger strike against God: when God apologized to the Jewish people for the Holocaust, I would repent of my supposed sins. I especially disliked the *Un'taneh tokef* (Let us acclaim), a central prayer on both Rosh Hashanah and Yom Kippur that images God as a judge who determines the fates of both humans and the hosts of heaven. "On Rosh Hashanah it is written and on Yom Kippur it is sealed," who shall live and who shall die, who by water and who by fire, and so on. The first shift in my attitude toward the *Un'taneh tokeh* came during the year my mother was dying when I realized that the power of the prayer lies less in its description of judgment than in its evocation of the inescapability of mortality and the uncertainty and ultimate uncontrollability of our lives. I have come to see the images of sovereignty that are so central to the whole of the High Holidays as essentially about our fragility, our need to surrender to the larger forces that govern our lives even as we claim the real power we do have to reshape ourselves and the world in which we live. One year, I decided to devote a particular Yom Kippur to seeing whether I could forgive my childhood rabbi for being opposed to the ordination of women, and I realized that Yom Kippur is not about repentance in the sense of beating ourselves up before a silent God but about the genuine possibility of *t'shuvah* (turning), the notion that it really is possible to turn the page and make a new beginning. In giving up the idea of a God who can or needs to repent, I have been freed to attend to the emotional undertones of various parts of the liturgy, the shifting stances toward a complex world that it seeks to evoke in the worshiper. Particularly in the last several years, since I discovered the power of High Holiday services at congregation B'nai Jeshurun on the Upper West Side of Manhattan, I can not only see around the Lord and King but actually value what these images say to me about my utter dependence on the source of life that fills and sustains me, enabling me to undertake the work I need to do in the new year.

I am aware as I write this that much of what I say would have evoked great indignation in an earlier version of myself. All well and good to find personal meaning in the liturgy, I would have said, but individual reinterpretation still leaves problematic images intact to be passed on and shape the imaginations of future generations. I find myself torn as I think about the question of what is worth transmitting and what is better forgotten. As someone who grew up with the Reform Union Prayer Book, I was very angry when I first encountered the traditional prayer book and realized how much of the Jewish heritage had been kept from me without my knowledge. The original reformers were thoroughly steeped in Jewish tradition and made thoughtful decisions about what to keep and what to excise that were both highly principled and deeply meaningful to them. But much as I understand the assumptions behind their choices and in many cases share them, I also feel that they took from future generations the right to make new and different selections, and to have the knowledge base to say what works and does not work for them.

On the one hand, it saddens me to think of my grandchildren and great-grandchildren needing to deal with the same problematic images and texts that trouble me and my contemporaries. On the other hand,

I think we can bequeath to them a Judaism in which such texts and images are only part of a broader menu of options. The question for me is how to hand on the liturgy—and indeed the tradition more generally—with all its complexity and problems and at the same time to give people the critical tools to interrogate and reshape it for each generation and community. My hope is that feminist critiques of liturgy and feminist liturgical innovations will become part of what is handed on as evolving Jewish tradition, that young people will be exposed to female and gender-neutral God-language, that they will encounter Marcia Falk's blessings and be encouraged to reflect on the very human process of "naming toward God" (to use Mary Daly's phrase).[7] I believe that, insofar as a multiplicity of images are integrated into a vibrant synagogue life, and insofar as communities grapple with metaphors of domination and violence in an ongoing way, problematic texts and images will lose some of their centrality and power and will be experienced simply as aspects of a rich and multifarious tradition. It will be taken for granted that Jews need to decide individually and as communities what aspects of tradition are merely of historical interest and which continue to be compelling. But that is not a decision that I or anyone else can make once for all; it must be made and remade over the course of a lifetime and in different historical periods and settings.

What brought me to want to write about the nature of God after many years of putting the subject aside was the opportunity to teach for the Wexner Fellowship Program. Each year, the Wexner Foundation brings together students who have received fellowships for graduate work in some form of Jewish professional leadership for four days of study and reflection around a particular theme. The theme for the year I taught in the program was God. As a teacher at the gathering, I was struck both by the difficulty that students from across the denominational spectrum had in speaking about God at all and by the numbers of highly intelligent Jews training for communal leadership

7. Mary Daly, *Beyond God the Father: Toward a Philosophy of Women's Liberation* (Boston: Beacon, 1973), 33.

who were still walking around with a Sunday-school understanding of divinity. One of the issues I raised in class was why, when so much of Jewish feminism has had a profound effect on the Jewish community, the question of female God-language has had little impact on liturgy and is currently barely discussed. It seemed time to reflect again on the nature of God and God-language, this time developing my own theology more fully and offering an alternative to the omnipotent father of classical theism.

Credo

My own beliefs about God can be stated very simply: I see God as the creative energy that underlies, animates, and sustains all existence; God is the Ground of Being, the source of all that is, the power of life, death, and regeneration in the universe. God's presence fills all of creation, and creation simultaneously dwells in God. In technical theological language, I am a panentheist: I believe in a God who is present in everything and yet at the same time is not identical with all that is. The part/whole analogy that I used in *Standing Again at Sinai* to describe both God and the world and the role of difference in community still expresses my understanding of the God/world relation. Just as a community may be more than the sum of its parts, so God is more than the totality of creation and includes and *unifies* creation. The idea of unity or oneness is particularly central to my understanding of God. To me, believing in God means affirming that, despite the fractured, scattered, and conflicted nature of our experience of both the world and ourselves, there is a unity that embraces and contains our diversity and that connects all things to each other.

In this concept of God, wholeness or inclusiveness is more important and carries more theological weight than goodness. The world as we know it has little use for human plans and aspirations. We can be stunned by the beauty of the raging waters of the sea and an instant later, find ourselves and the things we love annihilated by them. We can be astounded by the care, altruism, and intricate interdependence found everywhere in nature and also by its predation and violence. When we look at ourselves, we find the same, often ambiguous, mixture of motives and effects. Most people are capable of great kindness and also cruelty. Human beings have imagined remarkable ways to care for the most vulnerable among us and have also used our inventiveness to torture and kill. Moreover, there is not a straightforward relationship between our intentions and their outcomes. Things we mean for good frequently have unforeseen negative consequences, just as we can mean something for ill and yet good can come of it. To deny God's presence in all this, to see God only in the good, seems to me to leave huge aspects of reality outside of God. Where then do they come from? How are they able to continue in existence? How can we not see that the same amazing inventiveness that allows us to establish systems of justice, feed the hungry, and find cures for many diseases is present when we develop new weapons or build crematoria?

It is on this issue of the ambiguity of God that I see most clearly the continuing thread that has marked my perspective from adolescence to the present. On the one hand, my understanding of God has changed dramatically. I can no longer accept the notion of an omnipotent God who intervenes in the world or remains aloof according to standards utterly beyond our comprehension. Aside from the incoherence of the notion that God has all the power while we have none, why would we worship such an arbitrary tyrant? On the other hand, the words of Isaiah I cited previously—"I form light and create darkness, I make weal and create woe; I the Lord do all these things" (45:7) —still resonate for me as a profound metaphor for the ambiguity of the creative energy that pulses through the whole complex web of creation and sustains us in life.

I would maintain, however, though it may not seem so, that this notion of God provides significant grounding for ethical reflection and action. While the creative energy flowing through the world may have no moral purpose, the notion of a unity or *oneness* of being embodies a profound moral trajectory. To say that God is one, that the divine presence that animates the universe is one, is to say that we are all bound to each other in the continual unfolding of the adventure of creation. In the human family, for all our differences, we are more alike than we are unlike. All of us are faces of the God who dwells within each of us; the same standards of justice should apply to everyone. When we harm, diminish, or oppress any one of us, we harm ourselves. And this is true not simply of human beings, but of the whole of creation. We are linked to each other in a remarkably complex, intricate web of life, the individual elements of which are thoroughly interconnected. As creatures who have self-consciousness, who, in our better moments, are able to glimpse and appreciate our place in the larger whole, we have a deep ethical obligation to act in the interests of that whole and of the individuals and human and biotic communities within it. We are just one species on a small planet revolving around the sun in one solar system. Yet we have developed a unique capacity to overwhelm and poison the ecological system of which we are part. In the words of Deuteronomy, we are poised between life and death, blessing and curse (30:19). Our ability to "choose life" requires us to act on behalf of the flourishing of life, to participate in the unfolding of divine creativity as it manifests itself in the myriad forms of creation.

Why call the energy that animates and sustains the universe *God*? I am aware that there are people who call themselves secular who are equally humbled by the vitality and inventiveness of creation, and who joyously affirm the value of life and human existence.[8] Though my sensibility may not be so far from theirs, there are several reasons that I am unwilling to relinquish the word God for the power that brings everything into being and supports it in life. For one thing, the feelings evoked by this power and its manifestation in a beautiful and varied world are feelings traditionally associated with being in relationship to God: awe, gratitude, vulnerability, smallness, and dependence, but also significance in the sense of having a place and a calling in relation to the greater whole. "I believe a leaf of grass is no less than the

---

8. See, e.g., George Levine, ed., *The Joy of Secularism: 11 Essays for How We Live Now* (Princeton: Princeton University Press, 2011).

journeywork of the stars," says Walt Whitman, "and the pismire is equally perfect, and a grain of sand, and the egg of a wren." The reverence before each and every aspect of creation as an expression of God's infinite creativity, the notion that "a mouse is miracle enough to stagger sextillions of infidels" seems to me a profoundly religious attitude.[9] Second, the experience of being part of something larger than the self—"not separate at all"[10]—the notion that, in the midst of our ordinary lives, we can at moments glimpse a reality deeper and more fundamental, yet not separate from, those things we concern ourselves with every day, is quintessentially religious. That deeper reality is what various religious traditions call God, Goddess, the sacred, Brahman, Nirvana, the spirits, and many other names. Third, the idea that Oneness has built into it an ethical imperative, that to know the world as God's unified, ongoing creation is also to know that we are required to tend and care for that creation, coheres with and can make sense of the notion of "commandedness" that is central to Judaism and that finds expression both in specific ethical injunctions and the sanctification of daily life. There is no commander who issues orders from outside the web of creation, but there are obligations inherent in the interconnectedness of things that link our own self-interest to the preservation and prospering of all life. Fourth, as an engaged Jew, when I think of God as the ever-flowing wellspring of life, I am able to say what I mean when I pray, who or what I see myself as addressing. Indeed, imagining God in this way *enables* me to pray. To what else shall I speak other than to the reality that brought me and everything else into existence, that is an ever-renewing source of strength when I am troubled or downcast, and that challenges me to bear witness to the oneness of all things in the ways I act in the world?

The Book of Job

As I was working on this chapter, I found myself asking whether I could still find meaning in my once-loved book of Job, given that I have

9. Walt Whitman, "Song of Myself," in his *Leaves of Grass* (New York: Doubleday, 1940), 67.
10. Alice Walker, *The Color Purple* (New York: Harcourt, Brace, Jovanovich, 1982), 167.

come to a very different understanding of God from the one I held when I first encountered it. What in the book continues to resonate for me as for the girl I once was, and what must I read differently? I am no less moved than was my young self by Job's anger at the injustices of the world and by his gradually dawning, if incomplete, realization that others besides him suffer without reason. His vivid descriptions of the disconnection between human behavior and its just rewards appear to me no less breathtakingly brave or devastatingly accurate than when I first read them. "Men remove landmarks; they seize flocks and pasture them," he says. "They drive away the ass of the fatherless; they take the widow's ox for a pledge" (Job 24:2–3).[11] In the face of Job's refusal to put away his integrity and his demand for vindication, God's response had always seemed to me like an evasion, a deliberate attempt to change the subject by overwhelming Job with sheer might. Now, however, I find a different reaction to God's reply coming to the fore: an awareness of God's speeches as an extraordinary work of religious poetry. Here, in a more sustained way than anywhere else in the Bible, we find a description of the intrinsic value of nature apart from human purposes, a paean to the wonders of a strange and mysterious creation that preexists human beings and that has its own order and meaning. The natural world of God's reply to Job, like the waters of Iguassu, is unrestrained, turbulent, powerful, joyous, and beautiful. I had noticed this dimension of *Job* before but had dismissed it as irrelevant to the book's central problematic. I was never able to hold together my indignation at God's refusal to answer Job's question about justice and my love for the language of the "morning stars [singing] together," the horse pawing "in the valley, and [exulting] in his strength," and the Behemoth, made as God made us, eating "grass like an ox" (38:7, 39:21, 40:15).

But now it strikes me that, much as Job may not want to hear it, this *is* God's answer to his question. Right, the author of the speeches imagines God as saying to Job, the order of the universe is not founded

---

11. Quotations from *Job* follow the Revised Standard Version, which is the version I used when I originally studied *Job* at the University of Edinburgh.

on justice. It is not about you or your human standards. The world is about other things entirely: creativity, beauty, diversity, power, energy. It's about the amazing panorama of creation, the springs of the sea and the dwelling of light, the storehouses of snow and hail, the ostrich leaving her eggs on the ground to be trampled and the eagle making its home "in the fastness of the rocky crag" (39:28). This is a different reading from saying, as many have argued, that God's perspective is broader than ours, that if only we could see the world from God's point of view, we would understand the fairness of Job's suffering. The reality is that God's speeches show no concern for fairness, and, in any event, it makes no sense to talk about justice and at the same time assert that God's justice is incomprehensible.

But God doesn't stop there. The speeches are followed by the puzzling epilogue in which God turns to the "friends" who, throughout the book, have berated Job and told him he must have done something to deserve his misery. God says to them, "You have not spoken of me what is right, as my servant Job has" (42:7). What can this mean when God has seemingly been rebuking Job for the previous four chapters (Job 38-41)?[12] Can it be that the apparent contradiction between God's powerful speeches and this surprising conclusion holds the key to the book? God, the wellspring of life and creative energy that dwells within all that exists, is unconcerned with justice; indeed, the very word *concern* unduly personalizes the Ground of Being that sustains and enlivens all that is, good, bad, and indifferent. But it is *our* job to be concerned with justice. In my reading, Job has spoken well of God for two reasons: first of all, unlike the friends, he tells the truth. Lambasted by his supposed comforters, hemmed in on all sides, he still refuses to say what he knows to be false—that the good are rewarded and the wicked punished. Second, Job refuses to relinquish the yearning for the justice he fails to see in the world. Finding set before him life and death, first blessing and then curse, he chooses life in the form of speaking truth and demanding justice. This is our task as human beings

---

12. While many scholars see the book's prologue and epilogue as the work of a different author from Job's speeches—and I believe the author of the speeches must have been challenging a preexisting folktale—I also find it fruitful to engage the literary work as it has come down to us. Cf. p. 43n9.

in the face of an all-embracing God: to affirm the ties that bind us to each other and creation, and to *be* the justice required for creation to flourish.

PART II

Theological Conversations

9

───────

How Do We Think of Divine Power?

(Responding to Judith's Chapters in Part 1)

Carol P. Christ

When we began to discuss the nature of God while I was writing *She Who Changes*, you (Judith) questioned my view of Goddess as She who loves and understands the world. Yet you were able to read my book in a sympathetic way, to praise me when I got my argument right, and to point out where I needed to clarify it. When I asked how you could do this when you didn't agree with what I was saying, you responded with something like, "When I read what you write, I enter into it, and it is as if I believe it too." I feel similarly when I read what you write about God. This is not a simple matter of empathetic reading. There are many views of God I could not enter into, feeling as if I believed them too. For example, I do not believe that our knowledge of God comes through special revelation such as the Bible. I could not identify with the writing of someone who based her theology primarily on the Bible. I believe that many bad things as well as many good things have been done in the name of religious traditions, so I also would not empathize with the work of someone whose primary goal is to apologize for or to defend the history of her religious tradition. I do not believe that God is transcendent, omnipotent, or exclusively male. If I were reading the work of someone who did, critique would be my first response. A few years ago I read a feminist book on the Trinity. As I have never understood God to be three Persons, the assertions in the book about the relation of the Persons of the Trinity to each other made no sense to me. Rather than entering into the train of thought of the author, I found myself wanting to throw the book across the room. This was despite—or perhaps because—the author was arguing for a relational view of reality, a view that is central in my thinking as well.

Shared Theological Method

What this says about our conversations is that, though we have many differences, we share a great deal. Neither of us believes our views of God to be rooted primarily in revelation in the sense of written words or traditions handed down from the past. We both believe that we piece our understandings of God together out of a combination of personal experiences and the insights of others. In this process, you give more weight to inherited traditions than I do. But what makes it possible for me to talk with you about God is that you also insist traditions are not simply handed down, but that individuals and communities must choose which parts of traditions they will affirm, and which they will not. You situate yourself and your thinking within Jewish tradition, but for you Jewish tradition is a location and a resource, not the only or even the primary factor in your thinking about God. Indeed as a feminist, a lesbian, and a critic of the idea that the Jews are specially chosen by God, you stand in opposition to many strands of your tradition. The process by which you negotiate your relationship with Judaism is based on values that are not exclusive to Judaism, but that are shared in the larger human community—and with me.

The views of God that you and I articulate are also rooted in our individual personal experiences, both everyday experiences, and experiences that felt to each of us as if they had the force of revelation. Yet each of us would say that we must reflect upon our experiences. The criteria by which we reflect on them are also something that we agree upon. We understand that experience is not simply individual but that it must be able to be shared. I doubt that either of us would be building theologies on personal experiences if our experiences had not been affirmed by others, particularly by other women, in communities. This means that we must reflect upon all of the pieces that enter into the construction of our theologies, using criteria that are more than personal. These criteria are in the broadest sense rational. We ask, do the pieces of experience and traditions we use to construct our theologies help us to understand ourselves, our communities, and the larger world in which our communities are situated, which includes both other human communities and the web of life? Though our views of God are different, we agree that all views of God must be judged by their ability to make sense of the world we share.

You and I also agree with Christian theologian Gordon Kaufman that theologies can and must be judged by moral criteria. Like Kaufman we believe that humanity's capacity to destroy the conditions of life for human beings and many other species is an issue theology must address. Both of us have constructed our views of God with this question and other ethical questions uppermost in our minds.[1] In fact, however, we did not learn to judge theologies by moral criteria from Kaufman. We have long believed that theologies should address ethical questions. Early in our graduate years, we insisted that theology must help us to respond to social evils, including the Holocaust, racism, poverty, and war. We began our feminist theological journeys by calling traditions to task for the way they understood and treated women. We agree that theologies can and must be judged by feminist moral criteria: by their ability to help us to transform the system of male domination known as patriarchy and the historic oppressions it sanctions.

---

1. See Gordon D. Kaufman, *An Essay on Theological Method* (Missoula, MT: Scholars Press, 1979 [1975]) and *Theology for a Nuclear Age* (Philadelphia: Westminster Press, 1985).

Similarities and Differences in Girlhood Experiences

Rereading our first chapters, I find similarities and differences in the paths that led us each to study theology. We were serious children, for whom questions about religion seemed to matter more than they did to our peers. This was true for both of us as very young children—even before I had to face death or you learned about the Holocaust. After we each faced death and evil in different ways, this set us even further apart from other children. In that regard, we both experienced ourselves as different from other girls within our religious traditions and within the communities in which we were raised. A profound interest in religion, and the unwillingness of either of us to give it up, led each of us by different paths to Yale. Here are some of the contrasts I see in comparing the first parts of our spiritual autobiographies.

You define your earliest religious experience through a call to "lead the blind, heal the wounded, feed the poor," and state that for you the connection between God and ethics has always been central. I, on the other hand, spoke of my grandmothers' love and told stories about how they introduced me to the beauty and magical power of nature and, without words, to the power of prayer in their lives. In the churches I attended as a child, Christian ethics had more to do with treating one's near neighbors with love and kindness than with feeding the poor or fighting social injustices. Growing up in the relatively homogeneous world of the white lower-middle-class tract homes of southern California, I had very little direct exposure to injustice and no real concept of poverty. While your father was speaking passionately to you about the evil of racism, my father and his father were speaking critically in front of me about those who were "inciting violence" by trying to integrate schools in a faraway place called the South. Responding to what must have been a lackluster book report on *To Kill a Mockingbird*,[2] my high school English teacher said that someday something would make me really mad, and then my writing would be different. Though I did come to understand what poverty and racism

---

2. Harper Lee, *To Kill a Mockingbird* (New York: Grand Central Publishing, 1982 [1960]).

are and to oppose them just as strongly as you do, these convictions were not part of my upbringing. In the summer after my graduation from college, my newly liberal or radical views caused such a great rift in my family that I have ever since been perceived as a troublemaker and as the black sheep. My mother warned me never to speak about politics again to my father if I wished to be invited home. Though I connected ending poverty, racism, and war to the commands of the God of the Hebrew Bible, I did not come to my political views through my church or the Bible, but through conversations with a friend who identified his position as secular.

Like you, I read Anne Frank's *The Diary of a Young Girl* as a child, and I know it made a strong impression on me, but I am not sure what the nature of that impression was. It certainly did not inspire me to read about the Nazis or the concentration camps or to think about the social nature of evil. In my first year of college, I was assigned Hannah Arendt's *Eichmann in Jerusalem* and saw film footage of the concentration camps. However, I had very little actual comprehension of what I was reading or seeing because I did not have a context for understanding this information. Indeed, it was not until I read Elie Wiesel during the summer after my second year in graduate school that I began to think about questions about the nature of God and God's relationship to evil that you had already been thinking about for more than a decade. You think that you were the one who suggested that I read Wiesel, and I agree that this is likely, but as we were not friends at the time, I remember only that someone suggested it.

Three other differences stand out in our stories of religion in our lives before Yale. Despite the fact that I had very positive experiences with my grandmothers and a close and loving relationship with my mother, it never occurred to me as a child that God was anything other than a male figure, something like my father. The fact that my father was not only loving and kind, but also quick to anger and punishing, was no doubt part of what drew me into relationship with the God of the Hebrew Bible in college. The God of the Old Testament seemed more like the father I knew than the God who is love preached to me in church. It simply never crossed my mind as a child or as a young adult that God might be more like my mother or grandmothers than like my father—though this idea makes great good sense to me today. I also have no personal experience to compare with your desire to become a rabbi. Similarly, I could never have made a decision to get a PhD in religious studies by myself. Though I made the dean's list and Phi Beta Kappa at Stanford, I never met or even saw a woman professor, and the idea that I might become one was not something I could have imagined, had it not been suggested to me by an advisor. If I had been offered a proposal of marriage in college, I doubt that I would have gone to graduate school.

Meeting at Yale

Nevertheless, by the time we actually had a real conversation with each other at Yale, we had arrived by different paths at a place that seemed to us at the time to be very much the same. We had both studied the Hebrew Bible; we both found Martin Buber's *I and Thou* inspiring; we both loved *The Plague* by Camus; we both felt that God could be found in nature as well as in church or synagogue; we both were asking questions about God and the Holocaust; we both felt that theology should help us to make sense of our lives; and we both felt that theology should be relevant to social issues. We were also beginning to frame these questions within the question that was becoming uppermost in our minds: How had theology been shaped and deformed by the system we were beginning to name patriarchy or male dominance? It was very wonderful for each of us to have a sister who could share the struggle and help us to find the words to begin to write the kind of theology we wanted to read. The fact that I was a practicing Catholic at the same time you were exploring non-Reform Judaism was also something we had in common: we were both looking for a deeper and more complex understanding of faith and liturgy than we had found in the more rationalized religions of our childhoods.

Although our histories and our lives were different, at least for me, the sense of our sameness was uppermost in my mind during our last years at Yale and our first years of teaching. Even after I found the Goddess in California and you remained on the fence between Judaism and women's spirituality, we seemed more the same than different to me. We were both writing about the problems we saw in Christianity and Judaism, and we both saw our primary communities as feminist. We worked easily together on *Womanspirit Rising* and did not yet see how our paths would diverge after you found a renewed commitment to Judaism at the Havurah Summer Institute.

Choosing to Stay and to Leave

Your renewed commitment to thinking as a Jew about the questions we had heretofore been thinking about together was difficult for me to accept and understand. On the one hand, I understood that it was easier for me to leave Christianity than it was for you to leave Judaism, because, as you said, you would always be defined as a Jew in a Christian culture. On the other hand, I felt excluded when you began to organize retreats for Jewish women—to which I could never be invited—in which you would have your deepest insights and do your most profound thinking. Moreover, on an intellectual level, I could not understand why you would want to recommit yourself to a tradition in which God was not only imaged as male, but in which God's power was closely identified with images of warfare and violence. As you would later express it so well, Judaism's God was not only a male other, but also a dominant other.

For me, no longer identifying with Christian tradition had a great deal to do with belief. Though my childhood religion had focused on the love of God, in graduate school, I came to understand that Christianity defined itself through the doctrines of the Trinity, the incarnation, original sin, and salvation exclusively through Christ. These doctrines are expressed in the Nicene Creed, accepted by all Christians, and recited by the congregation at the beginning of the Roman Catholic mass and in some Protestant liturgies. As I never prepared for the ministry, I had not been required (as most of the students with whom we studied had been) to clarify or defend positions on these questions. Suffice it to say that I tended to think of the doctrines in terms of the overarching theme of God's love for the world and the human responsibility to improve it, and that both feminism and the Holocaust raised questions I had not resolved. In an interview at a Christian seminary early on in my career, I was asked to define my Christology or theory of salvation through Jesus Christ. My answer that feminism had put a question mark over all doctrines handed down through traditions crafted by men was not considered acceptable. I have been surprised that so many of our feminist colleagues have written books on Christology and Trinity. I wonder if this is because they have been challenged by their seminary colleagues to prove their doctrinal orthodoxy. Judaism, in contrast, is not a religion that stresses belief. Indeed, your husband Robert used to love to shock me and other Christians by saying that, for a Jew, belief in God was not required as long as he or she followed the law. Understanding this difference between Judaism and Christianity makes it clear that the question of belief in core doctrines simply was not as central for you as a Jewish theologian as it would necessarily have been for me as a Christian theologian.

However, my reasons for leaving Christianity did not only have to do with its core doctrines. For me, the issue that I call the power of symbols was equally if not more important. Once I began to understand the way in which the core symbols of the Bible had influenced people and cultures, I simply could not ally myself with traditions that continued to promote them in liturgies. I could not repeat the words nor stand in silence when God the Father, Lord, and King was celebrated in communal worship. On the one hand, my body revolted. On the other hand, my mind told me that, even if I could control the reactions of my body, the continued repetition of these symbols by others was influencing their individual actions and the actions of the culture they were legitimating through them—and these actions were hurting others. For me, images of God as a warrior in the Bible were just as important as the images of God as male. As I worked on my dissertation on the Holocaust, I also became intensely aware that the Christian story that the Jews rejected the Messiah helped to create the atmosphere in which the Holocaust occured. It was partly my friendship with you that made it impossible for me to participate in the Easter liturgies I had loved—once I perceived them as anti-Jewish.

Though we have discussed this issue many times, I have never in fact understood why the issue of the power of symbols is not as important to you as it is to me. Why does your body not recoil as mine does when images of God as a dominant male other and as a violent dominating other are invoked? Why does this imagery bother you less than it once did? What effect will this imagery have on your granddaughter and other girls? What about the ways the Hebrew Bible is fueling the militaristic and colonialist right wing in Israel? Or the ways in which the biblical tradition as a whole inspires young men to fight America's unjust wars around the world? You asked if you are becoming more conservative. Are you?

Ambiguity

Thinking back on your earlier chapters, I suspect that part of the answer to this question has to do with your understanding of what you call the profound ambiguity that underlies our world. I imagine that you might reply to me that, while you understand my desire to purify religious traditions of imagery that we both find offensive, you do not believe this is possible. Given that all religious imagery is created by human beings, it is just as likely, you might say, that newly created religious imagery will enshrine new injustices—or that, like the Reform liturgy that you found incomplete, new liturgies will deny the complexities of life. So, you might conclude, why give up a tradition and a community that has a long and in many ways meaningful history, when it is not likely that we can do better? I suspect that you may even enjoy and appreciate intellectually the ways in which Jewish tradition embodies and expresses the contradictions and ambiguities that are found within human nature and within life. My answer to the questions you would undoubtedly pose to me in reply is that I would prefer to ally myself with the Reform Jews who tried to purify their tradition of imagery they knew had done harm in the world. And even if I might agree with you that Reform Jewish leaders failed to create a fully satisfying liturgy, I applaud their attempt to try to create a set of symbols that would not harm others. This is a cause to which I have committed myself as well.

As you said in your chapters in the first part of our book, the theme of ambiguity has always been central in your work. I suspect that you believe that my view of God idealizes life. You might also say that attempts to create new liturgical traditions based on moral criteria are likely to fail because they too idealize life. You might even ask if my decision to leave my tradition behind because of my discomfort with traditional liturgies is based on idealization of life—on a belief that human beings can create communities and liturgies that are inclusive. Still, I would not say that my view of life as a whole is particularly idealized. Because of the experiences I had as a child, I have never denied that death, including the death of babies and death that involves great suffering, is a part of life. One of my brothers had undiagnosed dyslexia, which meant that he never did well in school. Despite the fact that my parents tried their best with him, he got into trouble as a teenager and became a teenaged father, and then by the time he was twenty, a single father. My parents had not one, but two children who disappointed them. As a teenager, I did not date, despite desperately wanting to, and as an adult I never found my true love. Though I did get married, I also got divorced. When my relationships failed, I found myself plunged into deep despair. Although I did not have a word for it at the time, my mother suffered a severe depression after my baby brother died. Through all of those experiences, I learned that, despite our best intentions and efforts, life does not always turn out as we hope it will.

In terms of the world beyond myself and my family, I have no illusions about the efficacy of human efforts to change or save the world. There was a brief and wonderful time in the 1960s and 1970s when, like others of my generation, including I think you, I believed that we could change the world. I still hope that we can make the world a better place. However, we have not done so well, so far. Your work and mine have helped women to find their voices and some things have definitely improved for some women. At the same time, the gap between the rich and poor has only gotten greater in the United States and the world as a whole. More people in the world are suffering from war than ever in the past, and the portion of the United States' budget devoted to war has increased. Looking at the rate at which the environment and species are being destroyed and at global climate change, I would have to say that I am not optimistic about the future of the human race and the future of the world we are destroying. I suspect that, in regard to life in general, we share a common vision that includes great ambiguity. Neither of us expects that the world as a whole will ever be as we would like it to be. At the same time, we both continue to hope that our efforts can help to improve the world.

As I reread what I have just written here, I can hear you saying, "Carol, you have spoken about ambiguity in the world, but you have not spoken about ambiguity in yourself. Do you see yourself primarily as one who suffers from the evil in the world, or as one who can perpetrate it as well?" Of course I know that I am not always loving and understanding. I also know that we all harm others all the time without knowing that we are doing so. I recognize that the limitations of my perspective may exclude others. I perpetuate evil every day when I do not protest loudly enough against the unjust social structures that shape my position in the world. On the other hand, the fact that I did not speak first about my own capacity to do evil or to harm does suggest a difference in the way we think about the world. Christianity taught me to think of myself and the world as sinful. It was a great breath of fresh air for me to begin to think of the world, my body, and myself in more positive ways. The Charge of the Goddess says: "Let my worship be in the heart that rejoices, for behold—all acts of love and pleasure are my rituals. Let there be beauty and strength, power and compassion, honor and humility, mirth and reverence within you."[3] I

---

3. Starhawk, *The Spiral Dance: A Rebirth of the Ancient Religion of the Great Goddess* (San Francisco: Harper & Row, 1979; 2nd and 3rd editions, expanded, 1989, 1999), 77 (1979 ed.), rewording Doreen

think love and joy are better motivators of ethical concern and action than the cycle of judgment and guilt familiar in biblical traditions.[4] I am not particularly interested in ritually confessing my sins. I prefer rituals that inspire me to enlarge the scope of my care and concern to include the whole world—or at least as much of it as I am capable of comprehending.

Am I an Idealist?

Despite not idealizing life, I do not choose to ally myself with a tradition, the Christian one, that I know has already done a great deal of harm in the world. And despite recognizing that religious idealists have generally failed to change the world as a whole, I guess that I am one. With your prodding, I am willing to own up to that. I will not participate in religious rituals that I feel are harmful to myself or to the world. I do have a choice about that. And if that choice isolates me, I am willing to pay the price. I recognize that separating oneself—myself—from communities that can provide sustenance and self-correction is not in all ways a good choice. As you know, I often feel lonely and long for communities that I do not have. I sometimes envy the Jewish community you share with your friends, family, and life partner. I do keep trying to create communities that I can feel part of. For many years, I have not had an ongoing spiritual community, though I find one for four weeks a year on the Goddess Pilgrimages to Crete. In my daily life I am working with the Green Party of Greece. I agree with the Green Party's four central principles: sustainability, social justice, no violence, and participatory democracy. The Green Party has been a feminist party since its inception, committed not only to equality between men and women, but also to ending the domination of "man over nature" and to eradicating all forms of violence and hierarchy. I can translate the Green Party principles as a spiritual commitment to human beings in the web of life that is the

Valiente, who reworded Charles Leland's alleged informant; Starhawk capitalized the "M" in "My."

4. I have discussed this issue in *Rebirth of the Goddess: Finding Meaning in Feminist Spirituality* (New York: Routledge, 1998 [1997]), chap. 8.

body of the Goddess, while recognizing that other members of the Green Party would not necessarily understand or agree with me on that. The Green Party is a small visionary party that is unlikely to become the dominant party of Greece any time soon.

When we take all of these factors into account, perhaps we can see that our difference with regard to affiliation with inherited traditions is not explained by my idealizing life while you do not. It also is not, as you suggested recently, that you choose community and I do not. Our difference is that I choose to situate myself within small visionary communities while speaking to the world, but you identify with a larger historic community known as Judaism as you also speak to the world. If we look more closely at our choices from this perspective, they are not as different as they may seem. Within the larger community of Judaism, you identify with the small visionary community of the havurah movement and the even smaller B'not Esh. My ancestral community includes a great-grandmother and a grandmother who rejected the Protestant traditions they inherited in favor of Christian Science. It also includes, as I have recently learned, Huguenots who fled France, Puritans who left England, and Quakers willing to stand against their culture in the name of their beliefs. Perhaps in rejecting inherited traditions because of my beliefs, I am not rejecting the paths of my ancestors, but following in their footsteps.

The Nature of Divine Power

In addition to having made different choices about inherited traditions and communities, we disagree about the nature of divine power. Before discussing our differences, I want to underscore the ways in which our views of divine power are similar, and in that similarity, different from traditional views of God in our culture. Neither of us believes in a God who is both omnipotent and good, who could prevent the evil in the world, but chooses not to do so. Neither of us believes that the things that happen in our world are meant to be because they are caused, determined, or sent to us as reward, punishment, or for our education by an omnipotent Goddess or God. We have both rejected the God "out there" of traditional theologies, defined as transcendent of the world. We have both found divine power in the world—in the body, in relationships, in community, in ethical decisions and activism, and in nature. We both use the term "panentheism" to define our views. We both affirm that the world is the body of Goddess or God. You speak of divinity as a power of creativity that underlies all life on our planet and in the universe. I speak of the powers of life, death, and transformation or birth, death, and regeneration that underlie all creative processes in the universe. We both experience Goddess in nature—in the crashing waves of the Pacific Ocean, in the gentle waves of the Aegean Sea, and in the sheer energy of the Iguassu waterfalls. We both experience the sacred in our bodies and in our bodies' participation in the larger rhythms of life that connect us both to other people and to the other than human world, traditionally called nature.

You and I both recognize that the power we call divinity is one, yet can be invoked with male or female and other names. As you said recently in a telephone conversation, we are both inclusive monotheists. We reject the exclusive monotheism that has spawned the idea that there is only one right way to worship, to think, or to act. We agree that inclusive monotheism affirms an intuition of the unity of being combined with the recognition of the necessity of a plurality of images to reflect all the diversity and difference in the world.

While we agree on divine immanence and inclusive monotheism, we understand the nature of divine power differently. In one of your chapters, you said that you suspected that most spiritual and religious feminists viewed divinity as both immanent and not personal. I agree that feminists are engaged in transforming the dualistic traditions that disparaged the body and nature—particularly the female body—and placed divinity outside the world. However, I think feminists and others divide on the question of whether Goddess or God is personal and cares about the world or is an impersonal energy or power of creativity. It is interesting to me that these were the two views I was unable to choose between when I wrote my Harvard lecture. This is one of the reasons why what you say about God makes perfect sense to me—except that it doesn't!

When we began to discuss the differences in our views about the nature of divine power, I brought up an argument expressed by Michael Novak in *Belief and Unbelief* that goes like this: if we sometimes love and understand, then there must be a source of our ability to love and understand—a God who loves and understands. To state the same argument negatively: If we love and understand, but God does not, does that not make us more than or better than God? As it does not make sense to say that the finite is more than or better than the infinite, does it not make sense to attribute intelligence and love to God?[5] I also brought up Charles Hartshorne's argument that a God who is to be worshiped must be worthy of worship. If love is the highest value in the universe, then God must be love, or more precisely an individual who feels the feelings of the world and understands them with perfect sympathy. To worship anything else is not to worship God. Hartshorne argued that traditional theology made the mistake of viewing unlimited power as the highest value. Theologians who defined God as "being itself" but insisted that God is not "a being" made a different mistake when they failed to understand that to be in relationships is a higher value than to be free of relationships, and that God must be an individual being in order to enter into (personal) relationships with the world.[6] These lines of reasoning do not for me prove the existence of God, but they do confirm that my experience and my belief that Goddess loves and understands the world make rational sense, at least from certain perspectives. However, these arguments made not the slightest bit of difference to you.

When Reason Fails to Convince

This suggests that the decisions that we make about the nature of God are based in experience as well as rational argument. Indeed, the fact

---

5. Michael Novak, *Belief and Unbelief* (New York: New American Library, 1965).
6. Charles Hartshorne, *The Divine Relativity: A Social Conception of God* (New Haven: Yale University Press, 1948); "omniscient sympathy," 48.

that you were not convinced by the rational arguments about God's nature that I proposed prompted me to conclude that these arguments only make sense to those who have a prior experience of God that confirms them. This suggests that arguments about God can help us to make sense of experience, but will not convince those who do not have certain kinds of experience. Then what is the experience or set of experiences that make the difference in the ways we each view the world and Goddess or God? If we look at our adult experiences, we could say that you have more reason to believe in the power of love and understanding than I do, because unlike me, you found a person who loves and understands you enough to want to spend a lifetime with you. In addition, you have never been alienated from your family to the degree that I have from mine, and you have a son and granddaughter who love you. Yet I am the one who says that Goddess loves and understands, while you say God is an impersonal and amoral power. Am I compensating for what I do not have? Are you denying the power of the love and understanding you do have?

There is also the question of health. I have always been able to take my health for granted and to fall asleep as soon as my head hits the pillow, while you struggled with health issues all your life and have trouble falling asleep. Do our different daily experiences of our bodies shape a sense of basic trust or lack of trust in the universe that affects our views of the trustworthiness or ambiguity of God?

Is history the decisive factor? Is it the fact that millions of Jews were killed in the Holocaust that leads you to deny that the great power of the universe is love? Is it the fact that I have no similar recent experience of my people being killed that enables me to believe the divine power is love? I do identify with the long history of the oppression of women, much of it violent, but I did not know this history as a child.

Or do we have different experiences of nature? You use the great and amoral energy of the Amazon waterfalls to construct your image of God, while for me the intelligent interest and perhaps even love of the spider monkey who chose to follow you when you got up early in the morning in the jungle might have seemed more significant. Yet I do not romanticize nature: I almost died in the Pacific Ocean's waves when I was seventeen.

I have written that I experienced a great power of love as my mother died. Would you have experienced the same power if you had been in the room when your mother died? Was I mistaken about what I thought I experienced? Or in the interpretation I gave to what I experienced?

There is one further issue, related to the others. In chapter 8 you said, "*For many of those with whom I spoke, the purpose of religion was to give expression to their highest aspirations, so that the notion of a God who was other than perfectly good simply made no sense. I, on the other hand, looked to religion to provide a map of the universe in all its messiness and complexity, and to furnish ways both to live with that messiness and, where appropriate, challenge it*" (172).[7]

Though you do not mention me in discussing this, you have captured perfectly a major difference between us. Another way of putting it is to say that we ask the question for whom God or Goddess is the answer in different ways. Certainly when Hartshorne or I say that a God or Goddess who is to be worshiped must be worthy of worship, we are aligning ourselves with the version of the question you reject. At the same time, this is a difference that cannot be resolved by saying that one of us is asking the wrong question, because, I would suggest, the two different versions of the question are situated in two different experiences of the nature of divinity.

The fact that we have discussed all of the various permutations of these arguments and questions over and over again and that neither of us has changed our minds is also significant. It seems that there is no way of deciding between our experiences. You can say that I am idealizing one aspect of life at the expense of others, but that is not really true, as I too recognize evil and suffering. I can say that you are failing to take account of something in your experience, but that also seems unfair, as you recognize the power of love—you just do not

7. Emphasis mine.

separate it from other less positive aspects of life. At the end of all our conversations, what we can fairly say is that each of us has constructed our view of Goddess and God based on different experiences and interpretations of the world we share.

We Feel the World Differently

I have said that the revelatory experience of love that I had when my mother died changed the way I experience the world. As I write, I experience the love of the kitten who is sitting in the crook of my arm with her paws on the edge of my laptop. You might point out that this kitten is just as likely to kill a bird as to cuddle up with me (and it turns out you would be right). Still, I insist that my experience with the kitten is one of the ways I experience love permeating the world. The love of Goddess is a constant presence in my life. When I attune my mind through prayer and ritual or through meditation or thought, I feel the love of Goddess always with me and in everything. This has changed my experience of the world in profound ways. Feeling love throughout the web of life and feeling loved by Goddess makes me more loving and gives me great joy. You might say that this means that, like Pollyanna, I do not see the presence of violence and conflict in the world. But I do.

You might say that your view helps you to keep the ambiguity of the world uppermost in your mind and that it prevents you from idealizing yourself or any group to which you belong. I feel the power of your view too. Does your view or mine make more sense of the world as we know it? I am not sure I can decide between them. Yes, life and death, good and evil, are intertwined. But would we be here today if something had not tipped the balance toward love and understanding? Which view helps us more to see the way to righting the wrongs we see in the world? I am not sure I can answer that question either. Your view underscores the capacity of every individual and every group to take life. My view provides a basis for choosing life.

When I read your chapters again in preparation for writing my response, your view of God made so much sense to me that I said to you, "I wonder if anyone will think my chapters make any sense at all, compared to yours." The idea that God is the power of creativity that undergirds human and other forms of life is appealing. Your arguments about the ambiguity of life and about the interconnections between life and death and good and evil in the world are compelling. I find your argument that recognizing the ambiguity of God requires us to recognize the tendencies toward good and toward evil within ourselves powerful. You are right when you say that viewing ourselves as only good is one of the reasons we fail to recognize the evil we do to others. The United States is a telling example of your point: despite a history of taking land from the Indians and building a new country on the backs of indentured servants and African slaves, most Americans perceive their country as always and everywhere good. And they continue to perpetuate injustice. When I read your story and your theology, I agree with you. And yet, when I step back into my own life, my story, and my reflection on it, my theology is the one that makes more sense because it more fully explains my experience. I believe that love really is the power that makes the world go 'round.

Two Ultimates

John Cobb's notion of the "two ultimates" offers a way of thinking about our different conceptions of divinity. He suggests that religions have defined the nature of ultimate reality in two distinct ways: as personal and as impersonal, as God and as the ground of being. God or Goddess as the personal ultimate is an individual interacting with other individuals in the world. This is the Goddess or God invoked in prayer and ritual in Christianity, Judaism, and Islam, as well as in popular devotion in Eastern traditions. The ground of being is the impersonal ultimate: the metaphysical principles that structure all of life, principles that he describes as creativity or the creative process. The impersonal ultimate is the God of some of the mystics and of many of the philosophers in Western and Eastern traditions. Some religions or strands within religions focus on relationship with or worship of a personal God, while other religions or strands within religions speak of divinity as the ultimate nature of reality as a whole. Cobb says that we do not have to choose between the two ultimates because (from his standpoint) both are real. Cobb also insists that the two ultimates should not be confused: the impersonal ultimate is not just another way of talking about the personal God, or vice versa.[8] In Cobb's view, the two ultimates are coeternal: this means that the personal God did not "create" the creative process, nor was the personal God "created" by the creative process. Rather, for Cobb, God as the personal ultimate, like all other individuals, participates in the creative process.[9]

The Creative Process

What then is the creative process? Although the term "creativity" has multiple meanings, in process philosophy it has a specific one. Whitehead's description of the creative process is rooted in the insight of modern science that the most basic components of our universe are particles of atoms that defy being categorized as either matter or energy, but seem to have elements of both and to change depending on their relationships. It is from the relationships of these tiny individuals that the evolutionary process of our universe began. The insight that the smallest particles of our universe are in movement and related to each other led Whitehead to recognize that the nature of reality or being is not fixed and static (as Western philosophers before him had concluded) but is always changing, or "in process" (as Buddhist philosophers have recognized). Whitehead's understanding of the creative process is summed up in his much-quoted phrase, "The many become one, and are increased by one."[10] The creative moment in the creative process (which is in fact every moment in the life of an individual) is the moment when the individual (whether particle of an atom, cell, animal, human, or divinity) in an act of creative freedom

8. John Cobb, "Being Itself and the Existence of God," in *The Existence of God*, ed. John R. Jacobson and Robert Lloyd Mitchell (Lewistown, NY: Edwin Mellen, 1988), 5–19.
9. David Ray Griffin clarifies this point in *Reenchantment without Supernaturalism: A Process Philosophy of Religion* (Ithaca, NY: Cornell University Press, 2001), 264–68.
10. Alfred North Whitehead, *Process and Reality: Corrected Edition*, ed. David Ray Griffin and Donald W. Sherburne (New York: The Free Press, 1979 [1929]), 21.

unifies the world (the many) into a new synthesis (the one): this new synthesis adds a new fact to the world (the many is increased by one). Freedom is expressed through the creative process, but freedom is not creation from nothing: it is always in relation to the world as it previously existed. At the same time, each creative synthesis introduces something new into the world. This is an abstract description of the creative process in its most basic form. Is this what you mean by the creative process or would you define it differently?

In fact, however, we do not experience the world in the abstract, but in the concrete. In this moment I (Carol) remember my past (many different Carols situated in many different worlds) as I shape this sentence (with my hands on my computer acting in concert with the feelings of my body and the thoughts that are flowing in my mind) and unite myself and my world in a new synthesis (which is this sentence). As I do so, I add a new fact to the world (the many are increased by one), a sentence that may be read by others in the future, therefore influencing their lives. The reader who reads my words reflects on them in relation to her or his memories and asks if what I am saying makes sense: in the moment that she or he decides if it does or it doesn't, a new fact is added to the world (the many are increased by one), an opinion that in turn may be expressed to someone else (the many is again increased by one), who in turn responds to it (the many is increased by one more). Though this description of the creative process focuses on mental actions, our mental processes are not divorced from our bodies and feelings, and the relations of mind, body, and feeling are complex. Thoughts are always influenced by feelings, and feelings arise from the body. In some creative moments, feelings are primary, while in others the body leads. This richer description of the creative process is still an abstraction. We do not generally experience life as a series of moments but as a flow in which one moment is indistinguishable from the others; nonetheless, we can recognize that our lives are made up of a series of moments in which we, along with others, create the world anew.[11] As we do so, we participate in the creative process that is the ground of being of our world.

Sometimes we take a longer and broader view of the creative process, recognizing patterns and cycles within the world we share with other than human life. Traditional peoples, for example, often speak of or invoke the creative processes of birth, death, and regeneration that are the basis of life on this earth. In our time, we speak of the evolution of the universe and our planet as an aspect of the creative process from which our lives have emerged.[12] These longer views are important ways of describing the creative process that is the ground of being because they situate human creativity within the creativity of the web of life.

The concept of the two ultimates suggests that you and I could resolve our differences by agreeing that each of our theologies focuses on one of them. I can recognize the Goddess as the personal ultimate, and the creative process as the impersonal ultimate. However, this solution works better for me than it does for you. While you recognize the metaphoric power of religious language that invokes a personal God, you do not believe a personal divinity exists. Unlike those who believe in a personal ultimate, you define God as the ground of being, as an impersonal power of creativity. Thus, while the notion of two ultimates can help us to situate our differences in a larger context, it does not resolve the question of the nature of divinity because you insist that the personal God is not ultimately real.

Judaism and the Personal Ultimate

Given that you do not believe in a personal God, I want to ask you again how you understand and situate your view of God in relation to the centrality of the biblical view of a personal God in Jewish tradition. If a personal God—whether loving and good or ambiguously involved in good and evil—does not exist, it would seem that it makes sense to

---

11. In this view, God did not create the world. Rather the world is cocreated by divinity and all the other individuals that participate in the creative process. I discuss this issue again in chap. 11.

12. Brian Swimme and Thomas Berry, *The Universe Story: From the Primordial Flaring Forth to Ecozoic Era—A Celebration of the Unfolding of the Cosmos* (San Francisco: HarperSanFrancisco, 1992).

rewrite Jewish prayers to remove all references to a personal God as Marcia Falk has begun to do. But that still leaves a very big elephant in the room: the Bible. Can Judaism survive without it? Can the Bible be rewritten from the perspective of God as an impersonal power of creativity? You often quote from God's speeches in the Bible to illustrate your views. How do you explain this? Would you argue that there is a need for a symbolic language that refers to God as a person, even though this symbolic language is not literally true? As I have said, I find this solution unsatisfying. Do the questions change if we ask them from the perspective of community rather than personal belief? What if we recognize that individuals in religious communities are likely to disagree about the nature of ultimate reality? If some members of a community believe in a personal ultimate and some in an impersonal one, should both be part of communal worship? However, we would not want to take this type of argument too far. If some members of a religious community believe that God is exclusively male or violent, or that God is totally transcendent of the world, we might view such conceptions as harmful. So I ask again: What do you do with the Bible's conception of God? If God really is not personal, should personal imagery work itself out of the picture? Could Judaism survive without the stories that involve a personal God? And if these stories remain central, will the personal God of Judaism always be male? And dominating? And violent?

10

Constructing Theological Narratives

(Responding to Carol's Chapters in Part 1)

Judith Plaskow

As I reflect on our accounts of our spiritual histories and theological development, the question that leaps out at me is how anyone comes to a particular understanding of God. What are the many factors, conscious and unconscious, that go into shaping an individual world view? You and I share much, even in terms of our histories before we entered Yale and certainly during our time there. And yet we have also parted ways on important issues: in our decisions about whether or not to work within the framework of the patriarchal traditions in which we were raised, in the language we use to talk about God/Goddess, and in our conceptions of the nature of Goddess and God. These are major questions, and we were in many ways unprepared to find ourselves in disagreement about them. What lies at the root of our differences: early childhood experiences? Basic temperament? Having been raised in different religious traditions? Does one of us have access to some

Truth that the other has refused to see? Are there other influences that we have not even thought to notice?

I do not expect to find an answer to these questions or that there is a single answer to be found. The narratives we have constructed—the incidents we have singled out as salient to our adult theological positions—are such a small selection from a vast sea of experiences that we cannot even know for certain whether we have described the factors that are determinative. We also can never be sure whether we have selected just those memories that cohere with our current standpoints or whether we remember certain things clearly precisely because they have deeply shaped who we are. But working on this project has made vivid to me the complex, and in many ways mysterious, origins of religious conviction, the admixture of emotional and intellectual influences, and the ways argument can serve ex post facto to explain and justify beliefs that are much more a product of nonrational factors than efforts to defend them would imply. My hope is that in describing what we see as our commonalities and differences, and in raising questions about each other's religious choices and theological outlooks, we can shed light on some of the many sources of our divergent theological understandings and, in doing so, invite readers to examine the wellsprings of their own convictions. Exploring our disagreements may also help to illuminate how our different theologies shape our ongoing experiences of ourselves and our world.

Childhood Convergences and Divergences

The first commonality that I find in our narratives—though it is hardly surprising given the course of our adult lives—is that we were both drawn to religion as young girls, more than might be expected from looking at our immediate families. I mentioned that my father grew up Orthodox, my mother Conservative; yet as a married couple, they joined a Reform congregation and, unlike their families of origin, chose not to keep a kosher home. Without breaking the familial connection to Judaism, they elected for it to play a less central role in their lives than it had for their parents. When my parents met my future in-laws for the first time, the four of them spent much of the evening reassuring each other that they had nothing to do with Robert's and my interest in religion. Clearly, my parents were bewildered at my having made choices that seemed so far afield from anything they had imagined or wanted for me. Your story is similar. Your parents were less religiously involved than your grandparents, and you mention pestering them to take you to church when they would much rather have stayed in bed on Sunday morning. You were viewed as thinking too much about things that did not bother other people and should not have concerned you. Your parents were also angry at your decision to go to graduate school in religion—though that seems to have been more a reaction to your wanting to continue your education than to your chosen field.

At the same time that our intense interest in religion may not have been fully explicable in terms of our backgrounds, we were both exposed to religious ideas and contexts, so that there was soil from which the seeds of our attraction could sprout. I went to synagogue with my parents on Jewish holidays and, as I grew older, Friday evenings, and I attended religious school for twelve years. Your parents too joined one or another Protestant church in Southern California, and you were also exposed to the greater piety of your extended family: the Christian Science convictions of your maternal grandmother, partially absorbed without being directly taught, and the Roman Catholicism of your paternal grandparents, through which you experienced the fascination of ritual. Did the Catholic Church also provide your first introduction to the Goddess in the form of Mary?

More striking than our attraction to religion, which makes perfect sense for girls who were to become theologians, we both began grappling with the problem of evil at relatively early ages. Your initial encounter with evil took the form of having to deal with many difficult deaths in your family, especially but not only the death of an infant brother when you were fourteen. This experience, which led you on a search for "the meaning of a life that included so much death" (6), was to shape the theological questions you have asked throughout your career. When you studied Old Testament in college, you found that God's on-again, off-again relationship with the Jewish people "seemed to hold a clue to the relation of life and death" (8). Your dissertation on the work of Elie Wiesel explored the problem of evil in relation to anti-Semitism and the Holocaust. It has also seemed to me that an important part of what you find intellectually satisfying about process theology's rejection of divine omnipotence is that it solves or dissolves the problem posed by traditional theologies of how to reconcile God's goodness and unlimited power with the evil in the world. Although I was fortunate in not having to confront death in an intimate way until my early thirties, my obsession with the Holocaust during my adolescence led me to ask many of the same questions that troubled you. Who and where was God? I wanted to know. How could God have allowed the Holocaust to happen, and what was it about human nature that made it possible for a supposedly civilized nation to perpetrate such an atrocity? For me as for you, these have been urgent questions throughout my life that have also shaped my adult theology. It is not surprising, then, that the relationship between God and evil has been a central topic of discussion and debate between us over the course of our friendship.

At the same time that the problem of evil was formative for both of us, however, the dissimilar ways in which it emerged in our lives point to crucial differences in our childhood experiences. For you, death was a close, personal reality that had an immediate impact on your life and family. My encounter with evil—and it was evil more than death that the Holocaust symbolized—came through my identification with the Jewish people. No one in my family was killed in the Holocaust or survived it in Europe. My grandparents immigrated to the United States at the turn of the twentieth century as part of the vast influx of Eastern European Jews. Yet as a Jew born immediately after the war ended, I could not help but be aware of the extermination of European Jewry as both a spoken and unspoken presence. I mentioned in my first chapter that my favorite Sunday school teacher had probably been involved in liberating the concentration camps. My family was also close to across-the-street neighbors who were survivors, and I overheard many conversations between them and my mother about their experiences. The fact that those conversations often were abruptly terminated when I came into the room only magnified their importance. I also remember dinner-time discussions about how much American Jews knew about the concentration camps during the war and whether they had done enough to pressure Roosevelt to intervene. I am not sure what the ultimate impact is of these contrasting ways of coming up against death and evil, but it cannot be irrelevant to the continuing importance of community in my life that I knew myself to be a member of a people who had a long and proud history, yet who, in my parent's generation, had been singled out for destruction. Though I grew up in a Long Island suburb where Jews were a substantial minority, I was always aware that Jews were outsiders in the larger culture. My parents told me never to ask anyone their religion, and though the reason they gave was only that it was "a personal question," I sensed that if I asked anyone their religion, they might ask me mine, and there was some undefined danger in saying that I was a Jew. The fact that I came of age as part of a minority and you as part of the religious majority surely had an impact on our ultimate religious choices.

Simultaneous convergences and divergences also mark other aspects of our youthful experiences. I was struck by the fact that we each independently singled out Camus's novel *The Plague* as an important influence and yet, at the same time, found somewhat different parts of the book compelling. You identified with Rieux's question of whether it is possible to believe in God given the pervasiveness of death and suffering. I too was interested in Camus's dramatization of this theological question, but I had asked it before. The moment in the book that jumped out at me was Rieux's paradoxical observation that it might be better for God if we refuse to believe in him, never looking up to the heavens where he sits in silence. There was something about that statement that felt deeply Jewish to me. It resonated with the stances of Job and Wiesel to which

I was drawn—their inability to stop believing in God even while they questioned God's goodness. Our different theological positions were thus foreshadowed fairly early on.

Connection to nature was another area of both similarity and difference between us in that nature was a more pervasive and powerful influence in your life than in mine, even while it was important to both of us. Some of your earliest memories are of peacocks screeching on the roof of your grandmother's house and strutting in your grandmother's garden. Your college thesis on nature poetry in Hosea and Second Isaiah was of a piece with your experience of walking in the arboretum that abutted your grandmother's home or your love of floating in the Pacific Ocean in a state of trance and feeling part of all that is. Buber was your favorite theologian partly because he affirmed that I-Thou relationships were possible with nature as well as with God and other human beings. As someone who grew up on suburban Long Island and loved nothing more than going into New York City, my relationship with nature was a more occasional thing. I have clear memories of ice-skating on a frozen pond and of speeding down hills on my bike with the wind flowing against my face and through my hair. Both these experiences made me feel at one with my body and the natural world and, in retrospect, were early tastes of the "power of the erotic."[1] When I first read Simone de Beauvoir's *The Second Sex* and came to the section where she talks about young girls feeling free in relation to nature in a way they do not in society, I knew exactly what she meant and thoroughly identified with her words. Yet these experiences were in some sense marginal to my life, out of the ordinary; they were not well integrated into my identity and certainly seemed to have nothing to do with my Jewishness. It is not surprising, then, that human embeddedness in the natural world has been a more central theme in your theology than in mine. It is a theme I value and identify with but that is largely absent from *Standing Again at Sinai*.

---

1. Audre Lorde, "Uses of the Erotic: The Erotic as Power," in *Weaving the Visions: New Patterns in Feminist Spirituality*, ed. Judith Plaskow and Carol P. Christ (San Francisco: Harper & Row, 1989), 208–13.

Becoming Feminists Together

Once we attended the first meeting of the Yale Women's Alliance, our paths converged much more fully. I do not remember whether I had suggested to you the previous spring that you read Wiesel, though given what I knew of your interest in religion and literature and your frustration with the department's lack of attention to Jewish theology, it seems highly likely. In any event, our friendship blossomed from the moment we repaired to a local hangout at the end of that first meeting and began to apply our budding feminist insights to our experiences in the department. We were both frustrated with the ethos of our courses, with the ways in which theological discussion was abstracted both from personal religious questions and the great political issues of the day. We both became involved in student organizing against the war in Vietnam and marched, picketed and boycotted classes. We wanted courses in Jewish theology, and in fact, that spring, we initiated a student-run course in modern Jewish thought. We began to notice and reflect on the significance of the fact that there were no readings by women in any of our courses. We wondered what that said about our presence at Yale and our future as theologians and asked ourselves how the substance of theology was distorted by the absence of women's perspectives.

I mentioned in an earlier chapter that much of my time at Yale is a blur, so it is difficult for me to remember when and how we came to particular insights. I know that you were out ahead of me for much of that first year in the sophistication of your thinking, both about theology and our needs as women students. It was you and Violet Lindbeck who brought a series of feminist speakers to the department, speakers who raised daring questions and modeled the possibility that women could be theologians. When you wrote a paper for a student-run seminar linking Karl Barth's statements about women with his view of the relationship between God and humanity, it took me a long time to grasp the full implications of your argument.[2] I was stuck in my

---

2. The original typescript of this paper written in 1970 is in the Alverno College Library Archives

anger at the misogyny of the theologians we were reading and was not yet able to think systematically about how that misogyny was related to the basic structures of their thought. By my third year at Yale, we were working more as a team both to prepare for our historical theology exam and to organize the other women in the department. We read Mary Daly's *The Church and the Second Sex*, and its second chapter on the sorry history of the Church's attitudes toward women provided us with many leads to patristic and medieval documents pertaining to women that we hoped—in vain, as it turned out—to discuss on our exam.[3] We spent many engrossing and sobering hours in the library collecting and reflecting on the history of contempt for women in Christian thought.

As important as our joint intellectual efforts were the ways in which we supported each other in dealing with a hostile academic environment. Many years after I left Yale, I met a woman who had graduated from the religious studies department some time before us who told me that more than half the graduate women who were with her at Yale had had nervous breakdowns during their time there. She said that several years after she graduated, a friend phoned her and told her excitedly about her involvement in women's liberation. As she listened, in a flash, she understood her experiences at Yale in a new light, and she began to cry and shake on the phone. We were incredibly fortunate to have had some language to describe what was happening to us while we were still in the midst of our time there. Having a vocabulary to name our experiences was crucial to our each being able to maintain some sense of self. Yet our feminist insights could not protect us against routine belittlement by our fellow students or ensure that our work would be taken seriously. In a situation that was traumatizing in ways we could articulate only in retrospect, our

and can be viewed online at https://feminismandreligion.files.wordpress.com/2015/07/barths-theology-and-the-man-woman-relationship-by-carol-p-christ-1971.pdf. A version of it distributed as "A Question for Investigation: Karl Barth's View of Women" by the Conference of Women Theologians, Alverno College, 1971, is also in the Alverno College Library Archives and can be viewed online at https://feminismandreligion.files.wordpress.com/2015/07/a-question-for-investigation-christ.pdf.

3. Mary Daly, "History: A Record of Contradictions," in her *The Church and the Second Sex* (New York: Harper & Row, 1968), 74–117.

validation of each other's ideas was indispensable to our getting through the program. We were a cognitive minority of two who worked hard to help each other maintain our alternative worldviews.

This mutual support did not end when we moved away from New Haven. The summer that you spent in Montreal was immensely important both to the progress of our academic work and in cementing our friendship. Although you were supposedly finishing your dissertation, in fact, when you weren't watching the Watergate hearings, you were working on a paper on women's spiritual quest in Doris Lessing's *The Four-Gated City*.[4] At the same time, I was writing about Lessing's five *Children of Violence* novels, of which *The Four-Gated City* was the culminating volume. Our projects were somewhat different in that I was less interested in the religious dimension of the novels than in their capacity to illuminate women's experiences in the mid-twentieth century. I agreed with and may have learned from you that literature gives concreteness to otherwise abstract questions and that novels by women provide insights into the texture of women's lives that, certainly at that point, were not available elsewhere. I thus decided to disregard the advice of my thesis advisor who was skeptical about my using literature and to immerse myself in the work of Lessing and other women novelists. *The Four-Gated City* especially became a touchstone for both of us for many years. Just as the rabbis say of the Torah, "Turn it and turn it again for everything is in it,"[5] so we mined that novel as a new Torah—the missing Torah of women's lives. Turning it over and over, we were repeatedly amazed at the light it shed on our own experiences as women living in a violent century and seeking to find a way beyond conventional roles.

After we left Yale, we continued to read and comment on each other's work, serving as informal mentors as we wrote our dissertations. My dissertation advisor remarked when he read my first chapter that my decision to use literature to define women's experience was "nutritive," but it was you who encouraged me to

---

4. This became the chapter "From Motherhood to Prophecy: Doris Lessing," in Carol P. Christ, *Diving Deep and Surfacing: Women Writers on Spiritual Quest* (Boston: Beacon, 1980), 55–73.
5. Mishnah Avot 5:22.

honor my conviction that it was necessary to my argument and who was willing to talk endlessly about the insights we gained from Lessing and other authors. I, in return, loved reading your work on Lessing, and I am probably one of very few people outside your committee and Wiesel himself who read your doctoral thesis. Indeed, there is little we have written over the past decades that the other of us has not seen, and so we have always followed each other's intellectual development and been influenced by it in a variety of ways.

Divides

Yet in the years after we graduated from Yale, we found ourselves at certain major intellectual and personal divides. Our partings of the way were gradual, and, certainly in the case of our religious choices, there were always obvious differences between us. The reality is that, even when I was angriest at Judaism and most frustrated by the absence of viable choices of a worship community, I never seriously considered becoming a "post-Jew." In fact, in writing these words, I am aware that the concept of "post-Jew" makes no sense to me: I *am* a Jew. As I have said, I could choose to affiliate with the women's spirituality movement and be a divided Jew, but I would still be a Jew. While, theoretically, I could have followed Starhawk's powerful model of someone who affirms and draws on her Jewish ethnic identity even as she defines herself as a witch and follower of the Goddess, this fundamental cleaving of myself never appealed to me. In his book *God's Presence in History*, Emil Fackenheim proposed a 614th commandment (beyond the 613 given in the Torah): never to hand Hitler a posthumous victory by abandoning Judaism.[6] While I find this idea very problematic for a number of reasons, I am sure that some such feeling nonetheless operated for me as I wrestled with integrating my feminism and my Judaism. Was it even a choice to leave Judaism when Hitler had defined a Jew as anyone with one Jewish grandparent? Thus at the same time that you and I were taking the insights we were

6. Emil Fackenheim, *God's Presence in History: Jewish Affirmations and Philosophical Reflections* (New York: New York University Press, 1970), 84.

gaining from the Yale Women's Alliance and applying them to our courses and the field of religious studies, I was also struggling with the question of what they might mean for my Jewish identity, a struggle that was probably less visible to you.

The fact that I was not the only Jewish woman raising these questions at the time undoubtedly helped me to remain Jewishly connected. I once heard Starhawk say that, had Jewish feminism taken off a few years earlier, she might never have become a witch. In my case, becoming a feminist coincided with rising ferment in the Jewish community around women's status and roles. Although I was lonely living in Montreal and later Wichita, Kansas when neither was a site of Jewish feminism activism (or, in the case of Wichita, much Jewish life at all!), I was certainly not alone with my critique. Yet the existence of nascent Jewish feminist community does not explain our different choices about whether to stay in or leave our respective traditions because there was certainly equal, if not more, ferment in the same period within both Catholicism and many Protestant denominations. Perhaps the greater centrality of belief in Christianity as compared to Judaism was a factor in your decision to leave, in that you could no longer affirm many central Christian doctrines. But it also seems as if your disagreements with other feminists were more vivid for you than a sense of participation in a shared project. The fact that not all feminists shared your critique of male God-language, for example, served to deepen your alienation from Christianity. You could not understand or sympathize with the desire of many women to gain acceptance within patriarchal traditions rather than to change them. I fully share your view on this last point, but of course there were always Christian feminists who *were* trying to change tradition and not just gain access, just as there have been a range of Jewish feminist positions on this issue. Your decision to walk out of the celebration of the irregular ordination of Episcopal women priests because you could not bear the traditional language was an important turning point in your journey from Christianity to the Goddess (86f). It seems to me, as I reflect on our different choices, that you have less tolerance for contradiction and imperfection than I do, that you demand greater purity of thought and action. I am not sure whether this means you are more principled than I am or just less able to bear disappointment. In any event, I see a connection between your unwillingness to remain part of a community with which you had serious disagreements and your desire for a perfect God, an issue I will return to below. For me, community trumps consistency, partly because I believe that all community—like all reality, including God—necessarily contains problematic and conflicting elements.

The complex and in some ways mysterious nature of the factors that led to my staying within and your leaving our patriarchal traditions is heightened by the fact that I was very much influenced by your critique of male God-language and warrior imagery and found your arguments for "why women need the Goddess" persuasive and intellectually compelling. As you were increasingly drawn to female language, I remembered my childhood experience of realizing that God might be a woman and my tremendous excitement at that thought. It seemed to confirm your thesis that female language validates female experience and female power; such language conveys the message that women are created in the image of God in ways that male language never can. When my son was about six, he and I had many conversations about God in which I talked about God being present in everything, and I said that we could think of God as female as well as male. "You think of God as a woman," he said. "I'm a boy; I'm going to think of God as a man." That was another moment that brought home to me the role of gendered God-language in solidifying and affirming identity.

And yet, while I was intellectually convinced by arguments for the necessity of female language, the Goddess never spoke to me on an emotional level. I remember very clearly the night that Anne Barstow presented her paper on Çatal Hüyük at the New York Feminist Scholars in Religion. I wondered whether there was something wrong with me that I was not attracted to female imagery and thought that, perhaps, if I journeyed to Çatal Hüyük and saw the many Goddess figures *in situ*, I might have an emotional reaction comparable to Anne's. When Nelle Morton wrote that the first time she was at a service with female language, she felt as if she had been punched in the stomach, I understood what she meant but, having been a participant in the same service, I had nothing like that response.[7] When you, my partner Martha, and I spent a wonderful ten days traveling around the Peloponnese together, visiting many ancient religious sites, each time we came to a site associated with some Goddess, you would go off and try to experience the energy of the place and get in touch with the earliest layers of Goddess history. For Martha and me, there was no difference between early Goddess sites and later patriarchal ones; for us, they were all Greek ruins! Yet Martha and I have been profoundly moved by the connection to our history we have felt at archaeological sites in Israel, even when that history is thoroughly patriarchal.

Today, while I still affirm the importance of female imagery as part of an adequate picture of God, I find the notion of a transgender deity more appealing than the idea of Goddess. I use the notion of transgender in the broad sense of challenging the gender binary, and I think the concept highlights both the fluidity of divine gender and the ultimately problematic nature of gender categories. To borrow Judith Butler's notion of gender as performance,[8] God can be seen as performing—that is, as present in—many forms of gender expression from the most conventional to the most provocative. The idea of a transgender deity builds on the feminist project of recovering the female aspect of God, but in a way that foregrounds the shifting gender of God and the instability of the gender binary. Part of the reason I argued for female imagery in *Standing Again at Sinai* is that introducing apparently conflicting gendered images for God—and especially introducing images that legitimate female power—disrupts the idolatry of the singular male image and concretizes the idea that God transcends gender. But I think the concept of transgender, which was not culturally available to me at the time, says this more clearly.

---

7. Nelle Morton, *The Journey Is Home* (Boston: Beacon, 1985), 156.
8. Judith Butler, *Gender Trouble: Feminism and the Subversion of Identity* (New York: Routledge, 1990), 24–25 and passim.

Female imagery remains an important aspect of the transgender deity, but as part of a panoply of images that emphasize the ways in which moving beyond exclusively male language challenges and transforms the very categories of gender. What should come to the fore is not the alternation of male and female imagery—which can keep conventional notions of masculinity and femininity in place by reifying certain gender-related characteristics—but the flexibility of and shifts in God's gender. We can think of God as masculine, feminine, female, male, both, neither, in various combinations, and in terms that have nothing to do with gender.

Embracing a Nonpersonal God

But I do not mean to depict the choice that confronted me as leaving Judaism and becoming a follower of the Goddess, or remaining Jewish and being stuck with male God-language. There are Jewish feminists for whom female language is a sine qua non of their feminism, and I certainly could have made one of their number. There is a deeper issue, however, that divides us: I do not think of God in personal terms, and I prefer not to use *any* personal language to describe or address God. Although it was only at my mother's funeral that I fully realized that God had become for me the creative ground of all being, the power of life, death, and rebirth, I suspect that this idea had been growing in me for a long time. Many years ago, you and I led a session at the American Academy of Religion on Margaret Atwood's novel *Surfacing*, and a particular image from the novel has stayed with me ever since: "Nothing has died. Everything is alive. Everything is waiting to become alive."[9] When Marcia Falk began writing blessings using nonanthropomorphic imagery, I immediately recognized them as the language I had been waiting for and began to incorporate them into my own practice.

Many people who are introduced to female God-language for the first time resist it, claiming that it discomforts them because it

9. Margaret Atwood, *Surfacing* (New York: Simon and Schuster, 1972), 182.

confronts them with the notion that God is gendered, whereas male language is so familiar and taken for granted that they don't perceive it that way. I have always found this response to female language irritating because, of course, the male God *is* gendered, and part of the value of female images is to get us to acknowledge that fact. But I must admit feeling something similar about female language as personal language: female language does not change the nature of God enough; it rubs my nose in problematic images of dominance in the liturgy and thus serves to activate and clarify my dislike of all personal language. I am quite aware that male language is also personal, and, of course, I have problems with it as well. But on those occasions when male language works for me, it is because its familiarity and resonance with childhood experience blunt the edge of my distaste and allow me to read it in terms of emotional states or stances toward the universe rather than as addresses to God as person. I find this act of translation more difficult with female language, both because of the way its unfamiliarity—especially in the Hebrew—calls attention to itself and because enjoying the notion of God as female is precisely the point of using such language. The God who is at the heart of my prayer is the ground of being. I know that many people do not see how one can pray to a nonpersonal reality, but I cannot imagine praying to anything else. What else holds and sustains me, connecting me to all that is? Starhawk's Tree of Life meditation in which people draw up energy from the ground that then streams out in myriad branches captures beautifully the way I understand the presence of God in my life.[10]

God and Evil

Why *not* think of God in personal terms? I cannot separate this question from the other great divide between us: the issue of the relationship between God and evil. This is a fundamental disagreement between us that we have been arguing about for over two decades. For you, personal female imagery is compelling because the Goddess is a center

10. Starhawk, *The Spiral Dance: A Rebirth of the Ancient Religion of the Great Goddess* (San Francisco: Harper & Row, 1979), 58.

of loving consciousness, or as you put it, "the intelligent, embodied love that is the ground of all being."[11] You thus combine the idea of the Goddess as ground with the notion of a personal power who cares about individuals and the fate of the world. I find this notion profoundly problematic for many reasons. First of all, in my view, to define the Goddess as loving consciousness contradicts the notion that she is the ground of *all* being. You have asked me on many occasions: how, if I am loving, can the Goddess be less than loving? This is a very crucial point in your understanding of the Goddess. But my response is, yes, I am loving, but that is hardly all I am. I am also judgmental, angry, envious, and other less admirable traits; I share the ambiguity of everything in the world that I have ever encountered. In the words of poet Penelope Scambly Schott, "Everything living is beautiful and ugly: the gelatinous egg sack / and the flexible, transparent quill of the squid."[12] If all we know of that exists is a mixture of the good and the bad, life and death, the ugly and the beautiful, if our creativity and the creative power that births and sustains the world brings forth both good and evil, *then how can the Goddess be less than ambiguous?* How can the Goddess be "the ground of *all* being" if she does not "form light and create darkness, make weal and create woe" (Isa. 45:7)?

Our difference on this point feels both deep-rooted and finally inexplicable, a fundamental temperamental disagreement in our stances toward the world. I certainly cannot say that you have less appreciation of evil than I do. Not only have you been grappling with death since you were a girl, but your deep identification with the characters and events in Wiesel's novels are part of what led you to reject Christianity. You have written powerfully about the evils of patriarchy and have worked all your adult life against many forms of injustice. But there is also a way in which, for you, evil finally has less metaphysical warrant or reality than good. I have had many experiences of being surrounded by love such as those you describe,

---

11. Carol P. Christ, *Rebirth of the Goddess: Finding Meaning in Feminist Spirituality* (New York and London: Routledge, 1998), 107.
12. Penelope Scambly Schott, "Caring for the World," *Journal of Feminist Studies in Religion* 22, no. 2 (Fall 2006): 123.

and I believe that they tell me something of great importance about the nature of reality. But they do not tell me *more* than the roiling waters of Iguassu or the horrors of the Holocaust. A colleague of mine once commented that it was deeply disturbing to him that people caught up in the power of Hitler's charisma described their experiences in remarkably similar terms to those used by people involved in great movements for social justice. To me, this points to the *power* of the forces of evil, indifference, and chaos, which are as solid and enduring as the positive aspects of existence. Where do they come from if they are not sustained in being by the creative energy of God or Goddess?

And this brings me to other problems with your position, a position that, ironically, despite the fact that you have rejected a patriarchal tradition and I remain within one, is in many respects more traditional than mine. It seems to me that your explanation for the existence of evil—and I say this partly tongue-in-cheek—comes down to the free-will defense. Many classical theologians, seeking to make a space for human freedom despite the omnipotence of God, have argued that God endowed human beings with free will so that they might freely choose to turn to him. With this gift, however, came the capacity to choose wrongly, and so the same theologians are able to reconcile God's goodness and omnipotence by attributing the evil in the world to human free will. You strongly reject the notion of divine omnipotence, which eliminates part of the motive for the free-will defense. But your rejection gives even more power to human evil in that the divine nature is such that Goddess could not intervene to stop or correct the wrongs that we do. So-called natural evils, you say, such as death, disease, and events like earthquakes and floods, are simply part of life. "The real evil in the world is not created by divinity but by human beings" (163).

I partly share and partly dissent from these statements, and I think our differences, though subtle, are significant. I certainly agree with you that human free will is responsible for much of the evil in the world. Even the catastrophic extremes of weather that have been so devastating and misery-inducing in the last few years, and that once might have been labeled natural phenomena (or "acts of God"!), are at least partly the result of human action. But I would not sharply separate out the forces of disorder that you say are just "part of life" from the impulse toward evil in human beings. I have always found the classical distinction between physical evils—those that are not humanly caused, such as disease, earthquakes, hurricanes, and so on—and moral evils, which have their origins in human free will, problematic but also compelling. On one level, I agree that it makes most sense to reserve the term evil for those destructive actions that are the result of deliberate decisions and for the social structures that result from the accumulation of such decisions over time, such as male dominance and white supremacy. Labeling as evil the basic conditions of human existence or the results of geological processes seems a misnomer that has had profoundly deleterious effects, as when the perception of death as an enemy leads to the association of women with death because all that is born must die. On another level, though, I find it hard not to name as evil the many impersonal forces that devastate human existence and the larger environment. I cannot say, as you do in *Rebirth of the Goddess*, that death of natural causes is never wrong or unjust.[13] I would perhaps distinguish between *evils* as a plural noun, denoting the many misfortunes that can befall us, and *evil* as an adjective describing behaviors and structures that stem from malicious wills.

I say all this because to me there is continuum between the brokenness and violence that exists in the world apart from human action and the human capacity for evil. Even if I accept the idea that most of the terrible injustices in the world come from human misuse of free will, I am still left with the question of the source of the capacity for evil in human nature. When I first realized I had stopped believing in a personal, good, and omnipotent God, I was delighted not to have to deal any longer with the classical problem of evil: with having to hold together God's goodness and omnipotence with the pervasiveness of evil. But then I realized that dissolving the necessity for justifying

---

13. Christ, *Rebirth of the Goddess*, 126.

God does nothing to solve the *mystery* of evil. I think that you fudge the question of where the impulse toward evil—what Jewish tradition calls *yetzer hara* (the evil inclination)—comes from. I find that the rabbinic idea that human beings are poised between evil and good inclinations (*yetzer hara* and *yetzer hatov*) makes good sense as a mythological way of speaking about observable human nature. The briefest observation of small children suggests that we are born with the capacity for altruism and for selfishness, kindness and maliciousness, ethical behavior and wrongdoing. It is not that the evil inclination must be expressed in any foreordained way or that society does not play an enormous role in both eliciting and shaping our feelings and actions. But you often write as if the impulse toward domination arose spontaneously at a particular moment in history, whereas I believe that, were the potential for domination not part of who we are, it would never have become manifest. I see both *yetzer hara* and so-called physical evils as part of the ambiguity of all things that is created and sustained in existence by a God who partakes of that ambiguity. To identify God only with the good seems to me to flirt with dualism in that it leaves the elements of chaos in the universe as an independent power coequal with God.

My greatest objection to your position, however, is that it feels to me like pure wish fulfillment. I understand the attractiveness of the notion of a good but limited God, and part of me would like to believe it. When I read *She Who Changes*, I found myself nodding in agreement with almost every page of the book.[14] I have long thought that it is necessary to reject one of the premises that generate the classic problem of evil. The notion that God is both good and all-powerful is not compatible with the existence of evil in the world. Letting go of God's power may well be the more religiously appealing choice in that it allows us the enormously gratifying and reassuring thought that we have a divine advocate within and around us who wills the best for all beings and lures all beings toward fulfillment. The process metaphysic

---

14. Carol P. Christ, *She Who Changes: Re-imagining the Divine in the World* (New York: Palgrave Macmillan, 2003).

articulated by Hartshorne and adapted by you essentially leaves intact the positive elements of the biblical God and eliminates the negative ones: divinity is a center of loving consciousness, related to and aware of all that happens, working insofar as is possible to bring good out of disorder, death and evil. In a riff on the childhood Christian song, "Jesus loves me," you seem to say, "Goddess loves me, this I know, for my experience tells me so."

In *The Future of Illusion*, Freud argues that the central doctrines of Christianity are the product of human wishes. He lays out an ironic sketch of dominant Christian beliefs: life in this world serves a higher purpose, difficult as it is to guess what that purpose might be; everything that happens in the world expresses the intention of an intelligence greater than ours, even if its ways are mysterious; good will ultimately be rewarded and evil punished, if not in this life, then in another—and so on.[15] He then points out how interesting it is that these ideas describe the world precisely as we would wish it to be. The reason this is so, he insists, is that religious ideas are *illusions*, "fulfillments of the oldest, strongest, and most urgent wishes of mankind [*sic*]."[16] Illusions are different from *delusions* in that they are not simply errors and may in fact be true. But they cannot be proved or disproved, and their central characteristic is that they are derived from human wishes. Isn't the notion of Goddess as embodied intelligent love a perfect instance of what Freud means by illusion—a wish fulfillment that can neither be proven nor disproven, yet, suspiciously, perfectly accords with the human desire for a cosmic advocate and friend?

As for me, I see nothing in the world as I know it that persuades me of the truth that Goddess is love. To be sure, there are signs of love and care written into the structures of the world, but there is also evidence of neglect and violence. I can only repeat that I know of no inventiveness that does not contain the potential for both creation and destruction. When I realized at my mother's funeral that I had come to see God as the power of life, death, and rebirth; the ground of

15. Sigmund Freud, *The Future of an Illusion* (New York: W.W. Norton), 23–24.
16. Ibid., 39.

being; and the rockshelf underneath everything that grows, what had changed was not my sense of God as the source of "weal and woe" but the idea of a personal will directed at groups or individuals. There is a Buddhist teaching story of people in a rowboat on a foggy lake who see another boat coming right at them and rail at the idiocy of the person steering the boat. Then they realize that the second boat is empty and their anger vanishes. So it was with me and God. If God is not a personal being with benign or malign consciousness, then it is possible to let go of anger and to stand in awe before the mysterious complexity of the world and the boundless creative energy that births its myriad forms and to accept the reality that all is a mixture of good and evil.

Why should you and I come to such different conclusions—and conclusions that seem impervious to argument in that we can understand and appreciate each other's positions without finally being persuaded by them? This is one of the places where I am most cognizant of the multiplicity of factors that go to make up a particular view of God. I cannot help linking your idealized picture of the Goddess with your frustration with feminists who do not share your critique of traditional God-language or, for that matter, with your decision to leave San Jose State. You long for and are not satisfied with anything less than the ideal, whereas I do not simply accept ambiguity but sometimes seem to revel in it. Why is this? Certainly it is significant that you learned as a child that God is love whereas no one ever spoke to me about the nature of God. My images came to me from liturgy and from the biblical stories I heard in synagogue or learned in Sunday school, and I was left to draw my own conclusions. The fact that I became obsessed with the Holocaust as an adolescent rather than as an adult certainly shaped my view of God and human beings; yet one can see that as an effect rather than a cause in that something in me was already drawn to the painful places in human experience. You describe the loving female faces that surrounded you from infancy and acknowledge that your relationship with your father was much more difficult. You also had a Christian Science grandmother from whom you may have unconsciously inherited a sense that evil is finally less real than good. My mother could be deeply loving, but she was also judgmental, inconsistent, and sometimes irrational. My father was more loving and tender with infants, but by the time we acquired language, he had difficulty giving himself over to pride or enjoyment and always focused on what was wrong or missing in any situation. I grew up in a household in which a ninety-five on a report card elicited a question about the other five points. Is my inability to look past the negative as simple as that? How formative were these childhood experiences in shaping our different worldviews?

Ethics

Given the divergences in our understandings of God, I find it both interesting and significant that our ethical perspectives are virtually identical. For both of us, the necessity to work for a transformed religious and social order is rooted in our sense of the interconnectedness of all things. This similarity, I would suggest, points to certain gaps or inconsistencies in the thought of each of us. I might expect that, given that you see Goddess as a locus of consciousness that transcends the world as her body, your ethics would be at least partly grounded in divine consciousness and will. But it is no voice outside creation but the notion of earth as the body of the Goddess that in fact shapes your sense of obligation to the web of life. One might think that my insistence on the ambiguity of God would make it difficult for me to develop an ethic and that I might take a quietist stance toward the evils in the world. But it is precisely the sense of the oneness of God as embracing the totality of creation that in my view necessitates human action on behalf of creation. We each have a thoroughly immanentist ethic that could be seen as partially in tension with other elements in our thought. This convergence stems in part from our joint rejection of the traditional view of God as lawgiver and judge, a view that often has been regarded as the foundation of ethics, but that we both believe has been far more conducive to intolerance and violence. But it is also a product of many other currents within feminism: the affirmation of relationship and connection, the shift from transcendence to immanence, the commitment to justice for women as part of a broader vision of social transformation. These things continue to unite us despite our disagreements.

In the end, I do not have a lot of questions for you. For the most part, I understand and sympathize with many of your choices that differ from mine. I can certainly appreciate the reasons a feminist would choose to turn her back on a patriarchal tradition, and I do not think that any amount of *argument* could persuade someone otherwise who was not already emotionally invested in remaining connected. I understand and intellectually agree with the importance of female language, and I feel some sense of loss that it does not speak to me personally. The place where I balk is the notion of Goddess as personal, loving consciousness. While I can perhaps comprehend the longing for an ideal at once within and beyond the conflictual nature of experience, I finally do not understand how someone with your critical brilliance can maintain a faith in an ideal so at odds with the world that we know.

11

If Goddess Is Not Love

(Responding to Judith's Chapter 10)

Carol P. Christ

I would be less than candid if I began my response to your last chapter without acknowledging the discomfort reading your criticisms caused me. I avoided reading your chapter for several days after you sent it. When on a first quick read I found you stating that my view of Goddess sounded like "what Freud means by illusion—a wish fulfillment" (236) and that "I finally do not understand how someone with your critical brilliance can maintain a faith in an ideal so at odds with the world that we know" (239), I found excuses not to reread your chapter for some time. Since I already knew we disagreed, I am not sure why I suddenly became so sensitive. In fact, views of Goddess and God are widely divergent among feminists and other thinking people, with our views being only two of many. Perhaps the combination of daring to speak of God and knowledge of our disagreement was too much to face—at least for a period of time.

Theology and Mother's Love

When I read your comparison of our views, I was glad that you acknowledged what has always seemed to me to be a critical factor in our differences—our different experiences of our mothers' love. You state that your "mother could be deeply loving, but she was also judgmental, inconsistent, and sometimes irrational" (238). I have described my mother and even more so my grandmothers as primarily loving to me. Over the years, I have often wondered if our different views of the nature of the world and of divinity come down to our earliest experiences with our mothers. There is no way of proving or disproving this, but having known your mother and mine, I keep coming back to them. I am quite certain that the love I received from my mother and grandmothers is one of the reasons Goddess imagery seemed immediately appealing to me. I also understand that my early experience of being loved is one of the reasons I continue to insist that the divine power is love. Conversely, your disinterest in female imagery for God could be linked to the ambivalent feelings your mother arouses in you; and there is no doubt that the way you describe the ground of being sounds very much like the way you describe your mother. You ask if my Roman Catholic grandmother's devotion to the Blessed Virgin and my Christian Science grandmother's devotion to the Father-Mother God made Goddess imagery seem natural to me. Of course! Still, neither of us are Freudians, which means that we do not trace everything back to early childhood experience. Whatever the origins of our views of God, our views have been shaped by later experiences, and we both are prepared to justify them theologically, philosophically, and morally by criteria that are not part of our early childhood experiences.

At the same time, I agree with you that our discussions have brought to the fore "the complex, and in many ways mysterious, origins of religious conviction, the admixture of emotional and intellectual influences, and the ways argument can serve ex post facto to explain and justify beliefs that are much more a product of nonrational factors than efforts to defend them would imply" (218). As I studied process philosophy and found views that seemed to me to answer questions we were both asking, I was surprised that rational arguments failed to convince you. Your response forced me to recognize that, though Charles Hartshorne claimed to derive and justify his views on purely rational grounds, other factors must have played an equally important role. Hartshorne, unlike other male philosophers, often made reference to his personal life. When he mentioned that he required no special revelation, but needed to look no further than his own mother to understand the love of God,[1] I concluded that his personal experience played a greater role in the development of his views than he acknowledged. Conversely, as I noted in chapter 9, I came to recognize that rational arguments probably will not convince anyone who does not have experiences that coincide with them.

Idealism and Community

As I think about your criticisms of my positions, there are a number of things you say that seem right to me and several that seem wrong or misleading. When you discuss the reasons I left Christianity while you stayed Jewish, I think you hit upon a crucial difference between us when you say that I am more idealistic than you are. I agree that this does not mean that I am more ethical than you are. When you say that I require more "purity of thought" (228), or perhaps, more purity of ritual symbolism, than you, I think you have hit the nail on the head. I cannot participate in a religious symbol system that I feel has done and continues to do great harm in the world. I reiterate that for me this problem is not limited to the ways in which the maleness of God justifies male domination—including violence against and rape of women. Equally important to me are the ways that religious symbolisms justify the violence of warfare and conquest. I will not and cannot participate in religious rituals that justify domination and violence in the name of God. If that makes me a purist or an idealist, I

1. Charles Hartshorne, *Omnipotence and Other Theological Mistakes* (Albany, NY: State University of New York Press, 1984), 125.

am willing to accept those terms. As John Lennon sang, "You, you may say I'm a dreamer, but I'm not the only one."[2] Dreamers have not fully succeeded in creating a better world, but I stand with them in their willingness to try.

On the other hand, I think you get it wrong when you say that I put purity or idealism above community. You are right that the path I chose was out of Christianity. But when you speak of my "unwillingness to remain part of a community with which [I] had serious disagreements" and add that for you "community trumps consistency" (228), I think you overstate your case. When you say that it "seems as if your disagreements with other feminists were more vivid for you than a sense of engagement in a shared project" (227), I think you get it just plain wrong. Your statement would be true if the choice had been between the courage of my individual convictions and feminist community. But that was never the choice as I saw it. When I chose to leave Christianity, I did not make that decision on my own. There were many other women—both inside and outside the academy—who were making it with me: Mary Daly, Naomi Goldenberg, Anne Barstow (when she was writing about Çatal Hüyük), Merlin Stone, Nelle Morton, Karen McCarthy Brown, Rita Gross, Starhawk, Z. Budapest, Ruth and Jeanne Moutaingrove, Hallie Iglehart, Kit Havice, Christine Downing, Charlene Spretnak, Mara Keller, the women in my ritual group, the five hundred women who came to the Great Goddess Re-emerging Conference, many of my students, and all the women who told me after my talks that my words had changed their lives. I counted these women as my community.

You may also remember that my disappointment with Christian feminists in the academy was not primarily over the fact that we chose different communities of faith. I worked for many years in the Women and Religion Section of the American Academy of Religion to promote dialogue among feminists in religion. I was never happier than when it occurred across traditions. My disappointment was not that Christian feminists failed to join me or follow me in leaving the church—though

2. John Lennon, "Imagine," official video, https://www.youtube.com/watch?v=yRhq-yO1KN8.

I might have wished more of them had. My disappointment came when large numbers of them decided to focus their discussions in-house. The day the women walked out of the Women and Religion Section in order to hear one of the "big guys" in liberation theology speak in a section where males were dominant was a watershed moment for me. When I later asked our colleague Beverly Harrison why she walked out of the Women and Religion Section, she answered that she left with her students because she believed they needed to be where the power was. That moment would not have mattered if it had not represented a trend among feminists in the field to close ranks as Christians. I suspect that several factors were at work. One was a desire to secure positions in a male-dominated and Christian-dominated field. Another had to do with what I called a contamination theory: Christian feminists may have feared (perhaps rightly so) that making common cause with post-Christians would taint them in the eyes of their male Christian colleagues. It is also possible, as a colleague once confessed to me, that Christian feminists feared that if they spent too much time in dialogue with post-Christians, they might be convinced to leave the church. And don't forget that the last nail in the academic coffin for me was the inability or unwillingness of the Harvard faculty women to engage in a scheduled discussion of my lecture.

When our differences are viewed primarily in terms of you choosing community and me choosing purity of faith or symbolism, several other key factors are left out. As I have already noted, profession of belief is not required of Jews, but it is of Christians. I feel somewhat jealous that you had more freedom in this regard than I did. Moreover, when you became a feminist, the havurah communities were already developing, which meant that you did not have to rely on larger, older, and generally more conservative synagogues to find Jewish community. Also, there has been very little opportunity for mainline Christians to decenter and reimagine worship as Jews have done in the havurah movement and in celebrations of the Sabbath and Passover in private homes. Christian feminists now gather in independent Women-Church groups to explore and create ritual, but these groups have no official status or sanction and have no direct influence on official Sunday services led by priests and ministers.[3] When Christian feminists openly experimented with female images for divinity, communities engaged in acrimonious struggles in which charges of heresy were lodged and careers ruined.[4]

Thinking back on my decision to leave Christianity in contrast to your decision to stay within Judaism, I recognize that my relationship to Christianity was more complicated than yours was to Judaism. My parents' mixed marriage meant that I did not have one Christian denomination to identify with—I had three. My father's decision to stop going to church meant that by the time I was in college my immediate family had no religious community at all. In addition, the class exclusion I experienced in the Presbyterian Church must have made me hesitant to join another Protestant community. Though it may not be evident to outsiders, mainline American Protestantism was and to some extent still is lived out within denominations with ethnic roots (Lutherans are often German or Swedish and Midwestern, Episcopalians tend to have English roots in the Colonial East Coast) that reflect divisions by class (Episcopalians tend to be upper class, while Methodists and Baptists are middle and lower class) and race (Sunday morning worship is more segregated than society as a whole). Denominational ties and loyalties are fundamental for mainline Protestants.[5] Yet I had none. My parents identified as Christian, never as Presbyterian, and I was taught to do the same. This allowed us to acknowledge the ethnic and religious diversity in our family and made it possible for me to practice as Catholic though I had been baptized as Presbyterian. But it also meant that, when I began to question Christianity, I had no clear family, ethnic, or class ties to bind me to a particular tradition. It would have required a positive decision to choose a Protestant community or to convert to Roman Catholicism,

---

3. Originally Roman Catholic, Women-Church groups are gradually becoming ecumenical; see Mary E. Hunt, "Response II to Rosemary Radford Ruether, 'Should Women Want Women Priests or Women-Church,'" *Feminist Theology* 20, no. 1 (September, 2011): 87.

4. Elizabeth Ursic, *Women, Ritual, and Power: Placing Female Imagery for God in Christian Worship* (Albany, NY: State University of New York Press, 2014).

5. H. Richard Niebuhr, *The Social Sources of Denominationalism* (n.p.: Kessinger reprint, 2004 [1929]).

and to make such a decision was complicated by the fact that I had serious questions about whether I believed in the central Christian doctrines. At the time, there were no Women-Church groups that I could have joined.[6] Finally, it seems pertinent to mention Nancy Vedder-Schultz's response to your articulation of your reasons for staying within the Jewish tradition. She said, "I think it's difficult for those of us who grew up in the hegemonic religion, i.e. Christianity, to understand the power of being an outsider religiously. . . . I believe that to leave one's oppressed minority religion would be very difficult. But to leave the hegemonic religion when you realize how oppressive it is—especially when you see it oppressing you personally—is easy."[7]

I have never regretted my decision to leave Christianity. Although I have a sentimental attachment to Christmas trees, Christmas dinners, Christmas carols, and some hymns, I miss little else about Christianity. At a distance of several decades, I find that I quite simply have no feeling for the Christian edifice of doctrines and rituals based on the life and death of a single individual. Jesus was a visionary, but there have been many others like him—including Martin Luther King, Elizabeth Cady Stanton, and Gandhi, all of them flawed, as Jesus must have been as well. A few years ago, I decided to participate in the Greek Orthodox Easter week services, because they are attended by so many of my neighbors. But while enjoying the company of the women who decorated the *epitaphios* (tomb for Jesus), the procession through the streets of our town on Friday night, and the lighting of candles at midnight on Saturday, I came to a clear understanding that the Easter drama is no longer my drama. During the Thursday night services, I realized that many of the women were openly grieving the death of Jesus. Though I could understand that the Easter drama allowed

---

6. According to Rosemary Radford Ruether, Roman Catholic Women-Church groups began forming in the late 1970s: "Should Women Want Women Priests or Women-Church?" *Feminist Theology* 20, no. 1 (September, 2011): 67. There were also no equivalent Protestant groups: the first Re-imagining Conference was held in 1993.
7. Nancy Vedder-Schultz wrote this in response to Judith Plaskow, "Deciding to Leave or Remain in the Religion of Your Birth, Part II" on Feminism and Religion, http://feminismandreligion.com/2013/05/20/9869/.

them to release pent-up emotions, I could not join them. I felt like an outsider looking in.

In leaving Christianity, I had gained the freedom to name the sacred in my own experience, confirmed my deep inner knowing about the human connection to nature, and found the power to create and participate in rituals that have meaning in my life. To listen to Alice Walker's words about the "green lap," "brown embrace," and "blue body" of "our beautiful mother"[8] on a mountaintop or to repeat Ntozake Shange's cry, "we need a god who bleeds now / whose wounds are not the end of anything"[9] at the mouth of a cave, moves me more than any passage from the Bible. Singing "Light and Darkness" in the depths of caves is an embodied act of reclaiming the womb as a symbol of creation and the darkness as a place of transformation.[10] I still enjoy singing the *Doxology* (Hymn of praise)—and doing so connects me to my history. But I now sing it in front of altars laden with summer fruits or winter vegetables and with words that express my spirituality:

> Praise Her from whom all blessings flow
> Praise Her all creatures here below
> Praise Her above in wings of flight
> Praise Her in darkness and in light.[11]

Symbols Again

This brings us to the substantive issues between us. One of them is female language for God. I understand that, if one does not believe in a personal God, then personal God language is not appropriate. This follows whether one is Christian, Jewish, or pagan. Theologian Paul Tillich's writing always seemed inconsistent in this regard: one

---

8. Alice Walker, "We Have a Beautiful Mother," *Her Blue Body Everything We Know: Earthling Poems 1965–1990* (New York: Harcourt Books, 1991), 459–60.
9. Ntozake Shange, "we need a god who bleeds now," *A Daughter's Geography* (New York: St. Martin's, 1983), 51.
10. See P. J. Livingston, "Goddess Pilgrimage to Crete with Carol Christ," a short video that includes the song "Light and Darkness" written and arranged by Jana Ruble and images of rituals in caves, https://www.youtube.com/watch?v=fljhKcbt-K4.
11. The new words are mine. See Carol P. Christ, *She Who Changes: Re-imagining God in the World* (New York: Palgrave Macmillian, 2003), 238, for a discussion of the meaning of the new words. Also see note 2, chap. 1.

moment he was arguing that "God" is not "a being" and the next he was preaching the God of the Bible. His notion that religious ideas must be expressed in symbolic language does not resolve for me the contradictions between the language of his theology and the language of his preaching. I agree with you that a religiously satisfying language can be developed that does not refer to God or Goddess in personal terms—or as conscious, caring, or compassionate. But if you do not believe in a personal God and still want to stay Jewish (or Christian), what do you do with the Bible? Is it enough to say, "I don't believe in a personal God, but I want to be part of a community that defines its history through the Bible?" You may feel that words that picture God as a dominating and violent male other are not hurting you personally because you pass over them or fill them in with images that make sense to you. But this does not resolve the question of the harm biblical words may do to others in your community, in other Jewish communities in the United States or in Israel, and in the Christian world. Are there no longer any women or girls whose self-image has been damaged by exclusively male language for God? And what about the people who are being hurt by Christians or Jews who believe God has authorized them to dominate others and make war in the name of God? For me this problem is not resolved by saying, "I as an individual member of a community don't take the words that image God as male or as a violent dominating other seriously." You may be correct that no religious community is likely to create a set of symbols that will engage the complexities of experience while creating only good in the world. But when we know that certain symbols have done and continue to do harm, I do not believe we can avoid the obligation to try to change them. Failing that, we can choose not to participate in rituals where they are used. You are right that I have less tolerance for living with contradictions in this regard than you have.

Though I am intrigued by your idea of a transgender divinity, I have a few questions. For me the most important reason to include female imagery for God or Goddess in worship is to give women and girls concrete evidence that we too are "in the image of God." Even if divinity is understood to be impersonal, women and girls still need female images to counter the deep hold of male imagery for God in the unconscious of everyone brought up in our culture. This is especially true in religions with sacred texts that consistently refer to divinity using images of God as dominant, male, and often violent. While I understand that you do not believe in a personal divinity, I find it puzzling that you can accept the maleness of God in traditional liturgies, yet struggle with female imagery—you say because it is unfamiliar. Why is it that male imagery and even male dominant imagery for God can make you feel that you are but a small part of a much larger universe, but female imagery cannot? Are you perhaps still affected by a lingering fear that female imagery smacks of paganism, even though you have written that this fear must be overcome?[12] Or, do female images of God evoke all of the problematic aspects of your relationship with your mother? In this context, I wonder if thinking of divinity as transgender might function to make the difficult, yet crucial, task of introducing female images into familiar traditional liturgies seem less important and less urgent.

Freud

You referred to Freud when you asked if my view of Goddess is a wish fulfillment. As you said, Freud's view of religion as an illusion is a critique of traditional views of divine sovereignty. If my view of Goddess is to be considered a wish fulfillment, it should at least be noted that it does not correspond to the three wishes Freud named: the wish that death is not the final end of individual life; the wish that a benevolent rational God is in control of the world; and the wish that the suffering of the innocent will be rewarded or redeemed. As you state, the only wish that is left is "the human desire for a cosmic advocate and friend" (236). That wish seems rather modest when compared to the three wishes articulated by Freud.

12. Judith Plaskow, *Standing Again at Sinai: Judaism from a Feminist Perspective* (San Francisco: Harper & Row, 1990), 147–54.

Ambiguity and Divinity

This brings us to the major philosophical issue that divides us: the nature of divine power and the relation of divine power to the world. It is fair to say that our major difference in this regard is whether the divine power is personal, conscious, intelligent, loving, and good. You ask, "If all we know of that exists is a mixture of the good and the bad . . . , if our creativity and the creative power that births and sustains the world brings forth both good and evil, *then how can the Goddess be less than ambiguous*? How can the Goddess be 'the ground of *all* being' if she does not 'form light and create darkness, make weal and create woe' (Isa. 45:7)? (232) This question lies at the heart of our differences and you have provoked me to clarify my view. Before discussing my response to this question, let me note that the quote from Isaiah you cite is not consistent with your view. Isaiah does not refer to an impersonal ground of being that is indifferent to good and evil, but rather to a God who is actively and consciously involved not only in supporting both, but in creating both. Leaving that issue aside, I will rephrase your question: How can the Goddess be the ground of all being if She is not equally supportive of good and evil, or more specifically, love and hate, healing and harming, making peace and making war? I return to this question at the end of this chapter. First, I will respond to some of your more easily answered questions.

Death and Evil

You ask whether "evil finally has less metaphysical warrant or reality than good" (232) in my worldview. The simple answer is no. This question calls forth another: What is evil? Is death or dying evil? Under what conditions? Is harming another individual always evil? Again, under what conditions? In my view, death and dying are not evil per se. Death and dying are among the conditions of finite life on planet Earth. Everything that is born will die. Some, like my baby brother, die before they have had a chance to live; others die after long and meaningful lives. Not having created the evolutionary process and recognizing that it was created by a multiplicity of individuals over the course of billions of years, I do not feel that I have the right to judge one death unjust and the other just. The death of finite individuals is for me simply a fact of life. Moreover, human beings and other animals must eat to live. Human beings can choose not to eat other animals, but they cannot choose not to eat animals and not to eat plants. The taking of life is one of the conditions of animal life, a condition that humans share with other animals. The fact that animals can live only by taking other lives is a fact of life in our world. It is also true that other individuals in this world live by feeding on us, not only on our dead bodies (the worms crawl in) but also on living bodies—sometimes the feeding of other individuals on living human bodies in the form of bacteria or viruses takes human life. This too is a fact of life in our world. I am not interested in denying these facts or in projecting a world where death is overcome. We also live in a world where, even in the best of circumstances, there are competing interests, many of which can be considered good in themselves. Do I really have more of a right to live than the plant or animal I eat or than the bacteria that are living in my body? All individuals in the web of life have a right to life, and no one of us can live without harming other individuals. I do not call these facts of life evil.

Skipping over what may be a number of steps in between, let us think about the harm that is done through domination in human relationships and communities. I do not believe that male domination over women, enforced through violence, is natural or inevitable. I do not believe rape, genocide, war, and slavery are inevitable. I believe patriarchy is a system of male domination created at the juncture of the control of female sexuality, private property, and war, in which the rape of women, the killing of people, and the holding of slaves are justified.[13] I am interested in the new research on egalitarian

13. See my "A New Definition of Patriarchy: Control of Female Sexuality, Private Property and War," *Feminist Theology* 23, no. 3 (2016), 1-12. I first articulated this theory in three blog posts on Feminism and Religion: Carol P. Christ, "Patriarchy as a System of Male Dominance Created at the Intersection of the Control of Women, Private Property, and War," part 1, http://feminismandreligion.com/2013/02/18/patriarchy-as-an-integral-system-of-male-dominance-created-at-the-intersection-of-the-control-of-women-private-property-and-war-

matriarchal societies, which are not the opposite of male dominant patriarchal societies because they are not based on dominance. These studies show that people can live very well without controlling female sexuality, without private property, without slaves, without domination, and without war. This new research is not a reiteration of nineteenth century theories of a golden age in prehistory, but rather is based on study and interpretation of living matriarchal societies.[14] Moreover, nineteenth and early twentieth century theories discussed matriarchy within an evolutionary framework in which it was necessary for matriarchy to be superseded by patriarchy in order for rationality and individualism, claimed to be the hallmarks of civilization, to evolve. In contrast, modern matriarchal studies is critical of patriarchy and does not view it as an evolutionary advance.

The Mosuo who live on Lake Lugu in the Himalayas are a prime example of a matriarchal society: their way of life may be a remnant of what were once more widespread cultural patterns.[15] The Mosuo culture honors mothers in a matrilineal and matrilocal clan system in which everyone continues to live in the maternal clan. Both males and females are encouraged to become as loving and generous as the mothers who raise them. In Mosuo society, men visit their lovers at night and return to their maternal homes in the morning. Love is free because it is not tied to property or the rearing of children, surplus wealth is shared, and systems of checks and balances are in place to ensure that everyone's voice is heard. Fatherhood is usually known, but not considered important: maternal uncles are the male role models for their sisters' children. Grandmothers and great-uncles together make the final decisions for the clan. The traditional

part-1-by-carol-p-christ/; part 2, http://feminismandreligion.com/2013/02/25/patriarchy-as-an-integral-system-of-male-dominance-created-at-the-intersection-of-the-control-of-women-private-property-and-war-part-2-by-carol-p-christ/; and part 3, http://feminismandreligion .com/2013/03/04/patriarchy-as-an-integral-system-of-male-dominance-created-at-the-intersection-of-the-control-of-women-private-property-and-war-part-3/.

14. Heide Goettner-Abendroth, ed., *Societies of Peace: Matriarchies Past Present and Future* (Toronto: Inanna Publications and Education, 2009); Heide Goettner-Abendroth, *Matriarchal Societies: Studies on Indigenous Cultures across the Globe,* trans. Karen Smith (New York: Peter Lang, 2012, 2013). Also see Peggy Reeves Sanday's discussion of the matriarchies of West Sumatra in *Women at the Center: Life in a Modern Matriarchy* (Ithaca, NY: Cornell University Press, 2002).

15. Goettner-Abendroth, *Societies of Peace*, 230–55.

spirituality of the Mosuo includes reverence for the Mountain Goddess Gemu, who is honored as a great and giving mother. The Mosuo believe the tears of the Mountain Goddess created Lake Lugu.[16] Mountains are sacred in traditional cultures not only because they are visible as the people go about their everyday lives, but also because rain and snow fall on them, creating rivers and streams that flow down to the valleys, providing the water that sustains life for the people who live below them.[17] It makes me very happy to know that the Mosuo culture exists. I believe that similar social structures must have been the foundation of the highly artistic, peaceful, egalitarian, settled, agricultural societies of Old Europe that worshiped the Goddess as the power of birth, death, and regeneration in all of life.[18]

The Mosuo culture shows that the suffering created by structures of violence and domination is not a universal fact of life on planet Earth.[19] I do not grant dominator societies the status of inevitability. That they are a possibility is obvious. I am quite willing to call structures of domination enforced by violence evil. In regard to systems of domination that have existed for the past five thousand or more years, I do not hold Goddess or God to be the cause of them, nor do I think Goddess or God has the power to undo the harm that has already been done. The power of the Goddess is the power to inspire us to create more harmonious ways of living together on our planet. I imagine Goddess is pleased that more and more people are learning about societies of peace.

The Free-Will Defense

You find it unacceptable that I do not view Goddess as the creator or metaphysical cause of evil. You state: "Your explanation for the existence of evil . . . comes down to the free-will defense" (233). I

---

16. See "Mountain Circling Festival: Pray[er] of Mosuo People, http://www.cits.net/china-guide/china-traditions/mosuo-mountain-circling-festival.html.
17. See my blog post, "Mountain Mother, I Hear You Calling," http://feminismandreligion.com/2014/07/07/mountain-mother-i-hear-you-calling-by-carol-p-christ/.
18. Marija Gimbutas, *The Language of the Goddess* (San Francisco: Harper & Row, 1989).
19. The Mosuo are discussed in Goettner-Abendroth, *Societies of Peace*, 230–55; and in Goettner-Abendroth, *Matriarchal Societies*, 108–15.

think you know that the traditional free-will defense goes something like this: existing on His own, without a world, an omnipotent and omniscient God understood that if He created creatures with freedom, they would probably do all of the evil things that have been done in the world (and possibly worse things as well), yet He decided to create them anyway, because it is better to have a world in which freedom exists than one where it does not. The corollary to this view is that, as an omnipotent, God could at any moment intervene to stop a rape, a murder, slavery, or even the concentration camps, but He chooses not to do so, because to do so would undermine human freedom that He believes is a higher good. As we are both well aware, this view creates the problem of evil expressed in the following questions: Why did God create the world if He knew that evil and suffering would occur in it? And why does a good God who could intervene not intervene when a child is being raped, when people are gassed in concentration camps, when people hold other people as slaves? Human freedom may be a good thing, but is it always the highest good?

The view of divinity on which the free-will defense is based is not my view. Process philosophy states that as relational, divinity is always in relation to some world. There never was a time when a divine power existed alone and decided to create this world or any other world to be in relation to. Thus, the divinity did not decide to create a world that includes human freedom and the possibility of evil or decide to continue to sustain a world that includes it. The impersonal ultimate, the creative process, is coeternal with the divinity. Divinity did not create it, and divinity cannot abolish it. Divinity did not create the world out of nothing as is commonly asserted, nor did divinity create the world at a moment in time out of pre-existing matter. Individuals other than the divine individual have always existed. Thus, omnipotence or all-power cannot be the kind of power Goddess has or can have. Divine power is always power-with the power of other individuals. Individuals other than Goddess really do have the power to choose; and they have the power to choose to do things that Goddess would not want them to do. The world has been influenced by Goddess, but the world has been cocreated by individuals, beginning with the atoms swirling in space that responded to each other and to Goddess. This view cannot be reduced to the traditional free-will defense of the omnipotent God. I think you knew that.

Perhaps what you meant to say is that, like those who invoke the traditional free-will defense of the omnipotent God, I attribute humanly chosen evil entirely to human beings—and not to the divinity. In this sense your point is well-taken. You say,

> I think that you fudge the question of where the impulse toward evil—what Jewish tradition calls *yetzer hara* (the evil inclination)—comes from. I find that the rabbinic idea that human beings are poised between evil and good inclinations (*yetzer hara* and *yetzer hatov*) makes good sense as a mythological way of speaking about observable human nature. . . . [Y]ou often write as if the impulse toward domination arose spontaneously at a particular moment in history, whereas I believe that, were the potential for domination not part of who we are, it would never have become manifest. I see both *yetzer hara* and so-called physical evils as part of the ambiguity of all things that is created and sustained in existence by a God who partakes of that ambiguity. (235)

In your statement, you fail to mention the fact that, for the rabbis, a prime instance of the evil impulse was the sexual urge or desire. By and large, the rabbis were not talking as you and I are about the impulse to dominate: in fact most of the rabbis did not have a problem with male domination of women, and they accepted the hierarchical authority of other rabbis and of tradition in ways you would not. However, you are right that I make a distinction between so-called natural evil that is a part of life, and the proclivity to dominate and violate that has become part of life under the conditions of patriarchy shaped at the junction of the control of female sexuality, private property, and war. As I said above, I believe that patriarchy, private property, and war, and with them rape and slavery, are the source of a great deal of evil in our world. I do not think these forms of evil are inevitable or necessary. I think they arose in human history and are caused by human beings. I dream that we can create a world where these specific forms of evil do not exist.

Is there an evil impulse in human nature? According to primatologist Franz de Waal, one of our closest primate relatives, the chimpanzees, created a primate culture based on male domination, enforced through violence—though not nearly so much violence as is found in recent human cultures. Some have concluded from this that "man" is the "naked ape" and that the will to dominate is innate in human nature or in human male nature. De Waal counters with another group of primates, the bonobos, who created a matriarchal primate culture that makes love not war. De Waal suggests that one of the lessons we can learn from our primate relatives is that the instincts we share with other primates are malleable: we have the capacity to create societies based on domination or to create societies of peace.[20] The recent studies of societies of peace like that of the Mosuo discussed above suggest that it is possible for human beings to create societies organized around the principles of love and generosity rather than domination. The "potential" for selfish, dominant, or violent behavior is always there, but it makes a big difference whether such behaviors are tolerated and rewarded or not. Societies of peace do not reward selfishness, hoarding, or any type of violent behavior. In contrast, patriarchal societies reward aggressiveness and accumulation of wealth and consider those who kill in the course of war to be heroes.

If another way is possible, then how did humanity end up in the sorry state in which we find ourselves today? What is the source of humanly created evil? This is not a question that can be answered in a paragraph or two. What I can do here is to sketch out the way I might answer this question at more length. I think doing some harm to other life forms in order to live is inevitable in human and other forms of life. Many traditional societies minimize the harm done to the lives of others through the principle of "taking only what you need." This principle is rooted in the understanding that life is interdependent. This principle is not consistent with domination or with hoarding private property. The interdependence of life is a fundamental

20. Franz de Waal, *The Bonobo and the Atheist: In Search of Humanism among the Primates* (New York: W. W. Norton, 2013), 81–82.

metaphysical principle that I affirm—and that is affirmed by process philosophy.

What went wrong? Are people inherently incapable of recognizing the interdependence of life and thus of curbing their desires to acquire more than they need? I don't think so. Many tribal groups and early agricultural societies were able to live without dominance, war, and unbridled acquisition—and without rape and slavery. What seems to be the case is that, once societies begin to be organized around male dominance, private property, and war, they perpetuate violence and domination in their own societies and spread them when they conquer others. Through violence and humiliation, they create an "evil impulse" in babies and children raised in cultures of domination. Alice Miller has written about the role cruelty in child-rearing practices plays in creating violent societies.[21] This pattern has occurred throughout patriarchal history. Nonviolent societies are not equipped to resist dominator groups. They must submit to conquest and exploitation or learn the ways of violent domination as they fight back. I cannot argue this interpretation of human history fully here, but this is the direction my argument would take. Death and dying, the necessity of taking other lives in order to live, and conflicting interests are inevitable in human life. These realities must be taken into account in any explanation of the world. Beyond that, I believe we have to blame human choice, not human nature, the nature of the world, or the nature of God or Goddess, for the great evils human beings have created and inflicted on each other and the other than human world.

Goddess and the Ground of Being

Having answered several of your other questions, I come back to the one I put aside: How can the Goddess be the ground of all being if She is not equally supportive of good and evil, or more specifically, love and hate, healing and harming, making peace and making war? Your question provoked me to rethink the central statement of *Rebirth*

21. Alice Miller, *For Your Own Good: Hidden Cruelty in Child-Rearing and the Roots of Violence*, trans. Hildegaard and Hunter Hannum (New York: Noonday Press, 1990 [1993]).

of the Goddess that "Goddess is the intelligent, embodied love that is the ground of all being."[22] When I spoke of Goddess as the ground of all being, my intention was to call attention to the immanence of the divinity in the world. John Cobb also questioned my identification of Goddess with the ground of being when he read the manuscript of the book. At the time, I was not familiar with his discussion of the two ultimates, so I did not grasp his point.[23] Now I realize that I made a mistake when I identified the personal divinity with the ground of being. Cobb speaks of the ground of being as the metaphysical principles that structure life; he calls these principles the creative process. You also speak of the ground of being as the creative process and as the whole of which we are a part.

Let us examine your notion that ground of being is the whole, in relation to the personal divinity. If the personal divinity is an individual, related to all other individuals who are living, have lived, or will live, then, the whole must be made up of the divinity and all other individuals. In a relational world, individuals have the capacity to affect each other. From this perspective, to identify the personal divinity with the whole is to deny the reality and freedom of the other individuals who, together with the personal divinity, make up the whole—or alternatively, to deny the reality and freedom of the personal divinity who is more than the sum total of the other individuals who constitute the whole. The relationship of the personal divinity to the whole is more accurately expressed in the process concept of panentheism that defines the divinity as "in" the world and the world as "in" the divinity. The personal divinity feels the feelings of the world and responds to them and takes the feelings of other individuals in the world into the life and memory of the divinity.

If the ground of being is identified with the metaphysical principles that structure all of reality, then I agree with Cobb that it is also a mistake to identify the personal divinity with the ground of being.

22. Carol P. Christ, *Rebirth of the Goddess: Finding Meaning in Feminist Spirituality* (New York: Routledge, 1998 [1997]), 107.

23. John Cobb, "Being Itself and the Existence of God," in *The Existence of God*, ed. John R. Jacobson and Robert Lloyd Mitchell (Lewistown, NY: Edwin Mellen, 1988), 5–19; discussed in chap. 9.

The personal divinity, like all other individuals, acts and expresses itself through the creative process, the metaphysical principles that structure the reality of a relational world. Process philosophers are fond of stating that the divinity is not an exception to the metaphysical principles, but the supreme exemplar of them. If creativity is a metaphysical principle, divinity is supremely creative. If relationship is a metaphysical principle, divinity is supremely related to all. If change is a metaphysical principle, then divinity changes with the world. And so on. The ground of being is the creative process through which all individuals, including divinity, interact with each other. The creative process appears to be, as you insist, indifferent to or equally supportive of weal and woe, healing and harming, good and evil. Then shouldn't we conclude, as you do, that divinity is the supreme exemplar of the metaphysical principles of good and evil? The reason I answer this question negatively is that relationship, creativity or freedom, and change are metaphysical principles, while weal and woe, healing and harming, and what we call good and evil are outcomes of the creative process. I underscore this point because it may be unfamiliar: *from a process point of view good and evil are not metaphysical principles; rather, they are judgments individuals (including I assume the divine individual) make about outcomes of the creative process and the acts of individuals and groups that created them.*

Though participating in the creative process, the personal divinity is different from other individuals in one significant way: the personal divinity always loves and understands and always desires and promotes the flourishing of others. This is one of the fundamental insights of process theology. Hartshorne calls this the principle of "dual transcendence." Dual transcendence means that while the divinity is "in" the world and is changed by relationships to individuals in the world, divinity is unchanging and therefore transcendent of the world in one fundamental respect: divinity will always respond to the world with love and understanding.[24] Individuals other than the

---

24. Hartshorne discusses the principle of dual transcendence in *The Divine Relativity* (New Haven: Yale University Press, 1948).

divine individual do not always love and understand and do not always promote the good, whether by choice or because of circumstances beyond their control. The personal divinity, in contrast, always inspires us to "choose life": to make choices that will enhance the possibilities of life and fulfillment for the greatest number of individuals, human and other than human. This is the framework within which I assert that individuals other than the divinity create the evil in the world, while the good in the world is cocreated by individuals including the divinity.

With this clarification in mind, I can see that instead of stating that "Goddess is the intelligent, embodied love that is the ground of all being," I should have said that *Goddess is the intelligent, embodied love that is in all being*. This change clarifies the relation of Goddess and all being, while preserving the insight that the love and understanding of the Goddess is in the world, not outside it. Hartshorne's concept of the world as the body of divinity[25] explains the intimate relationship of divinity and the world.

The idea of the two ultimates enables me to understand two different strands in my spirituality. I experience—feel and sense—the personal ultimate, the presence of Goddess as intelligent love in my body, mind, and spirit and in all bodies, minds, and spirits, as I go about my everyday life. She is always there: feeling the love and joy I feel; supporting and understanding me when things are difficult; inspiring me to share the grace of life with everyone and everything. I also feel the power of the impersonal ultimate, the creative process that supports the creativity or freedom of all individuals who interact with each other in the web of life. For me the two ultimates—Goddess and the creative process underlying the web of life—are both real. Though the two ultimates are separate in the abstract, in the concrete experience of those of us who affirm the personal divinity, they are intertwined. The personal divinity relates to others and is experienced by them through the creative process that is the basis of life. Thus, at one and the same time, I experience myself and divinity within

---

25. See chap. 7.

me, other individuals and the divinity within them, and the creative process and the divinity who is known through it. I can celebrate the creative process and its fruits, the powers of birth, death, and regeneration and the evolutionary process of our universe, as the ground of all being, as well as the Goddess I experience as a personal, intelligent, loving, compassionate presence who cares about me and all other individuals in the world.[26]

To Choose Life

I imagine that when you read what I have written here, you will conclude that I have clarified the contradictions you found in my earlier discussion of the relation of Goddess and the ground of being, but that you still do not agree with me, because you don't experience what I experience. For you, the command to choose life does not come from a conscious, intelligent, loving, compassionate divinity. For you the command to choose life is a conclusion that can be drawn or felt—and that you draw and feel—through reflection and meditation on the fact that each of us is but a small part of a much greater whole. For me as well, the command to choose life is a conclusion I draw in relation to the deep connection I feel to the whole web of life. I do not need the Goddess to tell me to feel those connections. But for me, the command to choose life is also felt in my heart and whispered in my ear by a conscious, intelligent, loving, and compassionate Goddess who is as close to me as my own heartbeat and breath.

When faced with differences of experience and differences in views of the world that cannot be resolved, we do not have to accept every worldview as equally valid. We have both provided rational justifications for our views of the world and of divinity. While these justifications will not be convincing to all, the process of making them means that we are willing to discuss our views with each other, and to submit our deeply held views to rational scrutiny by others. It is also

26. Stephen Hatch has a lovely description of the doubleness of his experience of nature itself and God/Christ in nature in "Christ and the Natural World: Two Ultimates," *Jesus Jazz and Buddhism* blog, http://www.jesusjazzbuddhism.org/christ-and-the-natural-world-two-ultimates.html.

important to both of us also to judge our views by moral criteria: to ask if they create weal and not woe, healing and not harming, good and not evil in the world. As you said, though we speak from different standpoints, different histories, different personal experiences, and different experiences of Goddess and God, the ethical outcomes of our positions are virtually identical. For both of us, the call to transform the world is rooted in our sense of the interdependence of life.

We live in an interconnected world. We must care for others and ourselves. We can take only what we need. No special revelation is required to teach us this. No particular community is the sole guardian of these insights. We have a come a long way through our differences to return to basic insights that we share and that motivate everything that we do.

12

Evil Once Again

(Responding to Carol's Chapter 9)

Judith Plaskow

First of all, I appreciate your account of the many things that we share. It has been my experience that disagreements between people who are actually quite close to each other on a broad spectrum of views often loom large and feel of great import. It is therefore important to remember our many commonalities, including that we are both looking for alternatives to classical theism, that we both seek God or Goddess *in* the world and through our bodies, and that we both believe that the beautiful and complex web of life of which we are part is the only world we will ever know. You are quite right that, for me, Judaism is a location for my thinking about God (194); it is the community within which I make my choices, but it does not determine my choices. I bring to bear on Jewish tradition values—such as the full humanity of women—that not only are not exclusive to Judaism but that are in tension with certain strands within it. I also want to underscore your point that we both acknowledge the need to reflect on and evaluate our experiences and to develop theologies that make sense of them and of the world in which we live. Despite the ways in which nonrational factors have shaped our theological differences, we each feel the need to develop a case for the plausibility and meaningfulness of our theological perspectives in terms that make sense to others. Indeed, making such a case is an important part of what it means to each of us to be a theologian.

Given the ways in which our theological positions have been affected by our dissimilar histories, I find very interesting the extent to which certain significant discrepancies in our childhood experiences have turned out *not* to matter. You are right that issues of social justice were absolutely at the center of the Reform Judaism I imbibed as a child and were also important within my family. The fact that you were unaware of problems of poverty and injustice and, if anything, learned prejudice in your home, lost significance when you became "converted" to fighting poverty and racism during the summer after you graduated from college. Similarly, the fact that you grew up in a world in which only single women worked, whereas my mother was a teacher who believed strongly in the need for women to have meaningful work outside the home, turned out not to be determinative for our life choices. As I said in my initial response to your theology, I am struck by the extent to which our ethical positions are virtually identical despite our theological differences, and now I would add, despite significant differences in our upbringings. But let me turn to the issues that you raise.

Core Symbols in Context

Your central question to me, which you pose from a variety of angles, is how I can commit myself to a tradition in which God's power is identified with images of war and violence when these images have harmed and continue to harm women and the world. How can I not recoil from using such images in worship? Why is the power of symbols less important to me than to you? (201)

The first thing I would say is that, like you, I find these images profoundly problematic, indeed, truly awful. One of the projects I undertook when I first retired was reading the Bible from cover to cover, and I was appalled in rereading all the prophets in a group at the amount of violence in their teachings. When I have spoken on the topic of dealing with difficult texts in the Jewish and Christian traditions—and it is a subject that is dear to my heart—I always discuss God's violence in addition to texts that demean women. I have on a number of occasions led discussions in my havurah about how we can read such texts as Torah. And, yes, I have sometimes asked myself how I can remain part of a tradition in which God is depicted in this way. So I do not at all disagree with your critique of this imagery, but obviously for me, it is not decisive. Why not?

I think, as you suggest, that the different status of belief in Judaism and Christianity is a factor (199f), though I'm not sure it is decisive—for either of us. In fact, though you say that your leaving the Christian tradition had a great deal to do with your inability to believe in the Trinity, incarnation, or other central Christian teachings, the reality is that most of our Christian feminist friends understand these doctrines in ways that have little to do with their original meaning in the Nicene Creed. To me, this says that your decision not to participate in the process of feminist theological reinterpretation ultimately had more to do with your revulsion at Christianity's core symbols than with its beliefs. That said, my experience of the importance of belief was very different from yours. Not only did I never feel pressure to affirm certain things about God or the origins of Torah, but also I was never asked to defend or even to articulate my convictions. I did ask the rabbi when I was in high school why we paraded around the synagogue with the Torah when we didn't believe anything that was in it, so I was always interested in belief and aware of certain inconsistencies in what I was being taught. But I also felt free to raise critical questions and, indeed, understood doing so as part of what it meant to be a Jew. While this may have been one of gifts of my Reform upbringing, within certain parameters, it also characterizes the Jewish tradition more generally. Disagreement and debate are central modes of religious expression in rabbinic Judaism. The Talmud preserves minority views and, in a famous passage, depicts a heavenly voice as responding to an ongoing dispute between two important rabbinic sages with the words, "These and these are the words of the living God."[1] (How's that for the theme of ambiguity?!) Perhaps the different attitudes of our traditions toward asking questions is more significant than the reasonableness or unreasonableness of any particular belief.

The rabbis' willingness to entertain multiple—even conflicting—theological positions speaks to a certain sanity in the Jewish tradition that I value a great deal. Indeed, not to deny for a moment the problematic nature of aspects of Judaism, I think that, on the whole, it is a saner and more realistic tradition than Christianity. Its central narrative is a narrative about slavery and freedom, about the formation of a community and the obligations that bind that community. While I have many problems with Jewish law, I appreciate what I see as its central purpose: to cultivate awareness of God's presence as we engage in everyday practices from eating to going to the toilet. Notwithstanding the existence of beliefs about an afterlife within Judaism, the tradition is more focused on living this one life that we have in community with others and in relation to the sacred. Thus, insofar as belief is an issue, there is less propelling me out of Judaism than was the case for you and Christianity.

Beyond the issue of belief, however, there are many aspects of Judaism that I find meaningful and enriching. Problematic core symbols do trouble me, but they are not all that matters. It seems to me that, in focusing on the damage inflicted by such symbols, you discount all the positive things that Judaism (or Christianity) offers its adherents. Although, when it comes to our understandings of God, I insist on God's ambiguity while you see Goddess as entirely good, when it comes to our traditions of origin, you dwell on the negative. Perhaps our different childhood experiences in relation to social justice do matter after all because it is important to me that my life-long concern about such issues came to me through Judaism. I certainly do not claim

1. Eruvin 13b.

that the value of justice is exclusive to Judaism, not at all. But the idea of being kind to the stranger because we were strangers in the land of Egypt creates a powerful link between the central Jewish narrative and the ongoing task of repairing the world. I find the Jewish story a powerful story—both the biblical account of exodus and wandering and the continuing three-millennia saga of the survival of a tiny, often persecuted, people, scattered across the globe. It feels like a tremendous gift to be part of that long history and at the same time to have lived through the immense changes wrought by feminism over the last forty years. These changes strengthen my conviction that Judaism is an evolving tradition, that it has repeatedly transformed itself and can continue to do so. I recently came across a quotation from Philip Roth that nicely captures some of my own feelings: "I have always been pleased at my good fortune in being a Jew. It's a complicated, interesting, morally demanding, and very singular experience, and I like that. I find myself in the historic predicament of being Jewish, with all its implications. Who could ask for more?"[2]

I also treasure both the theological importance of community in Judaism and the specific Jewish communities that have enriched my life. When I pray with my havurah or am immersed in the wonderful music at my synagogue, B'nai Jeshurun, I do not *experience* God as king or warrior. Rather, I feel God's immanent presence in community as we lift our voices together in song. My experience weighs as heavily for me as what you call the core symbols of the tradition. I love the rhythm of the Jewish year and the way in which many of the holidays connect the Jewish story with agricultural and natural cycles. You ask how I can continue to value a text—the Bible—that fuels the right wing in Israel and justifies its wars (201). I am aware, of course, that there are people who do horrible things in the name of Judaism, but I do not see why I should allow them ownership of the tradition more than the many Jews (of whom I am one) who oppose the occupation of Palestine and demand the dismantling of the settlements in the name of an alternative understanding of Jewish values.

2. Cited in *Lilith* with no bibliographical reference, 40, no. 1 (Spring 2015): 16.

You raise the question of how the image of God as dominating male other will affect my granddaughter and other girls (201). Thinking about my granddaughter, Hannah, puts me in touch with a whole dense network of symbols, other than those that trouble you, that is central to my experience of Judaism and that I hope will be part of hers. Already at fourteen months, when Hannah saw the table set for the Sabbath, she put a kippah on her head and pretended she was singing. True, her father recites the blessing over wine using male God-language, but is that more important than sitting with her family around the table for a relaxed meal, dipping her finger in the wine, or feeling the texture of challah in her mouth? At her first Passover Seder, she saw a table laden with symbols, tasted the crumbly matzah and dipped parsley in saltwater, combining a taste of spring with the tears of slavery. In a few years, she will be able to spill ten drops from the second cup of wine when we name the plagues as an expression of sorrow for the drowning of the Egyptians. Later, she will hear us wrestle with the Haggadah and try to envision what it would mean for one people to gain our freedom not at the expense of another. In the fall, she will taste apples dipped in honey for a sweet year, hear the eerie blasts of shofar, and a couple of weeks later, sit in a sukkah decorated with pine needles and laden with fruit and gourds. Certainly, none of these symbols individually is as central as the male, dominating God, but together they make a web of sensuous, embodied connections to what it means to be a Jew. She will have at least one grandmother who will talk to her about how God is in all things and can be thought of as a girl like her and not just as male. She will grow up in a family in which asking critical questions is part of what it means to be Jewish, and she will be taught to think about the stories and images she is being bequeathed. Do I wish that her parents used Marcia Falk's blessings instead of the traditional ones? Yes. Do I see her exposure to male language and images of domination as something to be discussed with her and questioned? Yes. Would I prefer that she be deprived of all these experiences because of the problematic nature of many images of God? Definitely not.

Ambiguity and Liturgical Change

You ask whether my attachment to ambiguity makes me doubt the efficacy of changing liturgy or the usefulness of revising it according to ethical criteria (201). I want to be absolutely clear that I never appeal to the ambiguous nature of all life as an excuse for failing to address injustice. Not only am I a firm believer in changing liturgy, but more than that, I would like to think that my work has been one of the factors that inspired the prayer book revisions undertaken by all the liberal Jewish denominations over the last decades. All the nonorthodox movements have added the matriarchs to the *amidah*—the central silent prayer—and have removed male God language in the English. My havurah used the Reconstructionist prayer book, the one that has gone furthest in changing English God-language and even some of the Hebrew and that includes many alternatives to the traditional liturgy, quite a few of them by feminists. And even then, the prayer book was only our starting point in the quest for meaningful connection with the sacred and each other. I acknowledge that I do not favor jettisoning the traditional prayer book altogether because of its long history and because it provides people familiar with it with access to Jewish communities around the world. But I believe that young people can learn about it as an important part of Jewish history and as one of a series of possible options, and I would hope that the awareness of alternatives will open up the Jewish imagination and erode the power of traditional images.

You are right, however, that my conviction that all human efforts are ultimately ambiguous makes me suspicious of efforts to create a tradition *de novo* with the hope that it will be purer than what went before. It is easy to see certain symbols as benign or transformative when those who advocate them are part of a small, marginalized group without social power. Early Christianity offered its followers in a hierarchical Roman Empire the promise of a world without Jew or Greek, slave or free, male or female. Some Asian Christian feminists have testified to the generative power of Christianity in their lives

271

in their overwhelmingly non-Christian cultures.[3] Conversely, Goddess symbols in the Greco-Roman world and in India have been used to support male dominance, and, in fact, you are as critical of many traditional Goddess myths and images as you are of the violent God of Judaism and Christianity. I want to affirm two truths at the same time: that it is important and necessary to challenge and change images that support male dominance and violence; and that transforming core symbols is not of itself sufficient to bring about religious and social change. Flo Kennedy once said that "if men could get pregnant, abortion would be a sacrament."[4] Gloria Steinem made a similar claim about the cultural valence of menstruation, arguing that if men menstruated, being "on the rag" would be the ultimate cool.[5] The point is that the characteristics of a dominant group will always be used to justify its dominance; while the characteristics of a subordinate group will always be used to justify its subordination. I believe that changing ideas and symbols is an important part of challenging structures of dominance, but I am also aware of the limits of such change. This sense of limits probably does contribute to my unwillingness to turn my back on Judaism because of its core symbols.

The Role of Community

You suggest that one possible explanation for our different decisions about whether to affiliate with an inherited tradition is that you choose to situate yourself within small visionary communities while I identify with a larger historic community (205). But, as you then go on to acknowledge, we are not really so different in this regard because I connect to the wider Jewish community through the smaller visionary communities of various havurot and B'not Esh. Throughout my adult life, I have repeatedly chosen to help create the kinds of Jewish

3. See, e.g., Kwok Pui-lan, "Claiming a Boundary Existence: A Parable from Hong Kong," *Journal of Feminist Studies in Religion* 3, no. 2 (Fall 1987): 121–24.
4. This quotation has been attributed to many people, but the earliest published reference attributes it to Florynce Kennedy. "If Men Could Get Pregnant, Abortion Would Be a Sacrament," Quote Investigator, http://quoteinvestigator.com/2013/09/11/men-pregnant/.
5. Gloria Steinem, "If Men Could Menstruate," *Ms.* (October 1978).

communities that I wanted for myself, and it is participation in these communities that has enabled me to continue working happily in a Jewish context. The new liturgies and religious forms you pioneer in a Goddess framework are not so different from the liturgical and ritual experiments we undertake in B'not Esh. I firmly believe in the contagious power and energy of small, experimental communities that provide models for what the larger Jewish community could someday be. But again, you could have participated in creating feminist communities such as these within the Christian tradition, so I think that where we find visionary community is more the result than the cause of our different choices.

I would thus reaffirm what I said in my original response: that the reasons for our different choices are complex and multifaceted. I agree with you that your view of life as a whole is not especially idealized. As I have said, I see a discrepancy between your clear awareness of social evil and your engagement in many struggles against injustice and your depiction of the metaphysical plane, where you imagine a deity who is perfectly sympathetic and loving. I also appreciate what you say about the destructive effects of the doctrine of original sin and how liberating it was to begin to think of the world, your body, and yourself in more positive ways. Despite never having been taught to think of myself as a "sinner," I do have a good helping of Jewish guilt—guilt for the many privileges that I enjoy and probably an attenuated form of survivors' guilt that goes back to my adolescent fascination with the Holocaust. I suppose that that sense of guilt feeds my view of the ambiguity of human nature. And while I recognize that a certain amount of my guilt is inappropriate and can get in the way of effective action, I still think it teaches me things about the inequalities in the world and the human capacity for destructiveness that are worth knowing.

The Power of Love

It is interesting that you raise the question of whether I would have had an experience of the power of love had I been in the room when my mother died (209). I cannot know, of course, because I was fifteen hundred miles away. But I suspect that, having watched the disintegration of my mother's intelligence and personality over a period of ten months, and having seen her several times as she lay in a persistent vegetative state for six months, I would likely have felt the same intense relief that I did from a distance. As to the "love" and curiosity of the spider monkeys (208), those same monkeys later broke through the mesh roof of our hotel room, ransacked and shredded our possessions, and poured out and ate some of our medications. Though we were aware at the time that the incident would be very funny in retrospect, in the moment, it was creepy and frightening. It made very clear that, though the monkeys were at the lodge as semipets, in fact they were wild animals and were best treated as such. This lesson was reinforced when another guest tried repeatedly to pet a monkey and was bitten. We would hardly have labeled the monkeys as loving; nor would I do so in retrospect.

These different interpretations of our experience are very much related to our different understandings of God. I recognize that, for you, the intelligent interest of the monkeys and softness of your kitten are manifestations of the love of the Goddess that you felt when your mother died. But to me—and here we are back to the same puzzle again—this is a view of the world that simply does not accord with my experience. I hear in your questions—if we love and understand but God does not, doesn't that make us "better than" God, and how can the infinite be better than the finite? (207)—shades of Anselm's ontological argument. Anselm argued that God is that than which nothing greater can be imagined, and since what exists is greater than that which does not exist, God must exist.[6] But as Kant pointed out, existence is not a predicate: the fact that we can imagine a perfectly loving and understanding being as existing does not mean that such a being exists. More importantly, I do not think that your question takes immanence seriously enough. If God animates and fills all that exists then God *does* love and understand: *through us.* If the world is the body of God, then

6. Anselm, *Proslogion: With the Replies of Guanilo and Anselm*, trans. Thomas Williams (Indianapolis: Hackett, 2001).

we are the part of God's body that loves and understands. The part has no qualities that the whole does not have because every part is an essential constituent of the whole.

The Two Ultimates

In thinking through the differences in our concepts of God, you turn to John Cobb's notion of two ultimates as a way of understanding and potentially reconciling one of our fundamental disagreements (211f). Cobb notes that the word God is used by people in remarkably divergent ways, and he is particularly interested in the distinction between the idea of God as ground of being or being itself and the personal God of the Bible and traditional theism.[7] Cobb believes that the concept of being itself indicates something real, but he does not think that it can be appropriately identified with "God" because it lacks the personal characteristics traditionally ascribed to God. Most significantly, being itself is not an object of trust and does not "act for the improvement and betterment of creatures."[8] Cobb thus recognizes the existence of two ultimates—a nonpersonal ground in which all beings, including divinity, participate, and a personal God as the object of trust and worship, a unique and unsurpassable individual. This distinction, Cobb says, sheds light on the tension found in many of the world's religions between a nonpersonal, inexhaustible, unknowable ultimate reality, such as *Ein Sof* (Without End) in Jewish mysticism, and a personal and personified being, such as the God of the Bible. In Cobb's view, both these ultimates exist and are mutually dependent, and, though different religious traditions may value one over the other, it is not necessary either to rank or to choose between them.

I agree with you that Cobb's argument is helpful in understanding the fundamental difference between us. Like Cobb, you affirm the existence of both these ultimates, whereas I recognize the usefulness of the distinction for understanding various concepts of ultimate reality

---

7. John Cobb, "Being Itself and the Existence of God," in *The Existence of God*, ed. John R. Jacobson and Robert Lloyd Mitchell (Lewiston: The Edward L. Mellon Press, 1988), 5–19.
8. Ibid., 14.

in the world's religions but do not believe that "God" in Cobb's sense exists. Thus, I reject Cobb's contention that being itself cannot appropriately be called God. I recognize that the concept of being itself or the ground of being lacks the personal characteristics most often associated with God in the West, but as I argue in chapter 8, I think there are nonetheless compelling reasons why this reality can be called God. It is the creative source of our being and of all beings; it is the object of the mystical longing for unity; it evokes feelings of awe, gratitude, and dependence traditionally associated with belief in God. Cobb says that it is doubtful that being itself can evoke worship, since it is neutral with respect to the creation of particular forms. But I do not see that worship can be separated from the sense of mystery and deep reverence that he acknowledges may be associated with the ground of being. Moreover, despite Cobb's insistence that moral experience must be rooted in a reality that guides us toward right choices in the expression of our freedom,[9] I believe that awareness of our interconnection with all beings in the web of life is a sufficient basis for ethical decision making and that, therefore, the concept of being itself does provide a foundation for making certain choices rather than others. I also think it is interesting that, unlike Cobb, you do not root your ethics in the love and understanding of the Goddess.

When I talk about God as ground of being, being itself (a term I rarely use because of traditional understandings of being as static), wellspring of life, or the creative energy that sustains the universe, I mean to point both to the totality of all that exists and the creative process out of which new forms emerge and develop. On the one hand, I use ground of being to refer to "the whole" —the astounding variety and intricacy of our world and the universe beyond, of innumerable life forms (animate and inanimate) in their particularity and their relation to each other. I agree with you that the fundamental religious experience associated with God in this aspect is the connection to all other individuals in the web of life and to the web of life as a whole. I would add that an important dimension of a religious attitude toward the whole is

9. Ibid., 16.

surrender. While that term can be easily misunderstood and misused, I mean by it acceptance of my place as but a tiny node in the great fabric of existence. Not everything is about me; I am not the center of the universe, and important aspects even of my own life are simply not in my hands.[10] While I have an obligation to do my part in repairing the world and creating meaning in the context in which I find myself, I must accept the reality that I cannot finally control the outcome of my actions. Part of the reason I find the High Holiday liturgy so powerful is that it reminds me of my vulnerability and smallness as part of a vast universe, at the same time that it points me to my responsibility for shaping my life in the year ahead. Rosh Hashanah and Yom Kippur are the only times in the ritual calendar when Jews prostrate themselves before God, and I experience this as a literal bowing, in Hamlet's words, "to the divinity that shapes our ends, / Rough-hew them how we will."[11]

On the other hand, as you have argued so well in *She Who Changes*, "the whole" is never static. Ceaseless birth, death, and regeneration characterize all of existence from the subatomic to the cosmic levels. God as ground of being and wellspring of life is both sum and source of the processes of continual development, collapse, and change. Our planet and universe have evolved over untold eons and will continue to do so, with or without our presence. The cells in our bodies are always dying and renewing themselves; our brains constantly create new synapses. The tides move in and out, altered in their courses by the alignment of heavenly bodies; stars explode and new ones come into being. Societies undergo transformation, changing their means of production and social relations, at one time descending into violence, at another finding a way toward peace and stability. We grow and develop throughout our lives, learning new skills and sometimes making decisions that send us in new directions. Our choices become part of the ever-renewing wellspring of life, creating ripples that expand out in many directions, whether for good or for ill. God as

10. Carol makes a similar point when she says that she has become a kind of Buddhist insofar as she has given up many of the desires of her ego (152).
11. William Shakespeare, *Hamlet*, act 5, scene 2.

the creative energy that moves through all things sustains and renews the ceaseless flow of life, expressing Godself in the countless forms that make up the universe and in their continual interaction and metamorphoses. Our human creativity, which we as a species have expressed in both remarkably fruitful and destructive ways, is a reflection of the divine creativity and is rooted in and nourished by it. Though I could not have articulated it as clearly, I find compelling the definition of creativity you propose in your initial response to me (212). I especially resonate with the idea that, in the creative moment, the individual unifies the world into a new synthesis. This captures very well my view that the world is created anew at every moment. I also strongly agree with you that creative freedom is never absolute but "is always in relation to the world as it previously existed" (213). One of the existentialist ideas I found most attractive as an undergraduate was the notion that we are not self-created but, at birth, are "thrown" into a particular historical and cultural situation, and we must then make choices about how we will shape our lives in the context in which we find ourselves.

Clearly, my acceptance of only one of Cobb's two ultimates is connected to another of our central disagreements, namely our views of the relationship between God and evil. Our quarrel on this issue—the fact that I see God as the source of both good and evil while you do not—can be traced directly to our different stances toward the two ultimates. We both agree with Cobb that the ground of being is infinitely fruitful and creative without regard to the moral character of what emerges from it. You insist that you do not believe that evil has less metaphysical warrant than good, that death is a part of life and a precondition for its existence, and that the necessity of taking life in order to live is a fundamental fact of our world. I agree with all these statements. But while for me, they describe both the nature of reality and of God as the ground of being, you also affirm the Goddess as personal, intelligent, loving, and compassionate, the source solely of good and not evil. Were you to leave aside this second ultimate—and

I realize that, for you, this is impossible—I do not think that our descriptions of the world would be that different.

Reconciling Personal Imagery and Impersonal Power

You end your response with several big questions concerning the present and future of the personal God of Jewish tradition (214f). How do I hold together the personal imagery so central to Jewish tradition with my concept of God as an impersonal power? If God is not really personal, should personal imagery work itself out of the picture, or does the fact that it has been so important in the Jewish past mean that it also needs to be part of the future? Let me begin by pointing out that I am hardly the first Jew to have a concept of God that seems to be in tension with the literal meanings of Scripture and liturgy. Indeed, this disconnection is probably the rule rather than exception among Jewish thinkers throughout the ages. There are many different understandings of God to be found in the Jewish tradition, and the popular image of a personal, male God above us in the heavens is only one of them. The Bible and liturgy both also contain the alternative view that God is found within the world and particularly the human heart. The great medieval philosopher Maimonides spent much of his *Guide for the Perplexed* insisting on the metaphoric nature of all anthropomorphic terms in the Bible. Kabbalists (an important group of Jewish mystics), building on a rabbinic schema, taught that the literal meaning of the biblical text was just the first of four levels, the deepest of which was the mystical layer. For them, God was the unknowable *Ein Sof* that revealed itself in ten emanations or *sefirot*, which are imaged in an extraordinary variety of ways. Hasidism, which both built on and transformed Kabbalah, goes furthest in the direction of panentheism, understanding God as found everywhere and in every moment of existence. Contemporary Jewish theologian Arthur Green, in many books and articles, lays out a Hasidically inspired nonpersonal panentheistic theology while continuing to affirm the personal language of Torah and liturgy.[12]

You find it inconsistent and unsatisfying to yoke personal images for

God with a theology that understands God as ultimately nonpersonal. You object to the fact that Tillich talks about the ground of being and the "God beyond God" in his philosophical works and then uses the personal language of the Bible in his sermons. Not only am I not troubled by this seeming incongruity but I find it religiously compelling and even necessary. Thus, you point out, quite rightly, that I frequently quote passages from the Bible that presuppose the existence of a personal God in which I do not believe! I do this both because I find the language of Torah "good to think with" and because I easily look beyond its literal meanings to the deeper messages conveyed. I repeatedly cite Isaiah's "I make weal and create woe," for example, because I believe the prophet's beautifully poetic language conveys something significant about the nature of reality. Obviously, I do not accept the idea that a personal God up in the heavens is raining down good and evil on the world, but I learn from the verse that the sacred encompasses the totality of existence in its positive and negative aspects. For me, the personal language is a rich vehicle for communicating deeper truths. It gives me something into which to sink my teeth; it challenges me to peel back the layers to uncover multiple meanings, even as I feel free to be critical of the language in which these meanings are conveyed.

I see a partial analogy between the personal language of Torah and our decision in writing this book to try to give depth and resonance to our theologies by rooting them in the stories of our lives. We could have stated what we believe in simple and direct language, and at moments in these pages, we do. But we felt that our theological ideas would make more sense to readers and would more likely stimulate their own theologizing if we made clear how these ideas emerged from concrete experiences. So, could I imagine rewriting the Bible so that God is consistently depicted as the impersonal power of life, death, and rebirth? No, because that would flatten the biblical text and make it unidimensional, just as our book would be flatter if we just

---

12. See, e.g., Arthur Green, *Radical Judaism: Rethinking God and Tradition* (New Haven: Yale University Press, 2010).

laid out our theologies without situating them in narratives. It would be like paraphrasing poetry and substituting the paraphrase for the original. Such a substitution would make it impossible to say of Torah, "Turn it and turn it again, for everything is in it," for it would lose its multidimensionality.

But I also could not imagine rewriting Torah for another reason: because Judaism is the religion of Torah. The narratives of the Torah are absolutely central to Jewish identity and are probably the most significant element binding Jews across time and space. Torah tells us who we are, and, of course, its stories are centrally about the relationship between God and the Hebrew people. God is a character in the narratives who acts, interacts, and changes. I understand these stories as *stories*—in Tillich's language, as broken myths, myths that we know to be myths yet that we continue to read and value because they are the orienting narratives in the culture. As I argued in chapter 8, I have found that these stories, precisely in their complexity and ambiguity, hold up a mirror to ourselves and our world that enables us to see ourselves more clearly. To give up personal language would be to give up *Torah*, and what would that even mean?

The case of liturgy, on the other hand, presents different possibilities because Jewish liturgy has continually evolved and changed. In fact, we might think of Torah and liturgy as representing contrasting aspects (poles is probably too strong) of Jewish tradition, one of which remains fixed even as interpretation changes, the other of which has been repeatedly challenged, transformed and updated. Broadening the images of God found in the traditional liturgy is a way of placing the Torah's picture of God in a larger framework so that it becomes just part of a wider repertory of images for thinking about God. As I have mentioned more than once, the communities in which I participate experiment freely with liturgy, using traditional prayer only as a jumping-off point for finding language and forms that reflect our experiences and beliefs more faithfully. In the context of personal prayer, I am most comfortable using nonpersonal language in speaking about and to God because it is the language that feels most "true" to me. I routinely use Marcia Falk's language of wellspring, source, and flow of life, as well her blessings evoking God only indirectly without naming or addressing God at all. But I must admit that I would not be satisfied with a Falk-only diet and that the use of personal language continues to be important to me for several reasons.

First, as I commented about the language of Torah, removing all personal images would remove too much of the powerful language of the liturgy. Certainly, there is much in the liturgy that is profoundly problematic, but it also contains soaring poetry. Like many others who have gone before me, Jewish and non-Jewish, I understand the literal layer of liturgical texts on the symbolic level. As I have already mentioned, I read personal images as metaphors evoking the many psychological states that human beings experience at different times in relation to the universe: awe, fragility, vulnerability, fear, protection, comfort, care, love (yes, love), energy, empowerment, and so on. But metaphors need a vehicle, and it is precisely the density of images—many, though not all, personal—and through them the careful construction of a certain picture of our place in the universe through richly evocative language, that brings me to experience these various emotional states. Simple description or direct invocation would not take me to the liminal space that ritual at its best can create.

Second, and this point is related, if God is present in all of creation—if the world is the body of God—then every aspect of creation has something significant to teach us about God. We are personal beings for whom relationships with other personal beings are not only constitutive of who we are but are some of the richest, deepest, most complex and difficult relationships that we have. How could we possibly not make use of the vast realm of personal experience in speaking about God? Surely God is as present in our relationships with other persons as in the wind or the seas. Naming God as lover, friend, parent, or enemy brings to the fore aspects of experience that are left entirely out of account when we use only nonpersonal imagery. This is where I agree with your point that the whole cannot be less than its parts: persons are an important part of the whole and should be represented in the whole. For this reason, I stand by my position in *Standing Again at Sinai* that, despite the dangers of anthropomorphic imagery, it appeals to places in our nature that cannot be reached by more abstract philosophical terms such as ground of being or wellspring of life.

Third, as you acknowledge in your questions to me, I am part of a community with a long history that includes people with many different theologies. Jewish liturgy has evolved over time and will continue to evolve, and I see myself as part of that evolution. At the same time, I would not want to cut myself off entirely from the Jewish past or completely disconnect the language of prayer from that of Torah. Even in the liberal community, not all Jews share my preference for nonpersonal language. While I am delighted with the move to nongendered language for God in the English of non-Orthodox prayer books, for some Jews, this has made God less vivid and real. Again, as I argued in *Standing Again at Sinai*, I am convinced that broadening our language for God to include female, male, and nongendered personal images, as well as natural imagery and direct designations such as God or the Eternal, is the strategy that makes most sense. Such a range of imagery best communicates the presence of God in all aspects of creation and clearly says that God is identical with no particular aspect of creation—including maleness. Does all this mean I have become more conservative? In the sense that I now want to conserve parts of the tradition that once I would have been ready to jettison, yes. But insofar as I am still a strong advocate for the continuing feminist transformation of Judaism—including images of God—I prefer to think that my views have become more nuanced over the years as I have come to a deeper appreciation of aspects of the tradition that my upbringing had closed off to me.

Your last question is, I know, for you the most telling: If, as I have argued, Judaism cannot survive without its stories involving a personal God, will God always be male? (215) I must acknowledge in all honesty that it will be very difficult to dislodge this image, important as it is to do so. To change the prevailing Jewish picture of God will require a two-pronged effort that involves both creating new liturgy and expanding the notion of Torah. I would like to see nonpersonal language such as Marcia Falk's incorporated into the Hebrew of mainstream prayer books, along with a full range of female and personal but nongendered images for God. Various prayer books of the Jewish Renewal movement offer the traditional blessing formula (Blessed are you Lord our God, King of the universe) in both masculine and feminine language, substituting *Shekhinah* for Lord and Queen for King. In alternating gender in this way, they reinforce the binary, while leaving intact the image of divinity as a dominant other. I believe there needs to be more experimentation with entirely fresh imagery that challenges the notion of God's power as dominance, and that may sometimes be grammatically feminine without being specifically or stereotypically female.

But new imagery will acquire weight and plausibility only as we begin to tell new stories. Jewish feminists have argued that Torah as it has come down to us is only part of the record of the relationship between God and the Jewish people because women's stories have not been told. As women create new stories and expand on traditional ones through midrash, God will be changed. I hope that, just as a broader range of images in liturgy can communicate a view of God as male, female, both and neither, so new midrash and stories can crack open and increase the reparatory of God as character. In the early 1990s, Maggie Wenig gave a sermon that has been widely reprinted entitled "God Is a Woman and She's Growing Older."[13] Representing just the kind of new narrative that we need, the sermon depicted God as an aging woman sitting at her kitchen table on Rosh Hashanah, looking through her book of memories at the accomplishments and failures of her children and longing for them to pay a visit home. For Wenig, the sermon represented just one of the many new stories we need in order to give life and substance to multiple images of God and provide some counterbalance to centuries of male language. The relationship between new narratives such as this and new liturgy

13. Maggie Wenig, "God Is a Woman, and She's Growing Older," *Reform Judaism* (Fall 1992): 26–29.

is mutually reinforcing in that using fresh images in prayer can encourage people to bring more critical eyes to the God of Torah, and new stories can generate a felt need for novel images. I do not claim that this will be an easy or a quick process, but Judaism has undergone enormous changes in the last forty years, and I see no reason to doubt that this process of change will continue.

I am aware as I reflect on your last questions of both the contradictions in my own thoughts and feelings and of your likely response. For you, it is obvious that the difficulty of dislodging the image of God as dominating and violent male other in Torah and liturgy is sufficient reason to leave a patriarchal tradition behind. For me, the situation is more complicated. On the one hand, I do not believe in a personal God; on the other, I am unwilling to eliminate all personal images from the language of prayer. On the one hand, I am highly critical of exclusively male language; on the other hand, I cannot imagine jettisoning such language entirely. On the one hand, it works for me to read the stories in the Torah and the images in the liturgy on a symbolic or metaphoric level; on the other hand, I am quite aware that doing so leaves the literal level intact to continue to do its destructive work in the world. On the one hand, I am deeply troubled by the idea of handing on to a new generation the stories and images I find so problematic; on the other hand, I want my granddaughter and her contemporaries to have access to the fullness of Jewish tradition so that they can wrestle with it in their own ways. I have no final word that can reconcile or dissolve these contradictions. They are the tensions I live with and even find productive. I can only say again that I try to hold together a love of Jewish tradition with a love of critical questions that I hope and believe will continue to push that tradition in a more open and inclusive direction.

Embodied Theology and the Flourishing of Life

Carol P. Christ and Judith Plaskow

We began this book by naming the obstacles people face when trying to speak with others about the meaning of Goddess and God in our lives. But that starting point begs a question: Why engage in a discussion that in many ways has no definite beginning and no final end? We hope our answer to that question has become clear: theologies matter because they situate us in the world and orient us as we act in it. Throughout our book, we have considered the widespread dissatisfaction with the God of traditional theologies who rules the world from outside it. We have suggested that this God no longer answers our questions about the meaning of life and does not provide the guidance we need as we face the urgent social, political, and environmental issues of our time. Traditional ideas about divine transcendence turn us away from this world, which is the place where our lives and decisions matter, while understanding divine power as omnipotence does not adequately explain the evil in the world or the nature of human freedom. In addition, traditional images of God fail to affirm diversity and difference and legitimize domination and oppression.

Grounding Theological Dialogue

Though our theological differences motivated us to write this book, in the course of working on it together, we have come to recognize that our common ground is as important as our disagreements. It is because of the convictions we share that we have been able to carry on a sustained theological conversation. If one of us had appealed to the authority of text or tradition or to personal mystical experiences as the single arbiter of theological truth, or if one of us had claimed that this life is simply a prelude to the next, our exchange would have come to an abrupt standstill. Our dialogue is possible because we share a set of interrelated ideas about the nature of life and the way to think about its significance.

We agree that the meaning and purpose of human life is to be found in this world, not another. For us, this means that divinity is to be found in this world, not the next. Whereas traditional theologians have appealed to a transcendent source of reason or revelation in justification of their assertions, we have situated the theological process in bodies, relationships, communities, histories, and the web of life. We have explored an embodied theological method based on three interrelated insights: theology begins in experience; authority is located in individuals and the communities they shape and that shape them; theologies can and must be judged by rational and ethical criteria, even when these criteria provide no final answers. Using this method to think about divinity in the world, we have found that the concepts of immanent inclusive monotheism and panentheisim provide compelling alternatives to traditional theism and exclusive male monotheism. Although we have introduced each of these issues in specific contexts in earlier chapters, here we review and discuss them together as the foundation for a wider theological conversation.

Our readers may not fully agree with either of us about the nature of Goddess or God, but we hope our embodied theological method, the assumption that the meaning and purpose of life is to be found in this world, and the concepts of inclusive monotheism and panentheism we have found useful in articulating our views of divinity will prove useful to others as they explore their own theologies in relation to the stories of their lives.

Theology in the World

The most fundamental assumption we share is that the purpose of theology is to help us to understand this world and to provide orientation in it. We believe that the world and the body are our true home; that divinity can and must be known in the world and in the body; and that this world is the one where we live out our lives and where our choices make a difference. This conviction, which underlies all of our theological insights, is so basic to our thought that we have largely taken it for granted. Yet, we acknowledge that to locate the meaning and purpose of human life in this world flies in the face of many traditional views, both Eastern and Western. Numerous traditional philosophers and theologians have argued that embodied relational experience is finally unreal or insignificant because the goal of human life is to escape the body and the finite world in order to unite with the infinite—a transcendent divinity or ultimate principle. Many Christians have been taught that they will be rewarded or punished in the next life for their actions in this one and that suffering in this world will be redeemed in heaven. For many Buddhists and Hindus, samsara—the repeating cycle of life, death, and rebirth—is ultimately unreal and unimportant when viewed from the perspective of enlightenment. But if the meaning and purpose of human life is to be found in embodied life on this earth, then many of the ways we have been taught to think about theological questions no longer make sense or provide the orientation we need.

Embodied Theology

The embodied theological method we propose as a new way of constructing theologies begins with the insight that theology is rooted in experience. While we learned to value experience through feminist criticism of theologies written by men, we know that many others, male and female, have come to recognize the importance of experience through different paths. Here, we highlight two aspects of our understanding of experience. First, while we are especially interested in women's experience as a critical principle that can disrupt traditional theological discourse, we insist that all theology begins in experience. We believe it is important that all theologians cultivate awareness of the particularities of their perspectives and make evident the experiential roots of their thought. Second, we assume that experience is embodied. It is through the body that we experience and respond to the world. This is true for all human beings. While women have been identified with the body in many cultures, and cultural devaluation of bodies and women are often linked, men also experience the world through their bodies. Revaluing the body is an important issue in contemporary religious thought, and we appreciate the work of theologians who have explored their body experiences from male and transgender perspectives.

But even as our bodily experiences seem to constitute the most irreducible and individual dimension of who we are, the body—like all experience—is socially interpreted. Cultural attitudes toward different types of bodies deeply shape our sense of our bodies in the world. This is because experience is relational. We are not—as traditional Western thought, New Age philosophies, and much of popular culture often tell us—isolated individuals who create our own reality through individual choices. We are born into a relational world through the bodies of our mothers. Without care, we could not survive into adulthood. Though we develop greater degrees of independence, freedom, and responsibility for ourselves over time, we remain part of an interdependent relational web. Traditional dualistic thinking defines women as relational and men as independent, but in fact, both men and women are shaped by relationships and exercise freedom within them. The experiencing self is molded but not determined by personal, cultural, social, and historical factors. Though we may challenge the roles and values we learn in our families, cultures, and societies, we cannot escape some relation to them even as we attempt to oppose or transform them. We are also related in positive and negative ways to history. We may choose to identify with or reject the histories we have inherited, but we are never entirely free of them. In addition, we are constituted by our participation in the whole interdependent web of life. Recognizing that we are embedded in relationships, history, culture, and nature is an important corrective in highly individualistic societies like our own that encourage people to imagine themselves as self-created.

The second insight that shapes our embodied theological method concerns the nature of revelation and authority. Texts and traditions are not handed down by divinity in any simple way, but are created by human beings situated in particular historical, gender, class, sexual, and other contexts. Similarly, all experiences, including mystical experiences felt to have revelatory status, occur in the bodies and social histories of human beings. While we may refer to texts and traditions or to revelatory experiences in support of our views, we—as individuals who are also situated in communities, societies, and histories—must decide how to interpret them. We choose which of our experiences we will make central and which we will simply acknowledge as part of a larger picture. Though we will inevitably appeal to certain strands within our traditions or to particularly powerful personal experiences in justification of the positions we reach, we must take responsibility for our views and provide reasons for them.

The idea that revelation is always received by finite individuals who interpret it through their own language and cultural constructs has been widely accepted by biblical critics and scholars of religion for more than one hundred years. Yet as we have noted, some progressive religious thinkers, including feminists, have argued that while texts and traditions contain elements that reflect the standpoints of those who wrote or received them, they still have an essential core that can be called revelatory. We reject this notion on the grounds that it is impossible to separate an authoritative core from the remainder of scriptures or traditions. The messages people find in sacred texts are affected by their standpoints: different groups within the same tradition often read their canonical texts in conflicting ways, making incompatible claims about what is central. Reflecting on this fact, we have come to understand that individuals in communities are the ones who may or may not find a meaning in inherited texts or traditions and who must make choices about which aspects of tradition to affirm or reject.

Some people appeal to their own mystical or other religious experiences to justify their theological positions. The appeal to personal revelation is more likely to be found among those who reject inherited traditions, but is not necessarily absent from the work of those who remain within them. We have both discussed moments in our lives that we consider revelatory. The peacocks in Carol's grandmother's garden, as well as the words she heard in her mind after expressing her anger at God and Goddess, and the feelings she had when her mother died, have shaped her understanding of Goddess. Judith's experience at Iguassu Falls in Brazil is central to her understanding of God. But while we draw on other-than-rational experiences in developing our theologies, we do not accept any experience without question. We recognize that revelatory experiences can break open entrenched power structures and challenge longstanding ways of thinking, causing us to reorient our lives. But we also know that many injustices and dubious ideas have been justified through appeals to revelation. Because of the complexity of these issues, we believe that it is important to reflect on revelatory moments in light of other beliefs, values, and experiences and to share them with friends and in community to see if they make sense to others. As there have been periods in both our lives when we felt quite alone in our spiritual journeys, we know that important truths can be rejected or ignored by wider communities. On the other hand, we both have learned that when we speak or write about experiences that are especially meaningful to us, our words resonate in the experiences of others. Sharing our experiences and opening ourselves to dialogue about their meaning is an important and necessary part of evaluating them.

The third insight that shapes our embodied theological method is that theologies can and must be judged by rational and ethical criteria, even though these criteria are never final. As Carol learned at Yale, we can judge theologies by the three C's of consistency, coherence, and comprehensiveness. To this list we add a fourth C, clarity. We agree that theological ideas should be clear and expressed in ways that can be understood by others. While this criterion is often ignored by theologians and philosophers who use vocabulary that is opaque even to their colleagues, we are committed to discussing difficult ideas in accessible language. The criterion of consistency means that theological ideas must hold together; what is said in one context must not conflict with what is said in another. The criterion of coherence means that theological ideas must cohere with or make sense of the world as we experience it. The criterion of comprehensiveness means that, in theory, theological ideas should be able to explain everything in the world. These criteria for judging theological statements are rational in the broadest sense. The fact that rational systems have been used to categorize women and other groups as less than human, and the rest of nature as mere matter to be used for human purposes, has caused many people, especially women, to distrust rational thinking altogether. On the other hand, every group seeking liberation has criticized previous rational paradigms and offered reasons for widening our understanding of who we value and what we consider important. We want to affirm both sides of this tension: rational consideration of ideas is critical; being able to explain and defend our ideas and judgments is part of what it means to engage with others in a common world. Yet because reasoning is a process that is situated in bodies and histories, rational arguments cannot resolve all theological disagreements.

Theologian Gordon Kaufman argued that the truth claims of theologies cannot finally be adjudicated by rational criteria because the truth of a worldview is not the same as the truth of a fact. The question, for example, of who spilled the milk on the floor is more easily answered than the question of whether or not the divine power is good or evil or a combination of both. Theological worldviews are not based on single facts but rather are paradigms or models we use to interpret and organize a great number of facts, in principle, all the facts in the world. We can discuss how some worldviews help us to make sense of the world as we know it, while others do not, but we will never find definitive proof that one worldview is right, while another is wrong. How then do we choose between different theological worldviews? As Carol has previously noted, Kaufman proposed that theologies must also be judged by criteria he called pragmatic and humanistic:

> The most a theologian can do is attempt to show that the interpretation of the facts of experience and life, which he or she has set forth, holds within it greater likelihood than any other for opening up the future into which humankind is moving—making available new possibilities, raising new hopes, enabling men and women to move toward new levels of humanness and humaneness, instead of closing off options and restricting or inhibiting growth into a fuller humanity.[1]

Responding to a challenge from feminist scholars to think about religion in relation to the threat of nuclear annihilation, Kaufman argued that the knowledge that "it is possible that we may utterly destroy not only civilization but humanity itself"[2] makes it imperative for theologians to rethink traditional theological concepts, including the idea of divine sovereignty. He argued that the belief that an omnipotent God is in control of the world discourages human beings from recognizing and taking responsibility for the possibility that

---

1. Gordon D. Kaufman, *An Essay on Theological Method* (Missoula, MT: Scholars Press, 1979 [1975]), 75.
2. Gordon D. Kaufman, *Theology for a Nuclear Age* (Philadelphia: Westminster Press, 1985), vii.

we—not God—are the ones who may destroy human and other forms of life. The theological criteria that Kaufman calls pragmatic and humanistic can also be called ethical or moral. We agree that we can and must judge theologies by ethical criteria, the most important of these being whether or not they promote the flourishing of life in the age of nuclear threat, environmental destruction, and widespread injustice. We also concur with Kaufman that traditional views of God's transcendence and omnipotence turn us away from the pressing issues facing human beings today. While we believe that theologies must be judged by ethical criteria, we recognize that these criteria are also relative to feelings, bodies, and histories. People will continue to disagree about ethical questions, for example about what constitutes justice or equality in particular situations and how best to achieve it, and about whether or not violence is ever justified.

Panentheism and Immanent Inclusive Monotheism

Thinking about divinity in the world using this embodied theological method, we both have found the concepts of panentheism and immanent inclusive monotheism helpful as we articulated alternatives to traditional theism and exclusive male monotheism. As we have discussed, pan-en-theism, meaning all is in God or God is in all, is the view that God is in the world and the world is in God—without reducing either to the other. Panentheism differs from classical theism in finding God *in* the world rather than outside or totally transcendent of it. Panentheism differs from monism and some forms of pantheism in its clear assertion that the two terms, God and the world, though related, are also separable. This means that divinity is not simply the sum total of everything that is, and that individuals other than the divinity, though finite, are real. From here, our interpretations of panentheism diverge. In Judith's version of panentheism, God is the impersonal creative principle that underlies and supports everything. This principle is in everything that has been, is, or will be in the world, yet it is more than the world in also being its ground. In Carol's view of panentheism, Goddess is a personal power of love and intelligence who feels the feelings of every individual in the world and remembers them forever. Though in the world so intimately that it is appropriate to speak of the world as the body of Goddess, Goddess also has an individual mind or consciousness.

In addition, we have both found the notion of immanent inclusive monotheism to be an important corrective to the exclusive male monotheism of biblical traditions. We have not rejected monotheism altogether because we agree with Marcia Falk and many others that there is a unity underlying the multiplicity and diversity of the world. We value her insight that the multiplicity of the world must inspire a plurality of images for divine power.[3] We name this view "immanent inclusive monotheism" in order to call attention to the presence of divinity in the world. We believe that the diversity of the world must be expressed through a wide range of anthropomorphic, zoomorphic, geomorphic, and other images for divinity.

Carol prefers to speak of and invoke the divine power as Goddess in order to affirm her own and all women's minds and bodies, and because the metaphoric power of female imagery for divinity challenges the classical dualisms that have structured the understanding of God, women, and nature in Western history. However, she considers divinity to be inclusive of all genders and recognizes the need for a wide variety of new male and transgender images that affirm the interconnection of life without sanctifying domination or violence. Carol loves the small Paleolithic and Neolithic statues of Old Europe in which the lines between humanity and nature are blurred, and divinity is bird, snake, and woman, as well as mountain and water. Judith continues to refer to divinity as God because for her the word God, although masculine, is also abstract, while the newness of female language foregrounds the personal aspects of divinity that she rejects. Judith views God as impersonal and values the natural imagery for divinity found in parts of the Bible and Jewish liturgy. Yet she also

3. Marcia Falk, "Notes on Composing New Blessings: Toward a Feminist-Jewish Reconstruction of Prayer," *Journal of Feminist Studies in Religion* 3, no. 1 (Spring 1987): 41; reprinted in *Weaving the Visions: New Patterns in Feminist Spirituality*, ed. Judith Plaskow and Carol P. Christ (San Francisco: Harper & Row, 1989), 128–38.

finds meaning in the Jewish tradition's use of personal language for God because it evokes emotional states such as gratitude and awe that she considers appropriate human responses to the universe in which we find ourselves. She believes that so long as Jews continue to use personal images for God, female images must be included among them. She is particularly attracted to the ways in which multiple images of divinity lead us to question gender and other binaries. Despite our different understandings of the nature of divinity and personal attraction to different images, we agree that an immanent inclusive theological imaginary must include images for divine power that are female and male, both and neither, personal and impersonal, and reflective of human and other than human life.

Reflecting on Our Differences

We have left our religious differences until last. We have lived so long with mutual respect for Judith's renewed commitment to Judaism and Carol's decision to leave Christianity for the Goddess, that our differences on this matter seem less important than they once did. Yet the decisions we made have shaped our lives in fundamental ways, not only determining the communities in which we situate ourselves, but also, in Carol's case, isolating her within the academy. On a daily basis and in concrete ways, our religious lives look and feel very different. Carol finds the Goddess in the contours of the volcanic island of Lesbos, in the birds, flowers, and tortoises in her garden, in icons of the Panagia (She Who Is All Holy), and in ritual connections to sacred trees, caves, mountaintops and histories on the Goddess Pilgrimage to Crete. She feels the Goddess as a loving presence in her body and all bodies, inspiring her to love and care for the world more deeply. Judith finds God in walks along the Hudson River and in the landscape of New York City, but also in the context of Jewish communal worship. She marks the Sabbath and Jewish holidays and reflects with others in her havurah and synagogue on the meaning of Jewish texts. She lives in a beautiful but indifferent universe, convinced that it is the task of human beings to discern the unity behind the apparent fragmentation of the world and to contribute to its repair.

Some feminists and other progressive thinkers have argued that those who stay in inherited traditions are brainwashed or deluded, or alternatively that those who leave them behind have not studied their traditions seriously enough, or are not sufficiently committed to community or social justice. We hope that our open exploration of our differences makes it clear that our decisions were not easily made, that neither of us is brainwashed, deluded, or ignorant of her tradition, and that we are equally committed to community and social justice. The reasons for our different decisions are many and complex and cannot be reduced to any simple explanation. We have sometimes wondered whether the Christian notion that God is love is at the root of Carol's view that Goddess is love. But if this is so, then how do we explain the fact that Carol is not moved by Jesus and the drama of sin and salvation so central to other Christians? We have also asked whether Judith is more likely to picture God as inclusive of good and evil because of the long Jewish history of arguing with God and holding God responsible for the evil in the world. Yet there are Jews who believe in a God of love, and Christians and post-Christians who cannot reconcile the notion of God's goodness with the evil in the world. We have thought about whether the notion of a personal divinity is more Christian than Jewish because Christians view God as incarnate in Jesus. But it could just as easily be argued that Christian theology has turned God into a philosophical principle, while the Jewish tradition never has lost sight of the personal God of the Bible. Finally, we have asked if it is easier to leave a dominant religion when you recognize the harm it has done to yourself and others, than to leave a minority religion with a long history of persecution. This is undoubtedly a factor in our decisions, but it does not explain why Christian feminists decide to stay in their traditions, or why Jewish women are prominent voices in the Goddess and Neo-pagan movements. Although the fact that one of us was raised Jewish and the other Christian clearly has influenced our theologies, it cannot fully explain them.

If our theological views cannot be reduced to the accidents of our birth, how do they fare when judged by the rational and ethical criteria we have articulated? Theologically, we disagree on two fundamental issues: whether divinity is personal or impersonal; and whether divinity is good or inclusive of good and evil. Is there any way to judge between our views? Does the notion of a personal or impersonal deity make more sense of our experience of the world? Carol argues that if consciousness and intelligence is a fundamental aspect of human existence and is found in varying degrees throughout the web of life, then it makes sense to think of divinity as also having consciousness and intelligence. Judith responds that the notion of a personal deity seems to her a holdover from the biblical picture of God and that she can find no evidence in her experience or reflection that a divine individual who is conscious and intelligent exists. We seem to be at a standoff here. There is some consolation in recognizing that this is a fundamental divide in the history of religions, but this insight does not resolve our disagreement. Does one or the other of our views offer better guidance in making moral decisions? Judith argues that her view places moral responsibility firmly in human hands, which is where it belongs. Carol agrees with Judith that humans and other individuals are the ones whose decisions will determine the fate of the world, and she believes that recognition of the interdependence of all things in the web of life is the ground for moral decision-making. But she would add that the love and understanding of a divine individual inspires her to love and understand the world and to promote its flourishing. Judith believes that the idea of one divine presence that enlivens and unites the universe is a sufficient basis for ethical action.

Our other major theological difference concerns whether divinity is good or inclusive of good and evil. Judith argues that if divinity is inclusive of the world, it must be inclusive of both good and evil. Carol counters that if divinity is reflective of what is best in ourselves and in other individuals in the world, then divinity must be good, not evil. Does one of our views provide better moral guidance? Carol argues that a divinity who is good inspires us to try to make the world better.

Judith replies that the notion that divinity is good leads us to idealize ourselves and to forget or deny our capacity to do evil. Carol feels that a clear focus on the world is sufficient to remind us of our capacity for evil. Does one of our views offer a more adequate account of the existence of evil in the world? Judith asserts that the idea that divinity is the ground of both good and evil provides a better answer to the problem of evil: the potential for both good and evil are inherent in the creative process that is the foundation of life. Carol believes that the world is created by a multiplicity of individuals, including the divinity. The capacity for good and evil is inherent in the creative process that structures the world. The divinity is good but not omnipotent. What we call evil is created by individuals other than the divinity. Judith replies that this view does not adequately account for the origin of evil.

One final question remains, and this has to do with the power of symbols. Carol refuses to participate in religious rituals that invoke ideas and images such as God the Father, Lord, and King, or God the Warrior, that have been and are being used to legitimate and promote violence and injustice, and she does not understand how Judith can continue to do so. Judith is also deeply disturbed by these symbols, but she thinks that they can provide starting points for grappling with the realities of injustice and violence and that they are part of a tradition that, on the whole, provides a rich, realistic, and meaningful way to live.

Is there any way to choose between our different positions? Each of us is firmly convinced that her view is clear, consistent, coherent, and comprehensive, that it takes full account of the complexity of human experience, and that it provides the moral orientation we seek. As our dialogue demonstrates, each of us has tried without success to win the other over to her perspective. In the process, we have gained a deeper appreciation of each other's views and clarified our own. This is as far as we have been able to go. We acknowledge that, in the end, we cannot know which, if either, of our theologies expresses the nature of ultimate reality or provides the crucial ethical guidance we need. Nor can we know whether there is more to be gained by working within inherited traditions to change them or by leaving them in order to discover or create alternatives. Our views have been shaped by our standpoints, including personal, communal, cultural, and historical factors, and this means that they are relative and partial. Because we cannot see into the future, we cannot know the long-term effects of either of our theological worldviews.

At the same time, we are unwilling to throw up our hands and declare that all theological perspectives are of equal value. We firmly reject the fundamentalist insistence that particular texts, traditions, or truths are universally and eternally valid. This position denies that people create and interpret traditions, and it has repeatedly led to intolerance and violence. We insist that traditional ideas of divine transcendence and omnipotence turn us from the world and our responsibility to ensure its flourishing. We concur that images of divinity must reflect the diversity of the human and other than human world. We believe that the views of divinity we have articulated make more sense of the world as we know it and provide better orientation as we face the problems of our time than the traditional views we have criticized. On the one hand, all theologies—and all worldviews—are relative to experience and limited by human finitude. On the other hand, they can be examined, evaluated, and debated in relation to their understanding of the world and the kind of life they make possible for both the self and others.

Inviting Theological Conversation

Although we hope that the two views of divinity we have articulated will have wide resonance, we recognize that there are other compelling views that we have not considered. Some people think of divinity both as unified and personal, as Carol does—and as inclusive of good and evil, as Judith does. This is one interpretation of the Great Goddess of Hinduism, and this understanding of ultimate reality has also been adopted by some Western Goddess feminists. Animists agree with both of us that all of life is sacred but do not attribute this sacredness to a single divine source. Some Native American and

African traditions are animist, and many Neo-pagans find that animism resonates with their experience of the world. Nondualists would not accept either of our conceptions of the relation of divinity and the world, because they believe that, in the final analysis, the idea of separate individuals is illusory. This is the central insight of Theravada Buddhism, which has many followers in the East and the West. Finally, polytheists agree with Judith that divinity includes good and evil, but argue that there must be more than one divine source for the multiplicity in the world. This view is found in some African and African-inspired religions, is one understanding of Hinduism, and is held by many Neo-pagans.

Recognizing the limitation of every standpoint including our own, we hope that others will be moved by the conversation we have begun here to share their own spiritual journeys and to reflect on their theological views in relation to the criteria we have proposed. Do animism, polytheism, nondualism, and other forms of monotheism call attention to important aspects of experience that neither of us has addressed? What do they contribute to the world we desire to bring into being? Where might we discover overlaps among worldviews that, on the surface, seem quite dissimilar, and where might we find unexpected divergences? What new insights might emerge if we were to engage in theological conversations at once committed and open, appreciative and critical, respectful and challenging? We will be delighted if our book inspires others to think deeply with us about how different views of the nature of divinity encourage or impede the flourishing of life on the planet we share.

List of Publications: Carol P. Christ

1970s

Book

Womanspirit Rising: A Feminist Reader in Religion. Coedited with Judith Plaskow. Harper & Row, 1979. Reissued with new preface, 1992. Japanese translation, Tokyo: Shinkyo Shuppansha, 1982. Korean translation, Daejeon, Chungnam: Chungnam University Press, 2011.

Essays

"Alternative Images of God: Communal Theology." Distributed by Conference of Women Theologians, Alverno College, 1971. Available online: https://feminismandreligion.files.wordpress.com/2015/07/alternative-images-of-god-carol-p-christ-emma-trout-1971.pdf.

"A Question for Investigation: Karl Barth's View of Women." Distributed by Conference of Women Theologians, Alverno College, 1971. Available online: https://feminismandreligion.files.wordpress.com/2015/07/a-question-for-investigation-christ.pdf.

"For the Advancement of My Career: A Form Critical Study in the Art of Acknowledgement." With Judith Plaskow Goldenberg. *Bulletin/Council on the Study of Religion*, June, 1972, 10–14.

"Shattering the Idols of Men: Theology from the Perspective of Women's Experience." With Marilyn Collins. *Reflection* (Yale Divinity School) Vol. 69, no. 4 (1972), 12–14.

"Story and Religious Sensibility." In *Teaching Religion to Undergraduates*, 202–7. New Haven: Society for Values in Higher Education, 1973.

"Explorations with Doris Lessing in Quest of the Four-Gated City." In *Women and Religion*, rev. ed., edited by Judith Plaskow and Joan Arnold Romero, 31–61. Missoula, MT: AAR & Scholars Press, 1974.

"Women on the Campus." *CrossCurrents*, Spring, 1974: 43–50.

"Whatever Happened to Theology?" *Christianity and Crisis*, May 12, 1975: 113–14.

"Feminist Studies in Religion and Literature." *Journal of the American Academy of Religion* 44, no. 2 (1976): 317–25. Republished in *Beyond Androcentrism*, edited by Rita Gross, 35–51. Missoula, MT: AAR & Scholars Press, 1977.

"Margaret Atwood: The Surfacing of Women's Spirituality." *Signs* 2, no. 2 (1976): 316–30.

"Women's Liberation and the Liberation of God." In *The Jewish Woman*, edited by Elizabeth Koltun, 11–17. New York: Schocken, 1976. Republished in Christ, *Laughter of Aphrodite*, 20–33 (1987).

"The New Feminist Theology: A Review of the Literature." *Religious Studies Review* (1977): 203–12.

"Some Comments on Jung, Jungians, and the Study of Women." *Anima* 3, no. 2 (1977): 203–12.

"Expressing Anger at God." *Anima* 5, no. 1 (1978). Republished in Christ, *Laughter of Aphrodite,* 2–33 (1987); *Women's Studies in Religion: A Multicultural Reader*, edited by Kate Bagley and Kathleen McIntosh, 101–5. Upper Saddle River, NJ: Pearson Prentice Hall, 2006.

"Heretics and Outsiders: The Struggle over Female Power in Western Religion." *Soundings* 3, no. 61 (1978): 260–80. Republished in *Feminist Frontiers: Rethinking Sex, Gender and Society*, edited by Laurel Richardson and Verta Taylor, 87–94. Reading, PA: Addison-Wesley Publishing Company, 1983; and Christ, *Laughter of Aphrodite*, 35–54 (1987).

"Why Women Need the Goddess." *Heresies (The Great Goddess Issue)* 5 (1978, reprinted 1982): 8–11. Republished in (not complete list): Christ and Plaskow, *Womanspirit Rising*, 273–87 (1979); *The Politics of Women's Spirituality*, edited by Charlene Spretnak, 71–86. New York: Doubleday, 1982; (German translation) "Warum FRAUEN die GÖTTIN brauchen." *Schlangenbrut* 8 (1985): 6–19; Christ, *Laughter of Aphrodite*, 117–32 (1987); *Current Issues and*

Enduring Questions, edited by Sylvan Barnet and Hugo Bedau, 700–713. New York: St. Martin's Press, 1993; (Spanish translation) "Por que las mujeres necisitan a la Diosa." *Del Cielo a la Tierra: Un Antologia de Teologia Feminista*, edited by Mary Judith Ress, Ute Seibert-Cuadra, Lene Sjourp, 159–74. Santiago: Sello Azul, 1994.; *Philosophy and Choice: Selected Readings from around the World*, edited by Kit Richard Christensen. Mountain View, CA: Mayfield, 2002; *Women and World Religions*, edited by Lucinda Peach. Upper Saddle River, NJ: Pearson Prentice Hall, 2002; *Sex and Gender: A Spectrum of Views*, edited by Phillip E. Devine and Celia Wolf-Devine. Belmont, CA: Wadsworth Publishing, 2003; *Traversing Philosophical Boundaries*, edited by Max O. Hallman, 583–92. 3rd ed. Belmont, CA: Wadsworth Publishing, 2006; *Women's Studies in Religion: A Multicultural Reader*, edited by Kate Bagley and Kathleen McIntosh, 163–74. Upper Saddle River: NJ: Pearson Prentice Hall, 2006; *She Rises: Why Goddess Feminism, Activism, and Spirituality?*, edited by Helen Hwang and Kaalii Kargill, 43–68. Adelanto: CA: Mago Books, 2015; *Reading Feminist Theory: From Modernity to Postmodernity*, edited by Susan Mann and Ashly Patterson, 113–15. New York: Oxford University Press, 2015; (French translation) *Feminisme et Écologie*, edited by Amandine Schneider. Paris: Cambourakis, 2016.

"Spiritual Power and Women's Experience." In Christ and Plaskow, *Womanspirit Rising*, 228–45 (1979).

"The New Scholarship on Women and Religion." *Bulletin/Council on the Study of Religion* 10, no. 1 (1979): 3–5.

"Homesick for a Woman, for Ourselves: Adrienne Rich." *Union Seminary Quarterly Review*, Fall and Winter (1979–1980): 65–74.

1980s

Books

Diving Deep and Surfacing: Women Writers on Spiritual Quest. Boston: Beacon Press, 1980; 2nd edition with new preface, 1986; 3rd edition with new afterword, 1995.

Laughter of Aphrodite: Reflections on a Journey to the Goddess. San Francisco: Harper & Row, 1987.

Weaving the Visions: New Patterns in Feminist Spirituality. Coedited with Judith
 Plaskow. San Francisco: Harper & Row, 1989.

Essays

"Another Response to 'A Religion for Women.'" *WomanSpirit* 6, no. 24 (1980):
 27–29. Republished in Christ, *Laughter of Aphrodite*, 57–81 (1987).

"A Religion for Women: A Response to Rosemary Ruether, Part II," *WomanSpirit*
 7, no. 25 (1980): 11–14. Republished in Christ, *Laughter of Aphrodite*, 57–81
 (1987).

"Images of Spiritual Power in Women's Fiction." In *The Politics of Women's
 Spirituality*, edited by Charlene Spretnak, 327–37. New York: Doubleday,
 1982.

"Symbols of Goddess and God in Feminist Theology." In *The Book of the Goddess*,
 edited by Carl Olson, 231–51. New York: Crossroad Press, 1983 Republished
 in Christ, *Laughter of Aphrodite*, 135–59 (1987).

"Feminist Liberation Theology and Yahweh as Holy Warrior: An Analysis of
 a Symbol." In *Woman's Spirit Bonding*, edited by Janet Kalven and Mary I.
 Buckley, 202–12. New York: Pilgrim Press, 1984. Republished in Christ,
 Laughter of Aphrodite, 73–81 (1987).

"Rituals with Demeter and Persephone." *WomanSpirit* 10, no. 40 (1984): 16–17.
 Republished in Christ, *Laughter of Aphrodite*, 199–205 (1987).

"Feminist Thealogy?" *Christianity and Crisis*, April 29, 1985: 161–62.

"Rituals with Aphrodite." *Anima* 12, no. 1 (1985). Republished in somewhat
 different form in Christ, *Laughter of Aphrodite*, 187–92 (1987).

"Vom Vatergott zur Muttergottin." In *Nennt uns nicht Bruder*, edited by Norbert
 Sommer, translated by Deborah Haubold, 282–87. Kreuz Verlag, 1985.

"What Are the Sources of My Theology." *Journal of Feminist Studies in Religion* 1,
 no. 1 (1985): 120–23.

"Virgin Goddess." "Lady of the Animals." In *Encyclopedia of Religion*, edited by
 Mircea Eliade. New York: Macmillan, 1986.

"Lady of the Animals" republished in *Encyclopedia of Religion*, edited by Lindsay
 Jones. 2nd ed. Macmillan, 2005.

"Daughter of the Father God." In *Daughters and Fathers*, edited by Lyda E. Boose and Betty Flowers. Baltimore: Johns Hopkins University Press, 1987. Also published in Christ, *Laughter of Aphrodite*, 93–102 (1987).

"Finitude, Death, and Reverence for Life," in Christ, *Laughter of Aphrodite*, 213–27 (1987). Also published as "Reverence for Life: The Need for a Sense of Finitude," in *Embodied Love*, edited by Paula M. Cooey, Mary Ellen Ross, and Sharon Farmer, 51–64. San Francisco: Harper & Row, 1987.

"The Initiation of an American Woman Scholar into the Symbols and Rituals of the Ancient Goddesses." *Journal of Feminist Studies in Religion* 3, no. 1 (1987): 57–66. Republished as "Carol Christ Is Initiated into Goddess Worship," *Major Problems in American Religious History*, edited by Patrick Alitt. Belmont: CA: Wadsworth, 2000, 2012.

"Toward a Paradigm Shift in the Academy and Religious Studies." In *The Impact of Feminist Research in the Academy*, edited by Christie Farnum, 314–25. Bloomington, IN: Indiana University Press, 1988. Republished in *Theory and Method in the Study of Religion*, edited by Carl Olsen. Belmont, CA: Wadsworth Publishing, 2002.

"In Praise of Aphrodite: Sexuality as Sacred." *Sacred Dimension of Women's Experience*, Elizabeth Dodson Gray, edited by Wellesley, MA: Roundtable Press, 1988, 220–27. Revised and reprinted as "In Praise of Aphrodite." *Woman of Power* 12 (1989): 70–73.

"Die Gegenwart der Gottin wird uberall wahrgenommen." In *Befreit zu Rede und Tanz,* edited by Angelika Schmidt-Biealske, 21–30. Kreuz Verlag, 1989. "Embodied Thinking: Reflections on Feminist Theological Method." *Journal of Feminist Studies in Religion* 5, no. 1 (1989): 7–15. Republished in *Constructive Theology in the Worldwide Church*, edited by William R. Barr. Grand Rapids: Eerdmans Publishing Co., 1996.

"Rethinking Theology and Nature." In Plaskow and Christ, *Weaving the Visions: New Patterns in Feminist Spirituality*, 314–25 (1989). Republished in *Reweaving the World: The Emergence of Ecofeminism*, edited by Irene Diamond and Gloria Feman Orenstein, 58–69. Sierra Club Books, 1990.

Interviews

"A Conversation with Carol Christ." Interview by Alix Evans, *Prospectus* (Vanderbilt Divinity School), 37, no. 3 (1985): 12–17.

"Darkness and Light: Visions of the Spirit," Interview by Lene Sjourup in *A Time to Weep and a Time to Sing: Faith Journeys of Women Scholars in Religion*, edited by Mary Jo Meadow and Carole A. Rayburn. Minneapolis, MN: Winston/Seabury, 1985.

1990s

Books

Odyssey with the Goddess: A Spiritual Quest in Crete. New York: Continuum, 1995.
Rebirth of the Goddess: Finding Meaning in Feminist Spirituality. Reading, MA: Addison-Wesley, 1997; paperback, New York: Routledge, 1998.

Edited Essays

"The Legacy of the Goddess: The Work of Marija Gimbutas." Six essays with introduction, coedited with Naomi R. Goldenberg. *Journal of Feminist Studies in Religion* 12, no. 2 (1996): 29–120.

Essays

"Mircea Eliade and the Feminist Paradigm Shift in Religious Studies." *Journal of Feminist Studies in Religion* 7, no. 2 (1991): 75–94. Republished in *Feminism and the Study of Religion*, edited by Darlene M. Juschka, 571–90. New York: Continuum, 2001.
"Gifts of the Goddess." *Anima* 21, no. 1 (1994): 5–9.
"Reluctant Guest at the Dionysian Mysteries." *Anima* 21, no. 1 (1994): 10–13. Republished in Christ, *Odyssey with the Goddess*, 60–69 (in slightly different form) and 39–42 (1995); and Christ, *A Serpentine Path*, forthcoming (2016).
"The Sacred Myrtle Tree." *Anima* 20, no. 2 (1994): 77–82. Republished in Christ, *Odyssey with the Goddess*, 33–35 (1995).
"The Serpentine Path (Dreams and Visions)." *SageWoman* 32 (1995): 50–53.
"'A Different World': The Challenge of the Work of Marija Gimbutas to the Dominant Worldview of Western Culture." *Journal of Feminist Studies in Religion* 12, no. 2 (1996): 53–66. Also published in *From the Realm of the*

Ancestors: Essays in Honor of Marija Gimbutas, edited by Joan Marler, 406–15. Manchester, CT: Knowledge, Ideas, and Trends, 1997.

"The Serpentine Path (Our Bodies)," *SageWoman* 33 (1996): 55–57.

"The Serpentine Path (Loving Partners)," *SageWoman* 34 (1996): 50–52.

"The Serpentine Path (Celebrating Diversity)." *SageWoman* 35 (1996): 54–56.

"The Serpentine Path (Our Children)," *SageWoman* 36 (1996): 52–54.

"The Serpentine Path (Mothers and Daughters)," *SageWoman* 37 (1997): 52–53.

"The Serpentine Path (Women and Animals)," *SageWoman* 38 (1997): 54–55.

"The Serpentine Path (Naming Ourselves)," *SageWoman* 39 (1997): 54–55.

"The Serpentine Path (Magick and Politics)," *SageWoman* 42 (1998): 58–60.

"The Serpentine Path (Ancestors)," *SageWoman* 43 (1998): 52–54.

"The Serpentine Path (Sacred Spaces, Sacred Places)," *SageWoman* 44 (1998): 54–55.

"Goddess Movement." In *Encyclopedia of Women and Religion*, edited by Serinity Young. New York: Macmillian, 1999.

"Religious Experience." In *Encyclopedia of Women and Religion*, edited by Serinity Young. New York: Macmillian, 1999.

"Jane Ellen Harrison." In *Encyclopedia of Women and Religion*, edited by Serinity Young. New York: Macmillian, 1999.

"Sappho." In *Encyclopedia of Women and Religion*, edited by Serinity Young. New York: Macmillian, 1999.

"Robert Graves." In *Encyclopedia of Women and Religion*, edited by Serinity Young. New York: Macmillian, 1999.

"The Serpentine Path (Breaking Free)," *SageWoman* 45 (1999): 54–56.

"The Serpentine Path (Welcoming the Muse)," *SageWoman* 46 (1999): 52–54.

"The Serpentine Path (Solitary Spirituality)," *SageWoman* 47 (1999): 48–50.

"The Serpentine Path (Magic in the New Millenium)," *SageWoman* 48 (1999): 48–50.

Interviews

"A Conversation between Mara Keller and Carol Christ." *The Salt Journal* 1, no. 2 (1998): 48–59.

"Life, Death, and the Goddess: The *Gnosis* Interview with Starhawk and Carol Christ." *Gnosis* 48 (1998): 28–35.

2000s

Book

She Who Changes: Re-imagining the Divine in the World. New York: Palgrave Macmillan, 2003.

Essays

"Divine Feminine." In *Encyclopedia of Feminist Theories*, edited by Lorraine Code. New York: Routledge, 2000.

"Earth/Gaia/Mother Earth." In *Encyclopedia of Feminist Theories*, edited by Lorraine Code. New York: Routledge, 2000.

"Pagan Religion, Feminist." In *Encyclopedia of Feminist Theories*, edited by Lorraine Code. New York: Routledge, 2000.

"Goddess." In *Encyclopedia of Feminist Theories*, edited by Lorraine Code. New York: Routledge, 2000.

"Goddess." In *Contemporary American Religion*, edited by Wade C. Roof. New York: Macmillan, 2000.

"'If You Do Not Love Life': Spirituality and Ethics in the New Millennium." *Concilium* 288 (The New Millennium issue) (2000) (published in five languages).

"Response: Feminist Theology and Religious Diversity" (Roundtable). *Journal of Feminist Studies in Religion* 16, no. 2 (2000): 79–84.

"The Serpentine Path (Welcoming Abundance)," *SageWoman* 49 (2000): 48–49.

"The Serpentine Path (Our Wise Blood)," *SageWoman* 50 (2000): 48–50.

"The Serpentine Path (The Crone)," *SageWoman* 51 (2000): 47–48.

"The Serpentine Path (Food)," *SageWoman* 52 (2001): 45–47.

"The Serpentine Path (Body and Soul)," *SageWoman* 53 (2001): 51–52.

"The Serpentine Path (Peace and Power)," *SageWoman* 54 (2001): 51–52.

"The Serpentine Path (Light and Shadow)," *SageWoman* 55 (2001): 53–56.

"Weaving the Fabric of Our Lives." In *Women, Gender, and Religion*, edited by Elizabeth A. Castelli and Rosamond C. Rodman, 34–39. New York: Palgrave, 2001.

"Reweaving." In *Women, Gender, and Religion*, edited by Elizabeth A. Castelli and Rosamond C. Rodman, 46–48. New York: Palgrave, 2001.

"Can We Ever Go to War with God on Our Side?" Guest editorial. *Journal of Feminist Studies in Religion* 18, no. 2 (2002): 79–82.

"Feminist Imaginings of the Divine and Hartshorne's God: One and the Same?" *Feminist Theology* 11, no. 1 (2002): 99–115.

"Feminist Theology as Post-traditional Theology." In *The Cambridge Companion to Feminist Theology*, edited by Susan Frank Parsons, 79–96. Cambridge: Cambridge University Press, 2002.

"The Serpentine Path (Coming Home)," *SageWoman* 56 (2002): 53–56.

"The Serpentine Path (Grounding and Centering), *SageWoman* 60 (2003): 61–64.

"The Serpentine Path (Sisterhood)," *SageWoman* 61 (2003): 55–57.

"The Serpentine Path (Courage)," *SageWoman* 62 (2003): 57–59.

"The Serpentine Path (The Journey)," *SageWoman* 63 (2003): 55–57.

"The Serpentine Path (Our Sister Moon)," *SageWoman* 57 (2002): 51–53.

"The Serpentine Path (Sexuality)," *SageWoman* 58 (2002): 53–57.

"The Serpentine Path (The Sea)," *SageWoman* 59 (2002): 59–62.

"What Process Philosophy Means to Me." *Process Perspectives* 25, no. 1 (2002): 14–15.

"Carol P. Christ: Leader of the Goddess Movement" (autobiographical reflections). In *Transforming the Faith of Our Fathers: Women Who Changed American Religion*, edited by Anne Braude, 97–113. New York: Palgrave, 2004.

"The Feast Day of St. Brigid." *Women's Journal* 11, no. 1 (Spring 2004): 13–14, 19–22.

"The Serpentine Path (Prayer and Invocation)," *SageWoman* 64 (2004): 55–57.

"The Serpentine Path (Truth and Beauty)," *SageWoman* 65 (2004): 49–50.

"Whose History Are We Writing? Reading Feminist Texts with a Hermeneutic of Suspicion." *Journal of Feminist Studies in Religion* 20, no. 2 (2004): 59–82.

"Does Feminism Need a Metaphysic? Toward a Feminist Process Paradigm." *Feminist Theology* 13, no. 3 (2005): 281–99.

"Musings on the Goddess and Her Cultured Despisers." *Feminist Theology* 13, no. 2 (2005): 143–49.

"Re-imaginando o divino no mundo como ela que muda." Translated by Monika Ottermann. "Re-imaging the divine in the world as she who changes."

(published in Spanish and English) *Mandragora* 11, no. 11 (2005): 16–28; 29–39.

"SIE verwandelt alles, was SIE berührt, und alles, was SIE berührt, verändert sich: Feministische Spiritualität im Lichte der Prozessphilosophie." *Schlangenbrut* 89 (2005): 19–22.

"Ecofeminism and Process Philosophy." *Feminist Theology* 14, no. 3 (2006): 289–310.

"Humanity in the Web of Life." With Kathryn Rountree. *Environmental Ethics* 28, no. 2 (2006): 185–200.

"Community and Ambiguity: A Response from a Companion in the Journey." *Journal of Feminist Studies in Religion* 23, no. 1 (2007): 29–34.

"Love in Process Philosophy." In *Encyclopedia of Love in World Religions*, edited by Yudit K. Greenberg. Santa Barbara, CA: ABC-CLIO, 2007.

"The Road Not Taken: The Rejection of Goddesses in Judaism and Christianity." In *Prophets, Patriarchs, and Other Villains*, edited by Lisa Isherwood, 22–36. Sheffield, UK: Equinox, 2007.

"Theological and Political Implications of Re-imagining the Divine as Female." *Political Theology* 8, no. 2 (2007): 157–70.

"'We Are Nature': Environmental Ethics in a New Key." *Creative Transformation* 16, no. 1 (2007): 2–8.

"Ecofeminism." *Handbook of Whiteheadian Process Thought.* Vol. 1, edited by Michael Weber and Will Desmond, 67–97. Frankfurt: Ontos Verlag, 2008.

"Embodied, Embedded Mysticism: Affirming the Self and Others in a Radically Interdependent World." *Journal of Feminist Studies in Religion* 24, no. 2 (2008): 159–67.

"We Are Nature: Environmental Ethics in a Different Key." In *Researching with Whitehead: System and Adventure*, edited by Franz Riffert and Hans-Joachim Sander, 481–502. Frieburg: Verlag Karl Alber, 2008.

Interview

"Interview with Carol P. Christ." By Ruth Mantin. *Feminist Theology* 11, no .1 (2002): 116–24.

2010s

Book

Goddess and God in the World: Conversations in Embodied Theology. With Judith Plaskow. Minneapolis: Fortress Press, 2016.

A Serpentine Path: Mysteries of the Goddess. (Revision of *Odyssey with the Goddess*). Cleveland, OH: Far Press, 2016.

Blog

Regular contributor to *Feminism and Religion*, beginning August 11, 2011. More than two hundred short essays as of spring 2016 on feminist theology, ethics, Goddess spirituality, ancient Crete, matriarchy, Greek folklore and religion, Green politics. Archive: http://feminismandreligion.com/author/ carolpchrist/.

Essays

"Whatever Happened to Goddess and God-She? Why Do Jews and Christians Still Pray to a Male God?" *European Society of Women in Theological Research Journal* 18 (2010): 43–60.

"The Last Dualism: Life and Death in Goddess Feminist Theology." *Journal of Feminist Studies in Religion* 27, no. 1 (2011): 129–45.

"Re-Imaging Goddess/God." In Creating Women's Theology: A Movement Engaging Process Thought, edited by Monica A. Coleman, Nancy R. Howell, and Helene Tallon Russell, 194–209. Eugene, OR: Pickwick Publications, 2011.

"Remembering Merlin Stone." *Goddess Thealogy* 1, no. 1 (2011), http://www.academia.edu/1193748/Goddess_Thealogy_An_International _Journal_for_the_Study_of_the_Divine_Feminine_Vol_1_No._1.1_A4_ December_2011. Also available: http://feminismandreligion.com/2012/02/ 20/remembering-merlin-stone-1931-2011-by-carol-p-christ-2/.

"Why Women, Men and Other Living Things Still Need the Goddess: Remembering and Reflecting 35 Years Later." *Feminist Theology* 20, no. 3 (2012): 242–55.

"Do We Still Need the *Journal of Feminist Studies in Religion?*" (Roundtable). *Journal of Feminist Studies in Religion* 30, no. 2 (2014): 139–41.

"Finding Ancestor Connection via the Internet." In *Feminism and Religion in the 21st Century*, edited by Gina Messina-Dysert and Rosemary Radford Ruether, 88–98. New York: Routledge, 2014, 88–98.

"Two Feminist Views of Goddess and God." With Judith Plaskow. *Tikkun* (2014): 29–32, 65–66.

"Foreword." In *The Mago Way: Re-discovering the Great Goddess from East Asia*, Vol. 1, by Helen Hye-Sook Hwang. Adelanto, CA: Mago Books, 2015, ix–xvii.

"The Life and Work of a Feminist Theologian." In *Foremothers of the Women's Spirituality Movement: Elders and Visionaries*, edited by Miriam Robbins Dexter and Vicki Noble. Amherst, NY: Teneo, 2015, 29–37.

"Can You Kill the Spirit?" and "She Who Changes." In *Jesus, Muhammad, and the Goddess,* edited by Trista Hendern, Pat Daly, and Noor-un-nisa Gretasdottir. USA: Createspace, 2016, 135–38, 263–64. Available online: http://feminismandreligion.com/2015/03/16/can-you-kill-the-spirit-what-happened-to-female-imagery-for-god-in-christian-worship-by-carol-p-christ/; http://feminismand religion.com/2012/05/21/she-who-changes-by-carol-p-christ/.

"A New Definition of Patriarchy: Control of Female Sexuality, Private Property, and War." *Feminist Theology* 23, no. 3 (2016): 1–12.

"Goddess Is the Intelligent Embodied Love That Is in All Being." In *New Reflections: Commemorating Two Decades of* Feminist Theology *at BISFT*, edited by Agnes Rafferty. Winchester, UK: ITP Publications, 2016.

"Environmental Activism in the Body of the Goddess." In *She Rises*, Vol. 2, edited by Helen Hye-Sook Hwang, Mary Ann Beavis, and Nicole Shaw. Adelanto, CA: Mago Books, 2016, forthcoming.

"Remembering Rita Gross." *American Buddhist Women.* Sakyadhita USA, No. 9, Winter 2016. Web, http://americanbuddhistwomen.com/winter-2016.

"The Mother of All the Living and Societies of Peace." In *Re-booting the Sacred Feminine for the 21st Century* (tentative title), edited by Karen Tate. Alesford, UK: Changemakers Press, 2017, forthcoming.

Interview

"From Scotland to the Aegean Sea: Diving Deep into Conversation with Carol Christ." By E.C. Erdmann. *Goddess Thealogy* 1, no. 1 (2011). Available online: http://www.academia.edu/1193748/Goddess_Thealogy_An_International _Journal_for_the_Study_of_the_Divine_Feminine_Vol_1_No._1.1_A4_ December_2011.

"Across the Generations: Interview with Carol P. Christ." By Elizabeth Ursic. *Journal of Feminist Studies in Religion*: forthcoming.

List of Publications: Judith Plaskow

1970s

Books

Women and Religion: 1972. Missoula, MT: American Academy of Religion, 1972. Revised edition, coedited with Joan Arnold Romero. Missoula, MT: AAR and the Scholars Press, 1974.

Womanspirit Rising: A Feminist Reader on Religion. Coedited with Carol P. Christ. San Franciso: Harper & Row, 1979. Reissued with new preface, 1992. Japanese translation, Tokyo: Shinkyo Shuppansha, 1982. Korean translation, Daejeon, Chungnam: Chungnam University Press, 2011.

Articles

"The Coming of Lilith: Toward a Feminist Theology." In *Women Exploring Theology at Grailville.* Church Women United, 1972. Reprinted in Christ and Plaskow, *Womanspirit Rising,* 198–209 (1979), and in *Women in a Male Church* (German), edited by Bernadette Brooten and Norbert Greinacher, 245–58. Kaiser Grunewald, 1982. Also in Plaskow and Berman, *The Coming of Lilith,* 23–34 (2005).

"For the Advancement of My Career: A Form-Critical Study in the Art of Acknowledgment." With Carol P. Christ. *Bulletin of the Council on the Study of Religion* 3 (1972): 10–14.

"The Jewish Feminist: Conflict in Identities." *Response* 18 (Summer 1973): 11–18. Reprinted in *The Jewish Woman: New Perspectives,* edited byElizabeth Koltun,

3–10. New York: Schocken Books, 1976. Also in *The Ethnic American Woman*, edited by Edith Blicksilver, 190–95. Dubuque, IA: Kendall/Hunt, 1978; and in Plaskow and Berman, *The Coming of Lilith*, 31–32.

"The Coming of Lilith." In *Religion and Sexism: Images of Women in the Jewish and Christian Traditions*, edited by Rosemary Ruether, 341–43. New York: Simon and Schuster, 1974. Reprinted in *Womanguides: Readings Toward a Feminist Theology*, edited by Rosemary Ruether, 72–74. Boston: Beacon, 1985. Also in *Four Centuries of Jewish Women's Spirituality*, edited by Ellen Umansky and Dianne Ashton, 215–16. Boston: Beacon, 1992.

"Carol Christ on Margaret Atwood: Some Theological Reflections." *Signs: Journal of Women in Culture and Society* 2 (Winter 1976): 331–39.

"Christian Feminism and Anti-Judaism." *Cross Currents* 33 (Fall 1978): 306–9. Reprinted as "Blaming the Jews for the Birth of Patriarchy" in *Lilith* 7 (1980): 11–12. Also in *Nice Jewish Girls*, edited by Evelyn Torton Beck, 298–302. Boston: Persephone, 1982. And in Plaskow and Berman, *The Coming of Lilith*, 89–93 (2005).

"The Feminist Transformation of Theology." In *Beyond Androcentrism*, edited by Rita Gross, 23–33. Missoula, MT: The Scholars Press, 1978.

"Bringing a Daughter into the Covenant." In Christ and Plaskow, *Womanspirit Rising*, 179–84 (1979).

1980s

Books

Sex, Sin, and Grace: Women's Experience and the Theologies of Reinhold Niebuhr and Paul Tillich. Washington, DC: University Press of America, 1980.

Weaving the Visions: New Patterns in Feminist Spirituality, coedited with Carol P. Christ. San Francisco: Harper & Row, 1989.

Articles

"Male Theology and the Experience of Women." In *The Challenge of Feminism to Theology* (Italian), edited by Mary Hunt and Rosino Gibellini, 100–125.

Querinina, 1980. Reprinted in English in Plaskow and Berman, *The Coming of Lilith*, 40–55 (2005).

"Women as Body: Motherhood and Dualism." *Anima* 8 (Winter 1981/1982): 56–67.

"Language, God, and Liturgy: A Feminist Perspective." *Response* 44 (Spring 1983): 3–14.

"The Right Question Is Theological." In *On Being a Jewish Feminist: A Reader*, edited by Susannah Heschel, 223–33. New York: Schocken Books, 1983. Preprinted as "God and Feminism" in *Menorah: Sparks of Jewish Renewal* (February 1982): 1–2, 6–8. Reprinted in Plaskow and Berman, *The Coming of Lilith*, 56–64 (2005).

"Anti-Semitism: The Unacknowledged Racism." In *Women's Spirit Bonding*, edited by Janet Kalven and Mary Buckley, 89–96. New York: Pilgrim, 1984. Reprinted in slightly different form in *Women's Consciousness, Women's Conscience: A Reader in Feminist Ethics*, edited by Barbara Andolsen, Christine Gudorf, and Mary Pellauer, 675–84. Minneapolis: Winston, 1985. And in Plaskow and Berman, *The Coming of Lilith*, 94–99 (2005).

"In Memory of Her: A Symposium on an Important Book." *Anima* 10 (Spring 1984): 98–102.

"Standing Again at Sinai: Jewish Memory from a Feminist Perspective." *Tikkun* 1 (November 1986): 28–34. Reprinted in Plaskow and Christ, *Weaving the Visions*, 39–50 (1989).

"The Wife/Sister Stories: Dilemmas of a Jewish Feminist." In *Speaking of Faith: Global Perspectives on Women, Religion, and Social Change*, edited by Diana Eck and Devaki Jain, 23–33. Philadelphia: New Society Press, 1986.

"Christian Feminist Anti-Judaism: Some New Considerations." *New Conversations* 9 (Spring 1987): 23–26.

"God: Some Feminist Questions." *Sh'ma* 17 (January 9, 1987): 38–40. And in Plaskow and Berman, *The Coming of Lilith*, 121–23 (2005).

"*Halakha* as a Feminist Issue." *The Melton Journal* 22 (Fall 1987): 3–5, 25.

"Religion and Gender: The Critical and Constructive Tasks." *The Iliff Review* 45 (Fall 1988): 3–13.

"Divine Conversations." *Tikkun* 4 (November/December 1989): 18–20, 85.

"Toward a New Theology of Sexuality." In *Twice Blessed: On Being Lesbian, Gay, and Jewish*, edited by Christie Balka and Andy Rose, 145–51. Boston: Beacon, 1989. Reprinted in *Redefining Sexual Ethics*, edited by Susan Davies and Eleanor Haney, 309–19. Cleveland: Pilgrim, 1991.

1990s

Book

Standing Again at Sinai: Judaism from a Feminist Perspective. San Francisco: Harper & Row, 1990. German translation, Luzern: Edition Exodus, 1992; Dutch edition, Amersfoort/Leuven: De Horstink, 1992.

Articles

"Beyond Egalitarianism." *Tikkun* 5 (November/December 1990): 79–80. Reprinted in *The Jewish Philosophy Reader,* edited by Daniel Frank, Oliver Leaman, and Charles Manekin, 519–22. New York: Routledge, 2000. Also in *Tikkun: An Anthology*, edited by Michael Lerner, 272–74. Oakland and Jerusalem: Tikkun Books, 1992. And in Plaskow and Berman, *The Coming of Lilith*, 128–33 (2005).

"Feminist Anti-Judaism and the Christian God." *Neukirchener Theology Journal: Church and Israel* 5 (German) (January 1990): 9–25. Reprinted in the *Journal of Feminist Studies in Religion* 7 (Fall 1991): 99–108. And in Plaskow and Berman, *The Coming of Lilith*, 100–109 (2005).

"Feminist Reflections on the State of Israel." In *Beyond Occupation: American Jewish, Christian, and Palestinian Voices for Peace,* edited by Rosemary Ruether and Marc Ellis, 88–98. Boston: Beacon, 1990.

"'It Is Not in Heaven': Feminism and Religious Authority." *Tikkun* 5 (March/April 1990): 39–40. In Plaskow and Berman, *The Coming of Lilith*, 124–27 (2005).

"Up against the Wall." *Tikkun* 5 (July/August 1990): 25–26.

"Facing the Ambiguity of God." *Tikkun* 6 (September/October 1991): 70, 96. Reprinted in Frank, Leaman, and Manekin, *The Jewish Philosophy Reader*, 510–12 (2000). And in Plaskow and Berman, *The Coming of Lilith*, 134–37 (2005).

"Jewish Anti-Paganism." *Tikkun* 6 (March/April 1991): 66–67. In Plaskow and Berman, *The Coming of Lilith*, 110–13 (2005).

"Transforming the Nature of Community: Toward a Feminist People of Israel." In *After Patriarchy: Feminist Transformations of the World Religions,* edited by P. Cooey, W. Eakin, and J. McDaniel, 87–105. Maryknoll, NY: Orbis Books, 1991.

"About Men." *Tikkun* 7 (July/August 1992): 51, 76. In Plaskow and Berman, *The Coming of Lilith*, 143–46.

"Appropriation, Reciprocity, and Issues of Power." *Journal of Feminist Studies in Religion* 8 (Fall 1992): 105–10.

"Creating a Feminist Judaism." *Manna* 37 (Autumn 1992), supplement.

"First Year Faculty." In *Guide to the Perplexing: A Survival Manual for Women in Religious Studies*, 45–67. Atlanta: Scholars Press, 1992.

"Promotion and Tenure." In *Guide to the Perplexing: A Survival Manual for Women in Religious Studies*, 45–67. Atlanta: Scholars Press, 1992.

"The Problem of Evil." *Reconstructionist* 57 (Spring 1992): 17–19.

"What's Wrong with Hierarchy?" *Tikkun* 7 (January/February 1992): 65–66. In Plaskow and Berman, *The Coming of Lilith,* 138–42 (2005).

"Anti-Judaism in Feminist Christian Interpretation." In *Searching the Scriptures: A Feminist Introduction*, edited by Elisabeth Schussler Fiorenza, 117–29. New York: Crossroad, 1993.

"Burning in Hell Conservative Movement Style." *Tikkun* 8 (May/June 1993): 49–50.

"Feminist Judaism and Repair of the World." In *Ecofeminism and the Sacred*, edited by Carol J. Adams, 70–83. New York: Continuum, 1993. Reprinted in Spanish in *From Heaven to Earth: An Anthology of Feminist Theology*, edited by Mary Judith Ress, 261–77. Santiago, Chile: Sello Azul, 1994.

"We Are Also Your Sisters: The Development of Women's Studies in Religion." *Women's Studies Quarterly* 21 (Spring/Summer 1993): 9–21. Reprinted in *Looking Back, Moving Forward: 25 Years of Women's Studies History. Women's Studies Quarterly* 25 (Spring/Summer 1997): 199–211.

"The Year of the Agunah." *Tikkun* 8 (September/October 1993): 52–53. In Plaskow and Berman, *The Coming of Lilith*, 147–51 (2005). Reprinted in Tirosh-Samuelson and Hughes, *Judith Plaskow: Feminism, Theology, and Justice*, 83–95. (2014).

"Dealing with the Hard Stuff." *Tikkun* 9 (September/October 1994): 57–58. In Plaskow and Berman, *The Coming of Lilith*, 114–17 (2005).

"Jewish Theology in Feminist Perspective." In *Feminist Perspectives on Jewish Studies*, edited by Lynn Davidman and Shelly Tenenbaum, 62–84. New Haven: Yale University Press, 1994. In Plaskow and Berman, *The Coming of Lilith*, 65–80 (2005); and in Tirosh-Samuelson and Hughes, *Judith Plaskow: Feminism, Theology, and Justice*, 45–67 (2014).

"Lesbian and Gay Rights: Asking the Right Questions." *Tikkun* 9 (March/April 1994): 31–32.

"Embodiment and Ambivalence: A Jewish Feminist Perspective." In *Embodiment, Morality, and Medicine*, edited by Lisa Sowle Cahill and Margaret Farley, 23–36. Dordrecht, Netherlands: Kluwer Academic Publishers, 1995.

"Im and B'li: Women in the Conservative Movement." *Tikkun* 10 (January/February 1995): 55–56.

"Sex and Yom Kippur." *Tikkun* 10 (September/October 1995): 71–72.

"Spirituality and Politics: Lessons from B'not Esh." *Tikkun* 10 (June/July 1995): 31–32, 85.

"What's in a Name? Exploring the Dimensions of What 'Feminist Studies in Religion' Means." *Journal of Feminist Studies in Religion* 11 (Spring 1995): 132–36. Reprinted in *Feminism in the Study of Religion: A Reader*, edited by Darlene Juschka, 405–10. New York: Continuum, 2001.

"Covenant." In *Dictionary of Feminist Theologies*, edited by Letty Russell and Sharon Clarkson, 59–60. Louisville, KY: Westminster John Knox, 1996.

"Feminist Theologies, Jewish." In *Dictionary of Feminist Theologies*, edited by Letty Russell and Sharon Clarkson, 102–6. Louisville, KY: Westminster John Knox, 1996.

"Progressive Homophobia." *Tikkun* 11 (March/April 1996): 65–67.

"Critique and Transformation: A Jewish Feminist Journey." In *Lifecycles: Jewish Women on Biblical Themes in Contemporary Life*, edited by Rabbi Debra Orenstein and Rabbi Jane Litman, 94–103. Woodstock, VT: Jewish Lights, 1997.

"Feminist Theology." In *The Sh'ma and Its Blessings.* Vol. 1 of *My People's Prayerbook: Traditional Prayers, Modern Commentaries*, edited by Lawrence Hoffman, 29 and passim. Woodstock, VT: Jewish Lights, 1997.

"Jewish Feminist Thought." In *History of Jewish Philosophy,* edited by Daniel H. Frank and Oliver Leaman, 885–92. New York: Routledge, 1997.

"Judith Plaskow's Un-orthodox Take on the Feminism and Orthodoxy Conference." *Lilith* 22 (Summer 1997): 4–5.

"Sexuality and *Teshuva*: Leviticus 18." In *Beginning Anew: A Woman's Companion to the High Holy Days,* edited by Judith Kates and Gail Reimer, 290–302. New York: Simon and Schuster, 1997. In Plaskow and Berman, *The Coming of Lilith,* 165–77 (2005).

"Spirituality." In *Jewish Women in America: An Historical Encyclopedia,* edited by Paula Hyman and Deborah Dash Moore, 1302–6. New York: Routledge, 1997.

"Indulgences for the Millennium." *Springfield Union News.* December 26, 1998.

"Innocent Victims." Religious News Service. May 1998.

"Sexual Orientation and Human Rights: A Progressive Jewish Perspective." In *Sexual Orientation and Human Rights in American Religious Discourse*, edited by Saul M. Olyan and Martha C. Nussbaum, 29–45. New York: Oxford University Press, 1998. In Plaskow and Berman, *The Coming of Lilith,* 178–92 (2005).

"The Academy as Real Life: New Participants and Paradigms in the Study of Religion." *Journal of the American Academy of Religion* 67 (September 1999): 521–38. Reprinted in *Women, Gender, Religion: A Reader*, edited by Elizabeth A. Castelli with Rosamund C. Rodman, 531–45. New York: Palgrave, 2001. Also in Tirosh-Samuelson and Hughes, *Judith Plaskow: Feminism, Theology, and Justice*, 27–43 (2014).

"The Danger of Women's Voices." *Springfield Union News.* July 24, 1999.

"Lilith Revisited." In *Eve & Adam: Jewish, Christian, and Muslim Readings on Genesis and Gender*, edited by Kristen E. Kvam, Linda S. Schearing, and Valerie H. Ziegler, 425–30. Bloomington, IN: Indiana University Press, 1999. In Plaskow and Berman, *The Coming of Lilith,* 81–86 (2005).

2000s

Books

The Coming of Lilith: Essays on Feminism, Judaism, and Sexual Ethics, 1972-2003. Edited with Donna Berman. Boston: Beacon Press 2005.

Heterosexism in Contemporary World Religion: Problem and Prospect. Coedited with Marvin Ellison. Cleveland, Pilgrim, 2007.

Articles

"Decentering Sex: Rethinking Jewish Sexual Ethics." In *God Forbid: Religion and Sex in American Public Life*, edited by Kathleen Sands, 23–41. New York: Oxford University Press, 2000.

"Expanding the Jewish Feminist Agenda." *Sh'ma* 30, no. 568 (January 2000): 12. In Plaskow and Berman, *The Coming of Lilith*, 157–58 (2005).

"Judaism and Feminism." In *Encyclopedia of Feminist Theories*, edited by Lorraine Code, 305–6. New York: Routledge, 2000.

"Authority, Resistance, and Transformation: Jewish Feminist Reflections on Good Sex." In *Good Sex: Feminist Perspectives from the World's Religions*, edited by Patricia Jung, Mary Hunt, and Radhika Balakrishnan, 127–39. New Brunswick, NJ: Rutgers University Press, 2001. Reprinted in *Body and Soul: Rethinking Sexuality as Justice Love*, edited by Marvin Ellison and Sylvia Thorson-Smith, 45–60. Cleveland: Pilgrim, 2003. Also in slightly different form in *Best Jewish Writing 2002*, edited by Michael Lerner, 189–98. New Jersey: Jossey-Bass, 2002. In Plaskow and Berman, *The Coming of Lilith*, 193–205 (2005); and in Tirosh-Samuelson and Hughes, *Judith Plaskow: Feminism, Theology, and Justice*, 69–82 (2014).

"God/Goddess in Jewish Feminist Perspective." In *Wordbook of Feminist Theology* (German), edited by Elisabeth Gossmann, et al, 254–57. Gutersloh: Gutersloher Verlagshaus, 2002.

"Whose Initiative? Whose Faith?" *Journal of the American Academy of Religion* 70 (December 2002): 864–67.

"Breaking the Silence about Class" and "Remembering Jewish Feminist Struggles." In *The Women's Seder Sourcebook: Rituals and Readings for Use at the Passover Seder*, edited by Rabbi Sharon Cohen Anisfeld, Tara Mohr, and Catherine Spector, 85, 172–73. Woodstock, VT: Jewish Lights, 2003.

"The Continuing Value of Separatism." In *The Women's Passover Companion: Women's Reflections on the Festival of Freedom*, edited by Rabbi Sharon Cohen Anisfeld, Tara Mohr, and Catherine Spector, 9–13. Woodstock, VT: Jewish Lights, 2003. In Plaskow and Berman, *The Coming of Lilith,* 159–62 (2005).

"Critical Theology and Jewish Sexual Ethics." In *Toward a New Heaven and a New Earth: Essays in Honor of Elisabeth Schüssler Fiorenza*, edited by Fernando Segovia, 487–97. Maryknoll, NY: Orbis, 2003.

"Dealing with Difference Without and Within." *Journal of Feminist Studies in Religion* 19 (Spring 2003): 91–95.

"Judith Plaskow: Jewish Feminist Theologian." In *Transforming the Faiths of Our Fathers: Women Who Changed American Religion*, edited by Ann Braude, 219–32. New York: Palgrave Macmillan, 2004.

"Why We're Not Getting Married." With Martha Ackelsberg. *Lilith* 29 (Fall 2004): 48. Reprinted in *Women: Images and Realities, A Multicultural Anthology*, edited by Amy Kesselman, Lily McNair, and Nancy Schniedewind, 274–75. New York: McGraw Hill, 2008.

"Womanist/Jewish Feminist Dialogue." *Union Seminary Quarterly Review* 58 (2004): 216–18.

"A Short History of the *JFSR*." *Journal of Feminism Studies in Religion* 21 (Fall 2005): 103–6.

"Three Steps Forward, Two Steps Back." *Nashim: A Journal of Jewish Women's Studies and Gender Issues* 9 (Spring 2005): 184–90.

"Jewish Feminism." In *Encyclopedia of Women and Religion in North America*, 3 vols., edited by Rosemary Skinner Keller and Rosemary Radford Ruether, 3:1220–29. Bloomington, IN: Indiana University Press, 2006.

"*The Coming of Lilith*: A Response." *Journal of Feminist Studies in Religion* 23 (Spring 2007): 34–41.

"Dismantling the Gender Binary within Judaism: The Challenge of Transgender to Compulsory Heterosexuality." In Plaskow and Ellison, *Heterosexism in Contemporary World Religion*, 13–36 (2007). Reprinted in *Balancing on the Mechitza: Transgender in the Jewish Community*, edited by Noach Dzmura, 187–210. Berkeley: North Atlantic Books, 2010.

"Feminist Theology." In *Jewish Women: A Comprehensive Historical Encyclopedia*, edited by Paula E. Hyman and Dalia Ofer. Jerusalem: Shalvi Publishing Ltd., 2007. CD-ROM and http://jwa.org/encyclopedia.

"Spirituality in the United States." In *Jewish Women: A Comprehensive Historical Encyclopedia*, edited by Paula E. Hyman and Dalia Ofer. Jerusalem: Shalvi Publishing Ltd., 2007. CD-ROM and http://jwa.org/encyclopedia.

"Gender Theory and Gendered Realities—An Exchange between Tamar Ross and Judith Plaskow." *Nashim: A Journal of Jewish Women's Studies and Gender Issues* 13 (Spring 2007): 207–51.

"Remapping the Road from Sinai." With Elliot Rose Kukla. *Sh'ma* 38, no. 646 (December 2007): 2–5. Reprinted in *Balancing on the Mechitza: Transgender in the Jewish Community*, edited by Noach Dzmura, 134–40. Berkeley: North Atlantic Books, 2010.

"Beyond Same-Sex Marriage: Social Justice and Sexual Values in Judaism." With Martha Ackelsberg. In *Righteous Indignation: A Jewish Call for Justice*, edited by Or N. Rose, Jo Ellen Green Kaiser, and Margie Klein, 195–205. Woodstock, VT: Jewish Lights, 2008.

"Contemporary Reflection" on *Vayeira*, *Yitro*, *Acharei Mot*, and *Ki Teitzei*. In *The Torah: A Women's Commentary*, edited by Tamara Cohn Eskenazi and Andrea L. Weiss, 107–8, 423–24, 696–97, 1187–88. New York: URJ, 2008.

"Embodiment, Elimination, and the Role of Toilets in Struggles for Social Justice." *Crosscurrents* 58 (Spring 2008): 51–64.

"Calling All Theologians." In *New Jewish Feminism: Probing the Past, Forging the Future*, edited by Rabbi Elyse Goldstein, 3–11. Woodstock, VT: Jewish Lights, 2009.

"Foreword." In *Ladies and Gents: Public Toilets and Gender*, edited by Olga Gershenson and Barbara Penner, vii–x. Philadelphia: Temple University Press, 2009.

"Foreword." In *Torah Queeries: Weekly Commentaries on the Hebrew Bible*, edited by Gregg Drinkwater, Joshua Lesser, and David Shneer, xi–xii. New York: New York University Press, 2009.

2010s

Book

Judith Plaskow: Feminism, Theology, and Justice. Edited by Hava Tirosh-Samuelson and Aaron W. Hughes. Leiden and Boston: Brill, 2014. The book consists of four of my essays, an interview with me, and an essay about me by Hava Tirosh-Samuelson.

Articles

"Foreword." In *Keep Your Wives Away from Them: Orthodox Women, Unorthodox Desires: An Anthology*, edited by Miryam Kabakov, xix–xii. Berkeley: North Atlantic Books, 2010.

"God's Pronouns." *Tikkun* (March/April 2010): 55.

"Beyond Sarah and Hagar: Muslim and Jewish Reflections on Feminist Theology." With Aysha Hidayatullah. In *Muslims and Jews in America: Commonalities, Contentions, and Complexities*, edited by Reza Aslan and Aaron J. Hahn Tapper, 159–72. New York: Palgrave Macmillan, 2011.

"The Bible on Homosexuality: A Problematic Question." *World Religions: Belief, Culture, and Controversy.* Santa Barbara, CA: ABC-CLIO, November 2011. http://religion2.abc-clio.com/Ideas/Display/1657588?cid=1657587.

"Remembering Oppression." American Jewish World Service, Chag v'Chesed, 2011. www.ajws.org/cvc.

"An Accidental Dialoguer." In *My Neighbor's Faith: Stories of Interreligious Encounter, Growth, and Transformation*, edited by Jennifer Howe Peace, Or N. Rose, and Gregory Mobley, 56–61. Maryknoll, NY: Orbis, 2012.

"Feminist Jewish Ethical Theories." In *The Oxford Handbook of Jewish Ethics and Morality*, edited by Elliot Dorff and Jonathan Crane, 272–86. New York: Oxford University Press, 2013.

"Wrestling with God and Evil." In *Chapters of the Heart: Jewish Women Sharing the Torah of Our Lives*, edited by Sue Levi Elwell and Nancy Fuchs Kreimer, 85–93. Eugene, OR: Wipf & Stock, 2013.

"Movement and Emerging Scholarship: Feminist Biblical Scholarship in the 1970s in the United States." In *Feminist Biblical Studies in the Twentieth Century: Scholarship and Movement*, edited by Elisabeth Schüssler Fiorenza, 21–34. Atlanta: Society of Biblical Literature, 2014.

"Two Feminist Views of Goddess and God." With Carol P. Christ. *Tikkun* (Summer 2014): 29–32, 65–66.

"Developing a Critical Consciousness: Feminist Studies in Religion." In *Writing Religion: The Case for the Critical Study of Religion*, edited by Steven W. Ramey, 96–113. Tuscaloosa, AL: University of Alabama Press, 2015.

Index

Columbia University, 45, 75

community: in Goddess feminism, 143, 169, 205, 244, 245; idealism and, 204–5, 243–44; in Judaism, 194, 205, 265, 269; of prayer, 176; presence of God in, 126–27; role of, 272–73; of women, 86–88, 126–27, 143, 244

Cone, James, 69, 75

Conference of Women Theologians, 28–29

consciousness raising, 56–57, 59, 114

contraception, 18

conversation. *See* theological conversations

covenant, 8, 21, 31, 39, 62, 69, 126

creative process, 177, 184–86, 211, 212–14, 255, 259–62, 276, 300. *See also* birth-death-regeneration

Crete: ancient Goddesses, 143; ancient ritual, 169; geology of, 165–66; Goddess experiences in, 101, 151, 153, 297; Goddess Pilgrimage, 151, 165–66, 167, 169, 204, 297. *See also* Paliani; Sacred MyrtleTree

Crites, Stephen, 26, 95

Culpepper, Emily, 110

Daly, Mary, 110, 112, 113, 114, 116, 134; on Be-ing, 157; on God as male, 28–29, 73; on God the

Verb, 59–60, 125, 144; on patriarchy, 51, 87; on sexism of Church, 224

dark night of the soul, 83, 95–96

death: anger and, 115; Carol's baby brother, 6, 8, 202, 219, 251; Carol's mother, 149–50, 153, 292; dealing with, 6; denial of, 105; evil and, 251–54; Judith's mother, 114–15, 119, 181, 209-10, 230, 236, 273–74; love and, 149–51; pervasiveness of, 9–10, 12

death of God movement, 69, 73, 131

de Beauvoir, Simone. *See* Beauvoir, Simone de

denominationalism, 87, 183–84, 246

de Waal, Franz. *See* Waal, Franz de

disability, 179

dissertations: on Holocaust, 200–201, 220; on Wiesel, 26, 30, 83–85, 220, 226; on women's experience, 58–59, 109

divine relativity, concept of, 68, 158–60

Divine Relativity, The (Hartshorne), 20, 158

Diving Deep and Surfacing (Christ), 26, 82, 91, 95–96, 98

divinity. *See* nature of God/Goddess

Downing, Christine, 29, 97, 98, 99, 134, 139, 152-53

Driver, Tom, 75

dualisms: classical, 72–73, 139, 145;